COUNSELING AN ADULTERER

A helpline for ministers & elders

SAVING A MARRIAGE

Dr. Wyveta Kirk, Christian Psychologist

This book is not intended to replace spiritual, psychological or medical advice from a professional. Readers are advised to consult with their minister or therapist regarding treatment for specific relationship problems. The author takes no responsibility for any possible consequences from any treatment, action, or application to any person reading or following the information in this book.

Copyright © 2018 by Wyveta Kirk
All rights reserved worldwide. No part of this publication may be reproduced, distributed, or transmitted in any form or by any means, without prior written permission by the author. The only exception is brief quotations in printed reviews.

Wyveta Kirk/ SuccesSteps Publishing
wyvetakirk@ymail.com

Scriptures taken from the Holy Bible, New International Version ®, NIV®. Copyright © 1973, 1978, 1984, 2011 by Biblica, Inc.™ Used by permission of Zondervan. All rights reserved worldwide www.zondervan.com The "NIV" and "New International Version" are trademarks registered in the United States Patent and Trademark Office by Biblica, Inc.™

Counseling an Adulterer; Saving a Marriage
Dr. Wyveta Kirk. -- 1st edition.
ISBN – 978-0-9971904-5-8
ebook ISBN -978-0-9971904-6-5

Cover designed by Maria Gandolfo from Italy. Contact her through www.Fiverr.com as renflowergrapx.

This book is dedicated to Toney Stowers, my former minister, who was humble enough to ask for help in knowing how to counsel with an adulterer.

It takes a special person to tackle such a demanding type of counseling as adultery, and Toney is one of those exceptional people. His love of the Lord is what makes others seek and trust his guidance.

"Our struggle is not against flesh and blood, but against the rulers, against the authorities, against the powers of this dark world and against the spiritual forces of evil in the heavenly realms."
(Eph, 6:12)

CONTENTS

NEED FOR ADULTERY COUNSELING	1
YOUR SPIRITUAL PROTECTION	15
HOW SEXUAL SIN PROGRESSES	33
INSIST HE STOP THE AFFAIR	53
INITIAL MEETING WITH THE WIFE	71
CONSEQUENCES OF HIS SIN	89
IF HE ENDS THE AFFAIR	101
TURNING POINT	119
HOME BECOMES ON-GOING DRAMA	135
GRADUAL RECONNECTION	151
GOD'S COMMAND FOR MARITAL SUCCESS	171
YOUR INVOLVEMENT AS THEY PROBLEM SOLVE	193
ASSESS THEIR PROGRESS	209
IF HE REFUSED TO END THE AFFAIR	221
HIS REACTION TO CONFRONTATION	235
PREPARE FOR CHURCH ASSISTANCE	247
TELING THE CHURCH	255
DIVORCE OR NOT?	267

CONTENTS CONTINUED

OTHER WAYS ADULTERY REQUIRES HELP   *278*

AGES AFFIARS ARE MORE LIKELY   *295*

LEGALLY PROTECT YOURSELF & THE CHURCH   *307*

Chapter 1

NEED FOR ADULTRY COUNSELING

"*Adultery is becoming a serious concern in our churches. I see more and more people trapped in this sin who come asking for help, and I have no idea what to do. Some come wanting to save the marriage, but others appear to want me to agree they have reason to leave their families. I asked another minister for advice, and he admitted that he too struggled with knowing how to respond.*" These could be the words of many of our ministers today. Yet, it is not a new concern. Satan has been attacking marriages of believers with this seductive sin forever. Adultery requires a challenging type of counseling. Often it proves as distressing for the counselor-minister as it does for the couple being ripped apart. This book offers help to the ministers and elders who face this difficult task because adultery is a sin that must be addressed by our churches. Jesus did. So must we.

In the US, it is estimated that more men (22-37%) than women (14-20%) commit adultery, and 17 – 20% of the divorces are the result of one party committing adultery. Because of the secrecy involved in affairs, accurate statistics are difficult to obtain. The reasons these marriages end with divorce differ for men than for women.

Chapman University polled 64,000 Americans and found that 54% of heterosexual men were gravely upset when adultery involved sex, but this was the primary concern of only 35% of the women. When the affair was limited to emotional infidelity 65 % of women reported extreme jealousy but only 46% of men. Research from Norwegian University of Science and Technology explains the differences. Men focus more heavily on the sexual aspect, and knowing his wife shared sex with another leaves such a huge bruise to a man's ego that his pride hinders his forgiving. A man is more likely to divorce his wife if her fling included sex, even if happened years earlier. However, women are more likely to forgive a sexual affair, especially when their husbands' fling 'meant nothing' and involved only sex with no emotional intimacy. Women focus on the emotional attachment, and the first thing that many ask is, "Do you love her?" More often, she forgives if his affair was all sexual, and he didn't emotionally bond with the woman

After an affair, men make more difficult counselees because, more often, they come to their minister-counselor seeking approval to divorce. More women come hoping to save the marriage. In addition, she has a built-in support system of other women who encourage her to 'hang in there.' Men have fewer, or no, friends who support their remaining with an unfaithful mate.

When a man learns of his wife's affair, he tends to view her unfaithfulness as the unforgiveable sin. A man is more likely to immediately seek a divorce attorney than a counselor, even if his wife's affair occurred years prior to his learning of it. Marital therapists find that a man's instant reaction to learning of his wife's unfaithfulness is an enormous flood of anger, not worry about the children or concern about the relationship, which become a woman's immediate focus. His instant alarm is a personal attack on his manhood. He can forgive himself for such indiscretion, but he does not forgive a wife for doing the same.

Some women will endure horrible treatment rather than divorcing and having to face living alone, being financially self-responsible, and becoming a single parent. In addition, many women's immediate reaction is to blame themselves for failures in the relationship. They have an attitude of, "something is wrong with me that had him wanting another." Most women want to save the relationship. Yet women initiate nearly 70% of all divorces. They attribute their divorce to overt conflicts and an overall dissatisfaction with the condition of their marriages, rather than their mate's straying. Women divorce for the same reasons they have affairs. They feel emotionally neglected and crave intimacy and romance.

ADULTERY BECOMES ADDICTIVE

Affairs tend to create a chemical reaction inside the person's brain. It matters not if the illicit partner is a live person, or a face on a computer screen of someone the adulterer will never meet, or a continual replaying of a sexual fantasy inside one's thoughts. The neurotransmitters inside the person's brain fire with each episode. With enough replays of these images, the brain rewires so that even a brief passing thought of the illicit party creates a feeling similar to having a fix of a strong drug. This emotional reaction provides positive satisfaction and an ongoing desire for more.

Drs. Tim Clinton and Eric Scalise, authors of *Addictions and Recovery Counseling*, explain that the human body is remarkably balanced chemically. But when the balance is disrupted, spiritual doors open to the soul. Only by discontinuing the use of what opened the door is a sense of equilibrium restored. This holds true whether it's sexual addition, a chemical-drug addiction, or even a food addiction.

It works because the process involves a form of pleasurable escape that removes the person's real feelings and replaces them with an obsessive-compulsive behavior. This leads to denial and lying, takes priority over issues that once were important, creates a psychological dependence, and becomes destructive to relationships. In Romans (7:14-25), Paul describes similar struggles and states that Christ is the deliverer for the person who has become a slave to sin.

SPIRITUAL DECLINE. 2 Kings 17: 16-17 describes the process of how the Israelites gradually deserted the Lord and committed what God called spiritual adultery. They forsook His commandments, worshipped man-made images, and served Baal. They burned their children as living sacrifices and practiced divination. Their evil practices provoked the Lord. Their estrangement and abandonment of the Lord was a progression that began with their own choices that ultimately had a generational impact. A similar sequence results from the choice to pursue an adulterous relationship.

The Israelites first chose to turn their backs on God and behave contrary to His will. They knew God's expectations but chose not to obey. While an immoral choice may later become an addiction that becomes difficult to control, each addict took a first step in the wrong direction by choice. Step one for an adulterer is to pursue a relationship with someone that is closer than that with other friends.

Next, the Israelites chose to make idols. They took the thoughts that were growing inside their hearts and made them into a reality. They deliberately set an image in front of themselves so they could engage their minds more and more with the objects. Adulterers create excuses and lies in order to spend more and more time with the illicit person who holds a dominate place in their thoughts.

Then the Israelites chose to worship what they had created. They idolized their choice. They gave their image more attention and respect than the Lord. They elevated their idol to a higher priority than God, and completely ignored the Lord's commands. They emotionally bonded with the image. For an adulterer, faithfulness to the adulteress becomes more important than being loyal to the Lord or to the spouse. They become so addicted they feel fully bonded with the illicit person, until they think they cannot live without this person. They ignore that Scripture calls adultery idolatry (Col. 3:5).

The Israelites progressed from worship of Baal to sacrificing their own children. Adulterers sacrifice their own spouses and children to have the good feeling that comes with being desired and valued by another. The Lord cautions in Malachi (2:15-16) that this turns the adulterer's children away from God. Adultery can only leave a negative and destructive impact on the lives of all impacted.

Thankfully, God's Word teaches how to address and stop such physical, emotional, and spiritual destruction. The return to the Lord requires the choice of godly sorrow, confession, and repentance. With God there is always a choice that can save the adulterer and his family. It requires some painful and trying times, but all things are possible with the Lord. Returning the heart home requires faith, a commitment to action, and continued prayer.

NOT A NEW PROBLEM

This book was written at the request a minister who lamented that he needed help in addressing this heartbreaking and disruptive sin. In fact, research finds that many Christian colleges and seminaries are graduating students to serve as ministers who feel unprepared for the types of counseling they face in the real world. Worse, many ministers do not know how to avoid becoming emotionally imprisoned themselves by a needy parishioner who sits crying in their offices.

One of the most trying and difficult challenges a minister-counselor faces is dealing with a couple where one partner becomes addicted to adultery. Adulterers feel certain they love the illicit person and no longer have positive feelings for their spouses. When the wounded mates are women who turn to the minister-counselor for help, their distraught and clinging behaviors make it extremely important for the minister-counselor to know how to keep an emotional distance from these women. Otherwise they can become entangled in too close a relationship. Without a conscious effort and commitment to remaining detached, a minister can become as easily entrapped in an affair as the person he hopes to help change. Few ministers leave their educational institution prepared for the temptation Satan presents. Research shows that it matters not if the minister-counselor is married or single. Satan tempts both, and he has been tempting such faithful believers since the beginning of time.

EXAMPLE. Peter Marshall, was a noted minister who moved to the US from Scotland, ultimately became Chaplain for the US Senate, and offered the prayer when Harry Truman was sworn in as President. After holding positions in large churches in Atlanta and Washington D.C., Mr. Marshall cautioned others about the many temptations a minister-counselor faces.

> "Here is a very real danger, which certainly ought to be stressed in Seminary more than it is. The minister seems to have an attraction for certain types of women. They will not only weary you with their problems– real or imaginary–but will often sorely try your patience and Christian grace."
>
> "You are caught in a dilemma. If you are short and abrupt with them, they can accuse you of being unsympathetic. If you are courteous, they will be encouraged and make life miserable for you in many feminine ways. Many a ministry has been ruined

because of the jealousies engendered among the women of the congregation."

Peter's wife, Catherine Marshall, wrote in her book, *A Man Called Peter,* that while a bachelor, Peter experienced a difficult time with the mothers of Atlanta debutantes because they considered him eligible husband material. Usually the mothers' opening attempt at matchmaking was a family dinner party followed by offering tickets for him to escort their daughter to some event. She described Peter as the target for feminine admiration, and it didn't matter if the ladies were nine or ninety. The effects were the same. Every congregation Peter served contained women whose hearts cried for something life had denied them, and they saw the minister through a romantic haze and wanted to do personal things for him like mending his clothes, bringing him flowers, and sending him notes and gifts. She quoted Peter as asking why Satan was always depicted as masculine when the devil was no fool by using women.

Mrs. Marshall shared the incident of a woman named Ruby who phoned Peter saying she had a broken collar bone, her maid had the day off, and her husband was out of town. Ruby insisted she was freezing, and she asked Peter to come build her a fire. Peter noted that she had not asked for the male janitor to come help. So Peter went, took along his secretary, built Ruby a fire, and he and his secretary left immediately.

Mrs. Marshall wrote that it was necessary for the minister and his wife to keep a sense of humor about this sort of thing or real trouble could result. Because in every church, the persons whom the preacher would most humanly like to avoid are the ones who most need help. This presents the minister with several dilemmas. He must find a way of helping these people, while at the same time protecting himself and his ministry from the harm they can do. When a woman asks to meet with the minister, even when he has good reason to suspect that she only wants an excuse for another contact with him, there is always the outside chance that she really is sincere, and does need help. And he can't risk failing anyone in need. She quoted Peter as saying, "*It isn't the fact of having temptations that should cause us shame, but what we do with them. Temptation is an opportunity to conquer. When we eventually reach the goal (heaven) to which we are all striving, God will look us over, not for diplomas, but for scars.*" (Pages 49-51). It appears that few of Satan's temptations have changed throughout the years.

SALVAGING THE MARRIAGE

After exposure of an adulterous relationship, if both spouses agree to work to save the marriage, they face a long, painful process. Proof-reading my book left my husband exhausted just thinking about all that's required for a woman to fully heal after her husband's affair. There is no quick fix and no fast technique to speed the recovery process. It can prove more challenging than some men can handle and they leave to avoid their wives' emotional episodes. Yet, all steps are mandatory for rebuilding trust and forgiveness. A couple has to want the marriage to succeed and be willing to work at it, even during the highly stressful, uncomfortable times. However, when they do devote the effort, the vast majority say it was worth the struggle, and they finish with a better marriage and closer relationship.

Counseling an Adulterer is written as if the adulterer is a man for three reasons. First, research finds the adulterous partner is more often a man, and after learning a spouse has been unfaithful, more women than men seek counseling to save the marriage. Second, having a man cooperate in counseling is intensely more challenging. If he wants to remain in the marriage, he expects his wife to 'just forget it' and begin again as if nothing happened, but few women can forget and forgive without knowing all specifics of his affair. Third, writing as if the adulterer is consistently one gender makes both reading and writing easier than using he/she and him/her.

If the unfaithful spouse is a woman and her husband wants to save the relationship, the same or similar steps are required. However, rarely do these men require step number 5 listed below. Few men want to hear the nitty-gritty details of their wife's affair. The majority of men who work to salvage the marriage can compartmentalize what she did and live as if it never occurred. They want frequent reminders that their wife loves them but ask that the particulars of what his wife and her lover shared together never be mentioned again.

However, dismissing his affair as if it never occurred is something few women can do. The vast majority of women must talk, and talk, and talk until she thinks every detail is exposed and resolved. Without discussing every intimate aspect, these women never fully forgive. Below are the required steps for saving the marriage.

PROCESS FOR COUNSELING AN ADULTERER (MAN) TO SAVE THE MARRIAGE

1. As the minister-counselor, protect yourself so you do not become trapped by a needy, emotional counselee, and understand how adultery relationships progress so you immediately recognize if you are being tempted and realize how the adulterer became entangled in an affair.
2. The adulterer needs to acknowledge his estrangement from the Lord and his ultimate spiritual destiny without change. You insist he ends the affair and tells his wife
3. If he ends the affair, he tells his wife and writes a complete history of the affair's progression and in your presence, he reads it to his wife.

4. He faces his wife's hurt and anger, as you work to help her control her emotions so she doesn't also sin and then move to marriage counseling to resolve their lingering issues.
5. If he refused to end the affair at your request (#2), the wife confronts his sin, and if he still refuses to end the affair, she shuns him in every way
6. If he ends the affair after being shunned by his wife, he writes a detailed letter of how the affair progressed and reads it to her in your presence.
7. He must show compassion to calm his wife's anger and heal her hurt as he answers her continual questions.
8. She must forgive and focus on their future
9. The couple discusses issues that contributed to the desire for an affair
10. The couple addresses lingering issues that have caused on-going arguments and marital dissatisfaction
11. If he refused to end the affair after being shunned by his wife, she takes two or three others to confront his sin
12. If he showed no indication of change after the group confronted him, the wife prepares for the worst.
13. She seeks support from an attorney, the elders, and the entire church
14. She decides either to divorce, or to wait and see if the affair's magnetism burns out by itself

15. If he wants to return home, she insists that he seeks personal counseling
16. She refuses to live with him until he is restored to the Lord
17. You counsel them using numbers 6-10

My prayers are for you as you begin this work. Counseling an adulterer and working to save the marriage will prove one of the most difficult counseling challenges you will face.

Rely on the Lord, and follow your head and heart anytime it tells you to depart from this provided process. Each person responds to assistance differently. If your efforts seem lacking, remember prayer still connects directly and personally with God, and praying is what Jesus told His apostles to do to avoid temptation. Also remember,

Satan attacks believers because
        non-believers already belong to him.

Chapter 2

YOUR SPIRITUAL PROTECTION

"*My husband was a minister. That is until he became involved with a woman in our church who came to him for marriage counseling. This woman would call our home at all hours crying and upset. I thought little about it because ministers receive a lot calls at home, and they feel obligated to take them. Caring for members of a congregation is a 24-7 job. But before I knew what was happening, my husband left me to live with this woman. He lost his job and our marriage. Our children were devastated. It hit them so hard they questioned if there even was a God. Eventually, he phoned, insisting he had changed and wanted to return home. I agreed, but two days before a month was over, he moved back to the woman's place and filed for divorce.*"

Unfortunately, this woman's story describes too many ministers. Too often our counseling-ministers deal with lonesome, desperate people without knowing how to keep the person's problems distanced from their own feelings. They become hooked emotionally and what began as helpful counseling develops into an attraction that results in an affair.

RESEARCH FINDINGS

Most ministers enter the ministry because they care about people, and they want to work full-time for the Lord. However, their concern for others can be their downfall if they become emotionally entangled with a counselee. To their ruin, many ministers receive no training in how to stay detached from an attractive woman who is lonely and distraught. Recent (2016) research by Dr. Richard J. Krejeir found 46.73% of the 8,150 interviewed preachers said they left seminary or Bible colleges unprepared to assume a ministerial role, and one of the primary voids listed was counseling.

Earlier research by Fuller Seminary found 90% of ministers felt they were inadequately trained to cope with congregational needs. While things have improved, they still reveal serous concerns. These ministers said it was due partly to so many churches no longer having open Bible studies and replacing it with the reading of books written by today's authors with little or no time left for studying God's word. Members prefer reading books that make themselves feel good and do not want to be challenged or hear about sin and its consequences. In many congregations, worship has become entertainment, not the good news of Jesus. What remains are lifeless or weak churches filled with fads, and divisions with no direction in life, no spiritual growth, or knowledge of the Lord, and young, inexperienced ministers have no idea how to implement needed changes. So instead of worshipping the Lord, they ignore that the focus becomes Self-Worship.

Or as I continue to hear during my continuing education counseling programs, instead of God centered families, the focus has become Child Worship. Little time, attention, or money is given exclusively to enriching the marital relationship but used for entertaining the children.

Dr. Krejeir's first research, conducted in 2006, found that ministers have no idea how to address the sin of adultery. He discovered 77% (808) of the 1,050 preachers surveyed reported having troubled marriages themselves.

In Dr. Krejeir's 2016 research, the minister's wives (26%) felt church was a prime source of stress for their relationships, and sixty-five percent (65%) of these women described feeling their family lived in a glass house. The study discovered 38% (399) of the ministers were either divorced or in the process, and almost the same number, (30%) admitted to either being in an ongoing affair or having had a one-time sexual encounter with a parishioner. Another contributing factor was that 58% had no supportive friend to help in a personal crisis or to ask for guidance when working with counselees bringing problems for which they lacked training.

The positive news is that when the 2016 study eliminated what Dr. Krejeir called mainline and 'dead' churches, the number of ministers who had committed adultery dropped to 3%, and another 16.5 % of the preachers admitted to being tempted but not acting on the urge.

MAINTAIN A SAFE DISTANCE

Keeping a safety net between yourself, as the minister counselor, and a needy counselee is a matter of maintaining aloofness physically and emotionally. It's refusing to carry another's problem home and only worrying about the person as you prepare for the next counseling session.

NO CALLS AT HOME. You can protect your family life by having your intake- admission form, include a comment in bold letters that says "I do not take counseling-related phone calls at home." Or post a large sign on your office wall. Accepting no counseling calls at home is applicable for both genders. Although you may serve as both a counselor and minister of a congregation, you are not required to respond to others 24/7. An explanation of this during your first meeting can eliminate needy counselees overstepping what must be a firm, healthy boundary. You can draw a line, and refuse to let others step over it. It's what people expect when they pay to see a licensed professional therapist. When you respect your time and home life the same way, so will others.

PREPARE EMOTIONALLY. By having counselees complete an intake-admission form stating the reason(s) they seek assistance, you can better prepare for working with them. You know which Scriptures are appropriate for their concerns and can do a computer search for research conducted on the issue. More importantly, advance knowledge can alert you to do small things that ensure you don't become emotionally trapped.

If a woman's intake-agreement form reveals she has experienced a serious loss, you need to prepare yourself for coping with her emotional condition. Otherwise, her crying and apparent helplessness can have you wanting to hold her as if she is a needy five-year-old little girl in serious pain. But you must remember that she is an adult, and it is never your role to fill her emptiness. You must remind yourself that, if you allow it, she becomes a target for Satan to attack you. Mentally repeat that you must remain detached -- not from her issue -- but from the woman and her pain so Satan doesn't trap you in an affair. You have to separate the problem from the person and ask yourself how you will address the issue. No matter the face of the person in front of you, she is not unique. It could be any woman with the same issue. The issue is what you work to remedy, not the woman's emotional state. Resolve the topic and it will help heal her pain.

Mentally repeat that you must remain detached

- not from her issue –

but from the woman and her pain

so Satan doesn't trap you in an affair

STAY FUTURE FOCUSED. Counselees, especially women, bring four basic types of issues that are more likely to hook you emotionally. Three involve serious loss and a fourth is an issue that gains her public success. Remaining detached from these people requires staying solution-oriented by focusing on what they can do in the present and creating plans that make their future better. This requires you to refuse to dwell on problems in their past. You may have to remind them several times to stop talking about prior happenings that cannot be changed. Keep focused on plans for today and tomorrow.

Virginia Satir, one of the world's most noted therapist, used four questions as she worked with families that may prove helpful in staying future focused:

What do you want?
How will you know when you have it?
What's stopping you now?
What do you need in order to get it, or what can you do that would get you what you want?

Virginia demanded that answers be very specific, and refused to accept vague generalization or abstractions. She believed people failed to see today's opportunities because they hid possibilities with their expectations of how others should have treated them in the past.

DEATH OF CHILD. Emotionally prepare yourself when meeting with a woman who has lost a child, because the death of one's child creates the deepest of all hurts. We live life expecting our children to bury us, not us them. With the burial of a child, she feels so hopelessly helpless that she will grasp at anything you say or do. Her reasoning and logic are not functioning well, and she thinks only in dark, deep, disturbing terms which can have her misinterpreting your offer of help. You must guard your words and actions so they cannot be misunderstood.

Remain focused on things she can do to feel better in control, not on how sad and empty she feels and looks. Take a stand that pushes her to find ways to be present for the loved ones she still has. If she has other children, press her to remember their needs and to understand the pain her husband shares at this time. Moving her forward in positive ways not only helps her to help others, but it keeps your focus off her current neediness.

DEATH OF HUSBAND. Be cautious when counseling a woman whose husband has recently died. Likely, she lives fearful of how she will manage the future alone and feels extremely vulnerable. You must guard yourself as you listen to her talk because you could easily begin identifying with her hurt, thinking how it could be you facing a similar fate. If so, you may find yourself wanting to offer comfort and support, but any attention you give her can easily be misunderstood. She feels desperate for relief from her pain and welcomes any kindness you provide. As she desperately reaches out to you for help in relieving her horrific grief, she could interpret your attention as more than simple caring, far more than you intend it to mean. Trying to supply this woman's emptiness has been the downfall of many ministers.

Remain emotionally detached from her emotional state, and insist that she become actively involved in learning more about her money, insurance, home maintenance, and auto care. The more you require her to take charge of routine daily details, the less opportunity there is for you think about her sadness or loneliness. And it prepares her to face the future alone. You are asking her to do as Paul said in Romans, *"Be transformed by renewing your mind so you can know what God's will is for you"* (12:2).

DIVORCE. For a woman going through a divorce, it feels like a form of death. Only with divorce, fewer people rally to support her. Instead, many whisper behind her back, wondering what she did wrong. There may be times when she thinks you are the only one who cares. If the divorcee's husband left for another woman, you can expect her to sit crying and sharing ways he mistreated her, and your heart may break. Perhaps, she has small children, no job, no money, and no family for support. Hearing her story can rip your heart. But you must also remember that she, too, failed her marriage in some ways, maybe many ways. At this point, she will gravitate to anyone who cares for her, someone who will give her what she missed all her married years, and she could easily believe your words and actions imply you want to do that.

For a while, you, as the counselor, may be the divorcee's only real friend, which places you in an even more susceptible position. If so, she may be clinging, and want to see you more often than you should allow. You may need to remind her that you cannot take her calls at home because you reserve your home exclusively for family time. If so, your actions must match your words, and if she calls, you must hang up without any discussion. No matter her issue, you must tell her to call you at work tomorrow.

Insist that she finds ways to involve herself with others. Have her not only make lists of things she might do, but do them. Keep directing her toward what is in her own control to do, because it empowers her to obtain the results that makes her life better. And encourage her to be with other women and join some women groups because she needs a strong support for a while, a long while.

HELP WITH PROJECTS. This is the woman who wants to tackle a worthwhile project, one you agree is an outstanding idea. It may be an endeavor your church or community would benefit greatly by implementing. Only she doesn't know how to execute the idea and needs your advice. This woman can make you feel like an expert, but she can also trap you emotionally, just as easily as the one losing a child. In her eyes, you become the knowledgeable authority on the topic, and let's admit it, we all like being able to direct and give directions on how to handle tasks we respect and think worthwhile. She may view you as her hero for helping her accomplish something that gains her respect and attention from others, especially if she thinks the task pleases the Lord. Perhaps for the first time in a long time, she feels successful, and she attributes it all to you. If this happens, it shows that you have allowed her to become dependent on you, instead of helping her grow on her own.

You need to take notice, if during group settings, she seems to always join your cluster of friends to talk, or if she lingers to ask you questions after others have left. This should clue you that you need to keep more distance from her and walk away the minute she comes near. Many a man has been entrapped at the end of a project when she grabs him and hugs him to thank him for his help. The goal of counseling should always be to help others become self-sufficient and need only the Lord's help, not yours.

> **The goal of counseling should always be to help others become self-sufficient and need only the Lord's help, not yours**

KEEP A SAFE DETACHMENT. Several small steps can help you avoid being overly committed to comforting these women during their distress. Most important is to protect yourself physically and spiritually by keeping a safe distance from a counselee of the opposite sex. Do not sit on a sofa beside her. Instead, stay behind your desk or if your room has a sofa and/or chairs facing each other, sit across facing her, and purchase a small coffee table to further separate the sofa and chair. Many therapists hold a notebook, not just to take notes, but to use as a psychological barrier between themselves and the counselee. However, most counseling notes are written after the person leaves.

When a distressed woman displays strong emotions, you may become overly sympathetic and feel like hugging and protecting her. But if you hug her when she is in this pit of despair, she can misinterpret your touch and define it as caring in ways you never intended. She could easily transfer her emotional hunger to you and attempt to depend on you beyond what a counselor should allow. So, above all else, do not hug, pat, or make any type of physical contact with these women, no matter how deeply they sob and tremble with grief. Instead, hand them a box of tissue and keep pressing them to think beyond the present problem. Stay focused on future possibilities.

Too often men do not understand the importance many women place on touch. To most women, a warm hug implies closeness and a form of intimacy. A man may have no idea that touching puts such ideas in her head, especially if he views it only as a way to say thanks or that he hopes things improve. I recently told my husband that if he had not hugged me in his office the first time we were alone, it's unlikely we would be married today. The interpretation I put on that hug was definitely different than he intended. . . until later. But for me, the hug initiated a special connection that has now continued many years.

IF SHE IS ATTRACTED TO YOU

A vulnerable time when touching might occur is when your counseling session ends. If she doesn't rise to leave, you need to stand, walk quickly past her, open your office door, and step into the hallway holding your notebook to your chest. This makes it less likely that she will attempt to embrace you as she thanks you for your help. Keep remembering that she is deeply distressed and will grasp at any glimmer of support.

If she initiates a hug, and you let it linger, or she presses her body too closely, she will have reason to believe you wanted the contact. If you push her away, she will likely apologize, saying she is sorry. Do not respond with, "It's okay, forget it," because what you say at this moment determines if she thinks you approved. Your words must show that you consider her actions as having stepped over the line. Any words that can be interpreted as condoning or rewarding her behavior ensure that her aggressiveness will be repeated.

You need to confirm she knows you have no romantic interest in her, and that you make it a practice of not touching those you counsel. Depending on her reaction, you may need to say, *"To ensure there's never any physical contact between us again. I am going to refer you to work with another. I will make the arrangements."* If she protests, which she likely will, you need to walk away without commenting further.

Actions communicate louder than words, and they show real feelings. Let your facial expression prove to her that you will not risk further contact after such an intimate situation. You must be strong because Satan stands ready to attack you too. You need to flee from all temptations Satan might throw at you.

To a needy woman, touching can imply you want to see more of her. Except for handshakes, you need to avoid all touching of a counselee of the opposite sex.

To a needy woman, touching can imply you want to see more of her

*"Brothers, if someone is caught in a sin, you who are spiritual should restore him/her gently. But **watch yourself, or you also may be tempted**"* (Gal. 6:1; my emphasis).

STRONGLY CONNECT WITH YOUR MATE

It's time to immediately begin putting more closeness, sexually and emotionally, into your own marriage because something you did or said had this woman thinking you would be receptive to her behavior. Perhaps, the counselee was testing to see your receptiveness, but it's a serious indicator that attention needs to be paid to your own marriage. If you doubt this, imagine your wife's reaction if she knew the woman hugged you, and you did nothing to stop it.

Take your wife on a vacation without the children, and share adult fun together. Do things you used to enjoy when you dated. Reconnect so you have no thoughts of another or what awaits you at home.

Many of the ministers in Dr. Krejeir's research described their marriages as lacking romance, sexual passion, and spiritual intimacy. They were more like a brother-sister than lovers. Their spiritual bond was disconnected, and they rarely prayed together or shared spiritual needs. Sadly, the longer they stayed in ministry work, the worse their marriages became. If this description fits your marriage, you need to withdraw from counseling women for a while and focus exclusively on regaining that spark of romance in your own relationship.

In Dr. Krejeir's study, the ministers who reported having illicit relationships said the affairs had little to do with sexual satisfaction but were a mental escape from a life of pressure, performance, and expectations. The 2016 study revealed 43% ministers described themselves as stressed, 26% overly fatigued, 54% overworked, 35% battled depression, and 9% burnout. A few admitted their affair was caused by being overcome by ego and success and having an arrogant attitude of entitlement. They reported having too little accountability of how they spent their time or where they went and this indirectly contributed to their moral collapse. They reported that when meeting with the elders or church board, the group never mentioned personal or moral issues, and when he strayed, the elders had no restoration plan to help. If the above description fits you, then you need to take a temporary break from doing counseling, refer those in need, and give your full attention to your family, especially to your spouse.

Minister counselors must take care of their families and put them before all others. They need to learn that it's a positive response to say no when they are already overloaded. They can't be all to everyone. They must have permission to say no to the members of their congregations so they can say yes to living as the Lord requires. And the first requirement is becoming one with their spouse and rearing believing children. Family comes before the job and before others. If a minister loses his own soul or that of his spouse what good has he done for the Lord?

> **Family comes before the job and before others**
> **If a minister loses his own soul**
> **or that of his spouse**
> **what good has he done for the Lord?**

IF YOU ARE ATTRACTED TO HER

Too many ministers and elders have been trapped by a needy woman who was an emotional strung-out mess, weeping in their offices. These women's stories can break your heart, but you must not let needy counselees destroy your own marriage and life.

If you feel the slightest attraction developing towards a female counselee, then you are failing her, her spouse, your own spouse, yourself, and the Lord. How Satan would enjoy that.

You must admit it to the Lord if you feel an attraction to a counselee, because that proves you are spiritually weak. You need to immediately refer this woman to someone else. Above all, DO NOT tell her that you find her attractive. Remember most women who suffer a loss or who rarely feel successful are hurting, emotional beings. Being starved for attention and support guarantees she would dwell on any comment that hints you find her appealing, and she might pursue you until you lose self-control.

Instead, it's time for you to say, "I am not qualified to deal with the issues you face, and I must refer you to another." And if you feel the least bit of attraction for her, it is true and accurate that you are no longer qualified for helping her.

You must do as Scriptures teach about avoiding sexual sin: *"Flee from sexual immorality"* (1 Co. 6:18). Flee! Run! Leave. *"The body is not meant for sexual immorality but for the Lord"* (v.13). The minute you realize you find a counselee appealing, your thoughts no longer focus on the Lord, nor of determining a healthy path she needs to pursue.

Remain firm, and direct her to another for counseling. Explain that you can no longer counsel anyone when you aren't qualified to help. If she chooses not to see another that is her decision, but it must not change your stance.

If after being referred to another, the woman phones you with a pretense of discussing what the new counselor says, you must refuse to listen. You are ethically, morally, and legally right to say, "I cannot talk with you now that you are seeing another counselor." Or, "Please remember, I take no counseling calls from those who are working with another counselor."

Kirk: Counseling an Adulterer Saving a Marriage

She needs to hear the phone go dead immediately after you say, "I have to hang up now", and not have time to protest or ask for 'just one small piece of advice'. You must hang up without further discussion because your own spirituality, and hers, depend on the phone click leaving a dead sound.

Chapter 3

HOW SEXUAL SIN PROGRESSES

"*I don't love my wife any more. I've met someone whom I'm sure God wants me to be with because of how compatible we are. I've never felt this loved before. Because God is love, He surely wants us to feel loved too, and I really do when I am with her. I haven't felt loved at home in a long, long time,*" said the man, offering a respond you will hear many times from those trapped in an affair.

Or he may walk in and blurt, "*I just don't love my wife any longer. We've grown apart and there's nothing left for us as a couple.*" Or, "*I like my wife, but I don't love her.*" Or, "*I just want to be happy, and I'm not at home.*" If you guess that these men are involved with another woman, you are probably correct. If not, it's a safe guess that he fantasizes about one, and probably will be involved with another very soon. He has likely convinced himself that he has a justifiable reason.

These are the types of messages counselor-ministers hear, and the expression on these men's faces prove they believe their actions are the fault of another. At least it's what they want to believe, even if they know their choices are contrary to every Scripture in God's Word.

No matter what you might say, expect this man to hold a justifiable excuse. *"I have good reason to act as I am. I wouldn't feel this way if only. . ."* Oh how we hate being confronted with our own sinfulness.

This man may have attended church faithfully since childhood, can relate every Bible story in the Old and New Testament, and may currently struggle with guilt. He may even be an elder or another minister, but at this moment, emotions and feelings over-shadow what he knows is Scripturally right. Remind him that regardless of his current thoughts and arguments, it is never acceptable with God for anyone to live contrary to His Word.

It is never acceptable with God for anyone to live contrary to His Word

Sexual immorality is a sin problem. It becomes highlighted and can no longer be ignored as it creates unavoidable marital problems.

These men faced temptation, and allowed Satan to rule their thoughts and behavior rather than turning to the Lord for escape. Some fell head-first into Satan's ploy smiling all the way; others lingered and required Satan's push. Satan blinded them to the consequences awaiting their actions and focused them on the good feelings of the moment. Having a new person find them attractive elicited notably positive feelings, and such strong emotions allowed them to ignore that their actions were sinful.

Even the most moral person can ignore an appropriate boundary and step over the line of safety, particularly if a couple has been arguing nonstop. Continual disagreements at home leave both spouses especially vulnerable to Satan's attacks.

To counsel people that Satan has ensnared in sexual sin, you needed to understand what contributes to their entrapment because sexual sins are a serious problem in the church.

SEXUAL-EMOTIONAL ADULTERY

Infidelity occurs when one partner takes emotional and/or sexual intimacy that rightly belonged to their partner, and gives it to someone else. After parts of their marital relationship has been shared with another, the wounded partner feels betrayed and considers the relationship contaminated. The marriage is no longer special and precious. It feels dirty. An affair destroys all the wounded partner believed about how their relationship would and should operate, and her destroyed assumptions leave her emotionally devastated and disoriented. More than about sex, infidelity is about betrayal by the mate crossing a boundary the partner assumed was protected.

In most adulterous situations, the man and woman never planned to be drawn to each other. Rarely, is the connection initially about sex. More often they enjoyed how their talks let them feel appreciated and valued. But sex became the inevitable outcome.

Women find emotional adultery more satisfying, but men tend to need the sexual intimacy. It's why a wife finds it difficult to believe her husband can be involved with another woman and not be emotionally connected, and why he rarely believes she can have an emotional fling without it being sexual. They judge each other based on their own desires.

Men are more likely to compartmentalize their relationships. Some men can love their wives, love their marriages, and still not turn down an opportunity for extramarital sex. Some men are even be more passionate at home while having affairs. However, these men are rarely the ones who once strived to live loyal to the Lord.

Affairs go through four serious stages: crossing a moral boundary, emotional intimacy, secrecy, and a sexually charged touching that lead to more. The affairs of most people who hold religious values begin in seemingly innocent ways.

Affairs go through four serious stages: crossing a moral boundary, secrecy, emotional intimacy, and sexually charged touching that leads to more

Affairs tend to begin by finding oneself captivated by the other person's ideas, and before they realize it, they have crossed the line from friendship to more. They likely told themselves they could have a cross-gender friendship, that there was no harm. And at first their relationships appeared innocent enough. They chatted and laughed and realized they appreciated each other's comments. They held similar ideas on an issue each considered important, one they agreed was especially significant.

When they were with a group, no matter how many others were present, they sought out each other to talk. Visiting with each other became all important as they slowly crossed the moral boundary. It may have been at work, church, a community event, or over the backyard fence. The pull to seek each other's opinions grew stronger and stronger until they were emotionally hooked.

Before long a new concern arose with the issue they shared. They telephoned each other with the pretense of discussing the matter. Finally, they decided to meet to discuss things more thoroughly, claiming not everything could be explained by phone. Most meetings began with at least one spouse being present. However, they eventually began meeting without their spouses' knowledge. Secrecy sealed their relationship.

Their talks became more frequent and gradually more personal. They bonded closer and closer because neither criticized nor showed disapproval of the other's ideas. They worked at making each other feel understood and discovered more and more topics where they agreed. Gradually they shared intimate details about their marital relationships, primarily negative concerns. By now they were emotionally hooked.

The newness of knowing another on a deeper level proved intimately exciting, and then they touched. It may have just been the hands, but the electrical, sexual charge moved their thoughts to more. Neither admitted they wanted to sleep together, but now they thought about it-- and often. Even when they made love with their spouses, their thoughts focused on the other person.

Then they kissed. The next time they caressed passionately, and it ended with intercourse. They swore it wouldn't happen again, but inside their thoughts, they knew they couldn't wait to be together again and again. They were bonded emotionally and sexually.

Along the way, their brains rewired. They were addicted to how exciting and alive they felt while with the other person. Without knowing the excited feeling was a hormone firing inside their heads, they created the positive feelings to the person. They called it love.

Human brains are wired to want to spend time with anyone who provides us pleasurable and exciting moments, and we tend to define the feelings that are created during these moments as love. Both parties in an affair seem possessed and lose all rational perspective on life. The feeling of love produces one of the strongest, most important emotions that humans have, and we will do practically anything to obtain it and then to keep it – even if it is sinful and no matter the cost. This is especially true of those who do not understand the Lord's love.

The feeling of love produces one of the strongest, most important emotions that humans have, and we will do practically anything to obtain it and then to keep it – even if it is sinful

Adulterers choose the sinful way because they fail to grasp God's love and how deeply He yearns for a one-on-one, intimate, bonded relationship with them. Satan has controlled their thinking until they have lost connection with the only genuine, trustworthy source of love. They also ignored that cross-gender relationships that exclude the spouse, without exception, are a setup for serious problems. They never work. These relationships allow people to cross the moral boundary without thinking about it.

cross-gender relationships that exclude the spouse, without exception, are a setup for serious problems

When did the relationship become adulterous? Jesus says it was wrong the moment he found her company so pleasurable he wanted to see her again because he enjoyed how they supported the same ideas. He ignored his clear desire to be with her by convincing himself he needed to ask her a question, or he had something he should explain. But his wanting time with her revealed the attraction that Satan put in his heart. The strong desire to talk each time they were in the same room moved them closer to the bedroom. Their talking let them continue seeking each other's company, and it required them to ignore the crossing of the moral ledge from being truthful to now lying. For some, part of the passion is the lying and feeling they have something forbidden. Regardless, an affair always requires compromising one's morals.

DETACHING FROM THE SPOUSE. Each conversation bonded the illicit couple tighter to each other and detached them from their mates. The more they shared with each other, the less they communed with their spouses. They no longer needed their spouses' feedback about their ideas, because they depended on another for emotional support of matters most important to them and now for sexual satisfaction.

While with the illicit partner, they mentally escaped daily concerns like overdue credit card bills, kids vomiting all night, or weeds overtaking the yard. Their time together centered on things enjoyable. Eventually, they believed they had more in common with each other than with their marital partners, and they did, because they stopped sharing the more important matters with their spouses. The spouse was used only for arguing about the daily unpleasant issues that every marriage faces. The affair let them escape the realities of daily living, and allowed them to live briefly in a problem-free fantasy world. The more they thought about the other, the more addicted to such feelings they became and the more they credited the other woman for how good they felt.

The adulterous couple ignored how strongly the Lord disapproved of their behaviors. Yet, God considered adultery such a severe sin, that He made it punishable by death. *"If a man is found sleeping with another man's wife, both the man who slept with her and the woman must die. You must purge the evil from Israel"* (Dt. 22:22). God didn't want tolerance of such sin because of the influence it has on others. He knew the devastating effect such sin had on the spouse, the children, and the larger community (today's church). He provided protection from such relational heartbreaks.

Paul includes those who are sexually immoral among the list of ones who, without confession and repentance, will not be allowed to enter the kingdom of heaven. He cautions believers not to deceive themselves by thinking God ignores their sins (I Co. 6:9-10).

PORNOGRAPHY & LUST

The September 2017 American Family Association Journal report by Luke Gibbons reveals that 68% of churchgoing men view pornography on a regular basis. A Barna Research study reports that 27% of people ages 25-30 admit to having viewed porn before reaching puberty. The youngest boy treated for sexual addiction was 12 years of age, and girls as young as five have admitted to watching sexually stimulating pictures. If you guessed that more Christian men looked at porn this month than read their Bibles, these reports find you would be accurate.

Adultery isn't just the outward, physical act. Jesus said it included thinking inside one's private thoughts about sex with another. Both the physical act and sinful thoughts of sex with another may affect people differently, but it remains sinfully offensive to the holiness of God. Jesus said, *"I tell you that anyone who looks at a woman lustfully has already committed adultery with her in his heart"* (Mt. 5:28). Fantasizing of having sex with another woman too often leads to the sexual act with her and to ignoring the spouse.

Some men daydream of a woman they liked years before meeting their spouses. The man's musing about this woman lets him escape being close to his wife. In his fantasies, he believes the other woman would satisfy all his desires, and he uses her to avoid creating intimacy at home. Satan traps him into believing he married the wrong person, and he spends hours lustfully thinking about the one that got away. The more he fantasizes, the more he masturbates, and the less he prays and reads his Bible. Soon he has less of a relationship with the Lord than he does with his wife.

As Jesus said in Matthew (5:28) both parties do not have to be present or involved for adultery to occur. Some men visit prostitutes, or view videos of them dancing, or watch them having sex with others. Many lust by masturbating as they watch people on pornography websites, many of whom they never meet. Or with a stranger they frequently chat with on Facebook and have yet to meet, but will likely arrange to do so – secretly. The availability of the internet makes porn available to everyone and everywhere.

Hiding behind a computer screen, he can act out any fantasy he wants. He can become any type person he wishes to project, and he can make his partner do and be anything he desires. The intimate details he creates super-charge the sexual chemistry involved and add to his excitement, and it matters not if what he says is true or a lie. If he quickly switches off the computer when his wife or child walks in the room, he has sealed his fate with secrecy. He has set in motion an affair with a woman he may or may never meet. It doesn't matter. He remains hooked. His heart has hardened. He no longer feels guilt. All he thinks about is satisfying his addiction.

As Cooper, Delmonico, and Burg report in the Journal of Sexual Addiction and Compulsivity, those viewing sexual activity on the internet accelerate rapidly from 'at risk' to 'addicted' and crave the high just as a heroin user does. They reach the point where just sitting down at a computer that is turned off gives them a sexual urge to want more.

Watching pornography or sexual fantasizing about another is a progressive sin that becomes addictive that is accompanied with pleasurable masturbation. If Satan made it painful, it would only occur one time, but Satan's too smart to do that. While watching porn, the powerful neurotransmitters released in the brain bond him to the sexual images, whether real or inside his thoughts, and his hormones fire automatically with each viewing. The more he watches, the faster his hormones fire and the quicker he becomes dependent. Eventually, porn becomes an addiction that he craves continually. As he increases his viewing to feel satisfied, his heart hardens, and he finds excuses to avoid admitting it is wrong. The more images he watches, the faster he loses all desire to have intercourse. He lives preoccupied with masturbation.

Lustful fantasizing is sinful. According to Paul, one's thoughts are where ideas of sin fight for control. He tells us to *"take captive every thought to make it obedient to Christ"* (2 Co.10:5). When Satan attacks with enticing thoughts of an illicit partner, the adulterer needs God's help for only the Lord controls Satan. He needs to pray the minute a sinful thought strikes his consciousness.

When a man dwells on lustful ideas of being with another woman, he forgets that God *"judges the thoughts and attitudes of the heart. Nothing in all creation is hidden from God's sight"* (Heb. 4:12-13). Adultery begins in the heart and mind. He must stop such thoughts, however pleasurable they seem.

IMPACT ON WIFE. The man addicted to porn loses all desires for sex with her. Porn is sinful because the woman in his thoughts isn't the wife, but another. If pornography viewing continues long enough, he reaches the point where he can no longer have intercourse with a woman, not with any woman.

If pornography viewing continues long enough, he reaches the point where he can no longer have intercourse with a woman, not with any woman

He no longer thinks about satisfying his wife's sexual desires. Satan snares him, and he can no longer obey God's commandments about sex between married partners (1 Co. 7:3-5). His body no longer belongs to his wife but to his lustful images. He simply cannot function the way God intended a man to be with his wife. Many porn addicts break faith with their wives by divorcing them, (Mal. 2:15), because they rarely agree to their needed therapy. They lose all desire to change as their hearts harden like stone. Others feel too ashamed to admit their sin and seek help.

This week, a minister, in a neighboring town where I lived for years, pled guilty to watching child pornography. Over the years, he served three different congregations in the area, and once his sin hit the newspaper and television, the destructive fallout was shocking. Appalling because as Christians we put on blinders. We hide from the truth of our fallen world and how strongly Satan desires to turn believers' hearts away from the Lord. Yet Jesus stands saying, *"Let him with eyes see, and him with ears hear."*

These people need our help, first condemning what they do, and then loving them so much they want to change and return to the Lord. But before that can happen, we have to make it okay to admit such sin and overcome their fear of asking for help. The immoral man operates with a strong, realistic fear because most people would condemn him and not think of helping him. If this preacher told his elders he watched child porn, he would be immediately fired, and how would he then feed his family or find other employment?

How about you? Would you carry him on a mat, tear open a roof, and carefully lower him down for Jesus' healing? If not, who else would help him return to the Lord? As a minister-counselor, you may be his last hope for help and change.

For a book on this subject, written by a pornography addict who changed, read Mark R. Laaser's book, *Healing the Wound of Sexual Addiction*. In it, Dr. Laaser mentions Golden Valley Health Center in Minnesota that specializes in helping people with sexual addictions. I have heard Dr. Laaser speak about the painful battle both he and his wife encountered as they worked to save their marriage. They faced a seriously painful, but successful, trial.

A DVD series, called Conquer Series, has proven success in working with groups of porn addicted men. When men first join these groups they think they cannot change because they believe the craving is embedded in their souls. But going through the series, as God unleashes His power in their lives, they acquire a flame of hope that shows they can change. It is available for purchase from www.conquerseries.com.

A counseling program that takes a Biblical approach for curing porn addiction that offers both residential and at home counseling is Pure Life Ministries.org. They also provide at home counseling for the wives. The goal always remains restoration, not unnecessary humiliation.

SATAN'S CONTROL. Without the Lord, pornography proves more powerful than many can resist. They fuel the passionate desires inside their thoughts until they become an unquenchable fire. They need God's help to stop Satan's attacks and be filled with the Holy Spirit so their minds stop playing enticing ideas of an illicit partner. Only by living by the Spirit can they stop sinful desires (Gal. 5:16). No man controls Satan on his own.

SEXUAL REJECTION

The steps involved in confronting an adulterer are also applicable for couples where one spouse refuses to have sex with their mate. Like the adulterer and the lustful fantasizer, the rejecting partner sins against the spouse and against God. The marriage covenant implies that sex is expected. When God created Adam and Eve, He explicitly told them to share sexually.

Spouses who withhold sex from their mate disobey the Lord, and to disobey the Lord is to be immoral, no matter how strongly they may argue otherwise. Paul explained that God values peaceful marriages more than remaining in a relationship where one spouse rebels, creates on-going disagreements, and refuses to follow the Lord's commands (1

Co. 7:15). Only true believers see reason to obey. Immoral partners do not.

Counseling these couples requires the same recovery process as working with a marriage overwhelmed with adultery. Both marriages suffer from a sin issue and a lack of intimacy. If a marital partner rejects sex with the spouse in order to punish the partner, the one refusing intimacy is attempting to set the rules for marriage rather than obeying God's commands. If it's because there's an illicit partner being substituted as the sex partner, that partner is guilty of sexual adultery.

God's word is straightforward about His expectations for sex between married couples. Scripture says sex is mandatory, and to withhold what God requires is sinful rebellion. To marry implies that sex is an obligation or due benevolence. The wife and husband are to meet the sexual needs of each other in order to protect the mate from Satan's temptation of an illicit person.

God provides only one acceptable reason for saying no to a spouse who desires sex and that is so both parties can pray. Even then, Scripture says the stoppage requires mutual consent, and it must remain a temporary delay (1 Co. 7:3-5). Never are the excuses, "I don't feel like it", or "She's/he's not being nice to me today," or "I'd rather watch videos and masturbate," acceptable with the Lord.

Certainly, if the partner is ill or they have a child dying, the spouse may be unable to be emotionally and sexually available, and both could share in prayer for the one who's ill. But to move permanently to another bedroom and lock the door, or announce, "*We're never having sex again*," or to use a substitute for sexual satisfaction is sinfully wrong. To say, "I'm very tired but will make it up to you if we can wait until morning" is usually agreeable to both, provided the one requesting the delay keeps her word. Believing men and women who love the Lord learn to work with their minds and bodies to obey God so there is no reason to sin in the sexual area of their relationship.

Rejection of marital sex is simply the reverse of adultery or the other side of the same sinful coin, and should be handled as such. Sexual rebuff reveals a relationship plagued with sin, and many times, this rejection creates more pain and frustration for the dismissed partner than sexual adultery does.

This sin should be addressed as explained in the following chapters to determine if there's a possibility of salvaging the marriage, or to learn if the rejecting partner's heart is so hardened, there's no possibility of change. If it's determined that change is possible, the couple needs to experience the process of developing intimacy and resolving problems plaguing the relationship (Chapters 10-12). If the rejecting partner still denies the spouse sexual satisfaction, the way to address such sin is the same as the sections on confronting an adulterer who refuses to change (Chapters 13-15).

God put the sexual drive in His creation, and it's an action that's intended to demonstrate love. Regardless of how people disobediently act out their sex drive, expect to hear all types of excuses to justify sinful actions. Most guilty parties blame their behavior on their mates, as if they have no other choice. But they need to remember no excuse makes disobeying God's command right.

OTHER ADULTERIES

I would be remiss to ignore that God speaks of other types of adultery, especially spiritual adultery. I think it is why Paul says if an unbeliever wants to leave that you are to let him and you are no longer bound. I counseled, one woman who fought constantly with her husband over her attending worship. He resented her involvement with other Christians, called her vulgar names, and made fun of her beliefs in public. Then one day when she returned home from worship, he punched her. She left him and filed for divorce. She tolerated things until she feared physical harm. Her husband left her emotionally, physically, and intellectually the day she accepted Jesus as her Lord and decided to put Him before all others.

Paul says that God values peace more than living in a marriage where one cannot focus on the Lord. If the Christian cannot serve the Lord because of constant marital conflict it is better that the believer leave and devote their all to the Lord (1 Cor. 7:15).

Your goal must be to shift your counselees' focus to the Lord's requirements. If they obey the Lord, their marriage relationships will automatically become important enough to try and save.

Chapter 4

INSIST HE STOPS THE AFFAIR

"*My wife is always on my case. I never do anything right. Then when I want to be loving, she rejects me, saying she doesn't feel close to me. I hear nothing but a long string of no's, and I'm tired of it. The other woman makes me feel loved. I just want to be wanted, and I'm not wanted at home.*" This is a typical remark a counselor will hear from one trapped in adultery.

As this man's counselor, you have to focus on his relationship with the Lord first and foremost. A man cannot develop intimacy with his wife while trying to remain true to two women or thinking he prefers the adulteress. You, as his counselor, face someone with a huge spiritual deficit. He needs you to kindly, but sternly, force him to address his eternal fate. If you don't, who will?

During your first counseling sessions, when the person admits to an adulterous relationship or an unacceptable attraction, focus exclusively on the person's sins, causes, and how he must change. Tell him that you expect him to end the affair, but continue focusing on his relationship with the Lord. Initially, the adulterer needs to view his options, not as saving the marriage or divorcing, but as spending eternity in heaven or hell. As Jesus said, he cannot serve two masters.

Initially, the adulterer needs to view his options, not as saving the marriage or divorcing, but as spending eternity in heaven or hell

Adulterers have lost sight of the Lord and need to hear the ultimate consequences of their sin and hear them said with kind, but stern, words that show genuine love for their souls. They must know all sexual ideas outside of marriage are wrong, and they need to hear it from someone they respect enough to see for counseling, and right now that's you. He has to make a choice: yield to the Lord and let Him weave his marriage together so he goes to heaven, or allow his heart to harden, resulting in him and his lover being eternally destroyed. As Solomon warned, *"So is he who sleeps with another man's wife; no one who touches her will go unpunished"* (Pr. 6:29).

FOCUS ON RESTORING HIM WITH THE LORD

Whether you see this man once or several times, your goal must always be to save his soul. If he fully and completely repents and lives for the Lord, saving his marriage will become his goal, and he will plead for his wife's forgiveness.

A marriage that's falling apart is simply a symptom of what's happening inside the heart of one or both parties. You can prove this by asking, *"How often do you currently pray for your marriage? How often do you pray for your mate -- and with your mate? How often do you study your Bible? How often do you have family Bible study?"* Sadly, too often the answer is, *"Rarely (or never), but I know I should."* Intellectually, Christians know that without God's help, they cannot control Satan's attacks.

DICUSS HOW HE DRIFTED AWAY. Few men deliberately plan to drift away from the Lord and from their spouses. They just allow worldly concerns to take priority. Many become so involved in advancing in their careers or mastering a sport (usually men), or even Christian work of helping others, or putting their children before their mates (some men but more often women), that they lose sight of how estranged their relationship with the Lord and with their mates has become.

Ask when and how he remembers first wandering from the Lord. Expect him not to know exactly. But press to see how long he has been drifting and pretending to love the Lord, instead of genuinely worshipping Him. Expect to hear excuses and rationalizations.

Some attempt to justify the activities that contributed to their estrangement. He may say, *"But this is how I work for the Lord, by being a good example at work."* If the adulteress is a woman, she may claim, *"I bake for the sick or keep other's children when needed."* Unfortunately, that ignores what's required to keep a personal, one-on-one relationship with God. Many have allowed religious and/or physical work to become more important than an intimate one-on-one relationship with God. They gave no thought to this being one way Satan sneaked inside their hearts. So when Satan arrived in full force, they remained easy prey. Ensure he sees how he substituted activities for closeness with the Lord.

Many allowed religious and/or physical work to become more important than an intimate one-on-one relationship with the Lord

You need to know how far he has drifted away from the Lord so ask about his involvement in other sinful activities. Ask if he watches porn, buys girly magazines, shares dirty jokes, gets drunk, uses drugs, etc. You need to know what sins he must address.

SATAN'S POWERFUL INFLUENCE. Explain that he, like many others, gave no thought to how powerfully Satan influenced his thoughts. Show how he has allowed Satan to help him find fault in his marriage rather than seeing his blessings. He will likely disagree, but try to help him realize that the adulteress is from Satan, and Satan has used her to pull him away from the Lord. Satan has assured him this new illicit person can and will satisfy his need for love, affection, and intimacy. Satan has him believing that he deserves this relationship and with this forbidden person.

Satan didn't care about his marriage succeeding or failing. That was not Satan's goal. Satan discovered that a lack of intimacy in his marriage was this man's weak area, and used it to separate him from the Lord. Satan wants everyone to abandon the Lord because of how deeply it pains God.

Adulterers have underestimated Satan's power and how difficult it is to remove his evil ideas once he has buried them in their hearts and thoughts. Rarely have they questioned their spiritual vulnerability. Instead, they want to spend your entire counseling session, describing how they no longer feel close to their mate, how their sex life is practically nil, and how they argue about the most trivial of issues. At this stage, about all these men discuss with their wives are their children, and even they often serve as another battleground.

Ask him to explain sin and how he thinks Satan operates in our lives. Help him complete and/or correct his understanding. Help him realize that adultery proves he is controlled by his sinful nature, not the Holy Spirit.

Sin is a lack of relationship with the Lord and trying to control our lives instead of depending on God. Sin becomes a gradual degenerative process where Satan convinces the adulterer that he is evil and contemptable – but has a valid reason. If he believes Satan, what difference does it make how he behaves? While he may not admit it, he likely thinks others do not like him and that many take advantage of him. Yet he desperately wants to be liked and loved. He has convinced himself that his affair fills this void.

Sin is a lack of relationship with the Lord and trying to control our lives instead of depending on God

Satan wared inside his thoughts and convinced him that he was no longer worthy of God's grace. In response to this negative idea, he turned to another and attempted to satisfy his craving to prove himself desirable. But it can't fully satisfy when his proof is a substituted, illicit sex partner. Even with the illicit partner he does not share what he really thinks or how he honestly feels about things. The use of sex distracts from his empty loneliness. Soon he feels so resentful and angry because of how cheated he thinks his life has been that he practically hate God. Who else can he blame besides the spouse and the Lord? And when this happens, Satan has won.

Adulterers must find a way to reconnect with God who loves them beyond any other. But attending church often increases their shame and leaves them more frustrated. So many run away from the Lord and religion altogether. Yet, they want to hold enough of a connection that the Lord won't ultimately punish them in hell. Although few listen at this stage, he needs reminding what John (1 Jn. 2:15-17) says: *"Do not love the world or anything in the world. If anyone loves the world, the love of the Father is not in him. For everything in the world – the cravings of sinful man, the lust of the eye and the boasting of what he has and does – comes not from the Father but from the world. The world and its desires pass away, but the man who does the will of God lives forever."*

Adulterers have to address their individual spiritual issues before the marriage can be saved. That's not to deny there are weaknesses in the marriage and many problems are contributed by the mate. But during the first few counseling sessions, it's the adulterer who needs immediate change. He must be challenged to understand God's love and to continually do what's right.

However, the adulterer may not be ready to change. Instead, he attempts to convince himself that God put this person in his life so he would be happy. At this point, he values pleasure more than obedience. People trapped in adultery often rewrite their history and forget the love they once shared with their spouses. They claim they have never before felt so loved. They feel justified in their current detachment from their wives and can offer a long list of reasons why their marriages are finished. So today, their cry is not for help but to announce they can never be happy with their spouses. They come seeking your help or approval to leave their mates.

His heart has hardened against his spouse and their marriage. And while he won't like admitting it, his heart first deadened against the Lord. As Jesus explained, Moses granted divorces because their hearts were hard (Mt. 19:8). But it should be noted that Moses did not command the couple to divorce. He only permitted it. Many could have saved their marriages, just as this man, hopefully, can too.

WHY THE ADULTERESS SEEMS SO ATTRACTIVE

When an unfaithful husband comes alone to see you, then you can expect your first session to be a continuous stream of problems in the marriage that seem impossible to correct. Likely, he will want to tell you about his wife's every failure and their many disagreements. However, the problem is that he has expected his spouse to satisfy needs that only God can provide. He wanted his wife to fulfill his deep longings to feel significant, affirmed, desirable, and wanted, but only God fully completes these needs. Then when the wife failed, he felt rejected and often created reasons for them to argue. Instead of addressing the marriage's weaknesses that leave him feeling empty, he sought approval in other people and places.

He may never have shared his feelings completely with anyone before meeting the adulteress. Perhaps his early childhood was formed in a family where true feelings were ignored, laughed at, or shamed. He married desperately wanting to be wanted and craves more than a shallow marriage. The adulteress offers him a semblance of acceptance and understanding, something he tries to convince himself never existed with his wife.

Perhaps, the affair partner is an exact opposite of the spouse. If the spouse is steady and stable, she may seem boring at times, while the illicit partner may act exciting and daring. Or the marital partner may be demanding and the adulteress be timid and needy. The affair lets the adulterer act out another side of himself, a side he likes but has missed. Satan tricked him into thinking the adulteress provided relationship qualities that he needed and were unavailable in his marriage.

At home, he expects and looks for continued disappointments and regular arguments. He focuses only on the negative situations that every marriage faces, while describing the affair as stimulating and rewarding. This has allowed him to ignore how shallow his adulterous relationship actually is and how few demands it makes of him. He has ignored that his hidden relationship doesn't have time or place to develop genuine depth. So for him, the affair feels safe and comfortable, an exact opposite of how he describes his marriage.

INSIST THAT HE RETURN TO THE LORD

The way to salvage his marital relationship is to convince him to turn to the Lord, allow God to soften his heart, and then plead for his wife to forgive him. However, at this stage, he may not care that his wife hurts, what the church thinks, or about his own spiritual life, not if it costs him the new lover. He is addicted to his new and exciting emotions that he has when he is with the adulteress, but he fails to see that such feelings are proof that Satan controls him.

He has forgotten that the reason Satan was kicked out of heaven was because he thought he knew more than God. Satan stood judging God, believing his ideas could replace the Lord. To his eternal destruction, he ignored that the Lord always has the ultimate victory. This adulterer's heart shows that Satan is using him to continue challenging God.

This man may have come for counseling to pacify his parent, or sister, or to keep his best friend off his back. Or occasionally the illicit woman will insist that he go for counseling so they know they have done all they could to save their marriages. But at this point, she doesn't want it saved any more than he does.

He needs to hear you say that in his current condition he is hell-bound. He knows it, but he keeps the truth pushed to the deepest crevices of his mind.

REQUIRE HIM TO END THE AFFAIR

To be right with the Lord and with his wife, he must sever all ties with the other woman and agree to give every lustful thought to the Lord. The minute he thinks of the other woman, he must immediately stop, confess his sinful thoughts, seek God's forgiveness, and ask Him to replace such thoughts with wholesome, moral ones. He must ask the Lord to help him flee youthful lusts, just as Paul explained to Timothy (2 Ti. 2:22).

DESCRIBE HIS THOUGHTS AS SINFUL. To do this, he must view each thought about another woman as sinful, which is why you first talked with him about every sexual thought and activity outside of marriage being wrong. Explain that James says when anyone is tempted, it is his own sinful desires luring him into doing wrong (1:14). Paul says he must *'put off'* such fleshly thoughts and be renewed in how he thinks (Eph. 4:22- 23). He needs to realize that controlling his thoughts is a commandment, and only the Lord can help him do this. This is necessary because without immediate prayer, each thought of the other person sears his conscience more, until his sin no longer bothers him, and he loves the sin. Then his heart hardens permanently, and he lives eternally lost.

Consider having him read what Joseph did when tempted by Potiphar's wife (Gen. 39:7-12), and how God blessed Joseph for acting strong. Remind him that because Joseph did what was right, that God saw him as a good person and showered him with blessings. Explain that God will see him as good when he, too, does what's right even if he doesn't feel like it. This man needs to believe that God cares about him, loves him deeply, and asks so little of him in return. But now he has to change.

CHANGING HIS BEHAVIOR, CHANGES THOUGHTS
Explain to him how controlling and changing his behaviors will change how he feels about the adulteress, what he thinks about himself, his spouse, and the Lord. If he stops all contact with the adulteress and treats his wife as he does the illicit woman, he will again love his wife.

EXAMPLE: Ask if he ever got up at 2:00 a.m. to feed his infant son. Did he want to get out of bed? Was he sleepy and hated hearing the baby cry? Did he hesitate in hope the child would go back to sleep? Did it take a few minutes to force himself to go warm the bottle of milk? But once he fed the baby and was changing the diaper, and his son looked at him with a huge smile, how did he feel? Was he glad he had gotten up? Looking at that tiny child, he felt good because he did what's right as a father. When we do what's right, we feel good. We tell ourselves we did good. We tell ourselves we are good. And we know God sees us as having done good too. To do what's right, always tends to demand that we choose to do what's harder.

To do what's right, always tends to demand that we choose to do what's harder

Tell him that he was good to respond as the child needed. Insist that God finds him a good man for doing what's right and for facing the challenging task of putting the child's need above the easier option of going back to sleep and letting him cry. And once this man ends his affair, which right now will prove harder than running from God and his family, he will again feel good about himself, his wife, their relationship, and his relationship with the Lord.

Once he stops seeing and thinking of the other woman, his emotions will change. When he stops his sinful actions, his feelings for the adulteress change too. Ending the affair will be difficult because he has become emotionally addicted to her, but he doesn't love her. He doesn't know her well enough to love her. He only knows her in secret, hidden, sinful moments.

Intellectually and emotionally, he needs to accept how God loves him even though he has committed a horrible sin. Remind him that while all are still sinners, God loved us enough that He sacrificed His only Son. And Jesus loved us enough to die for us. God's love is neither deserved nor earned.

It's freely given. Just as when he crawled from a warm bed to feed his hungry child, he didn't leave his bed because he expected something in return. Feeding his child was a pure, unselfish gift of love. At that moment, he loved his son as God loves him. Open the Bible and let him read aloud Scriptures that prove God's love. Show how we cannot earn it. He likely knows all of these, but hasn't read them in a long time.

After you have explored his spiritual condition as deeply as it seems possible, it's time to demand that he end the affair. Your insisting that he end the sinful relationship is where you have been headed with every meeting. You just needed to gain his trust before asking this of him.

INSIST HE END THE AFFAIR

Ask him to use your phone to call the adulteress and tell her they will never talk or see each other again. Promise you will help move his emotional and sexual desires onto his wife.

Give him a note to read so he cannot add more comments or give the adulteress time to respond. If his call turns into a discussion, he will be hooked emotionally and unable to tell her they are finished. His comments must be brief, to the point, and say only what's necessary. He should say:

> **Our adulterous relationship is over, and we will never again meet or talk**
> **I love my wife, and with my minister's help, I am going to tell her everything**
> **Don't ever contact me or my family**

GIVE HIM HOMEWORK

If he phones the adulteress and ends their affair, make an appointment for him to return with his wife to tell her about the affair and assign him Scriptures to read. Insist that he must dig into God's Word so his thoughts and attitude are challenged (Heb. 4:12). Scriptures remain the only place he will find strength to stop seeing and thinking about the illicit woman. Give him Scriptures to read that are based them on things he shared with you, and ideas that he needs God's word to challenge. Remind him to pray immediately with every thought of the other woman, so God controls his thinking.

As Solomon told his son, planting the seeds of Scripture into his thoughts helps him avoid temptations, *"My son, keep my words and store up my commands within you. Keep my commands and you will live, guard my teachings as the apple of your eye. Bind them on your fingers, write them on the table of your heart. . . they will keep you from the adulteress, from the wayward wife with her seductive words"* (Pr. 7:1-5).

He may value from reading the following Scriptures about adultery that show God's stand on sin and the consequences for those involved. Genesis 20:6-18; Leviticus 19: 20-22; 20:10; Deuteronomy 21:10-15; 22:13-30; Job 24-15; 31:9-12; Proverbs 5:3-23; Matthew 5:27-28; John 8:1-11; Romans 2:22; 7:3; 1 Corinthians 6:9; 7:1-6; Galatians 5:19; Hebrews 13:4; James 2:10-12; 2 Peter 2:14; Revelation 2:22.

In addition, he needs to study descriptions about hell and realize that a few sneaky sexual encounters are not worth a tormented eternity. Remind him that if he stays in the current extramarital relationship that torment is all that awaits him. As James explained, desire gives birth to sin and sin to death (Jas.1:15). He also needs an in-depth study of God's forgiveness and care for those who repent. Suggest other Scriptures that seem appropriate based on his comments.

At first, he may feel like a phony, because in his heart, he still isn't sure he has a relationship with the Lord. But ask him to fake it until he believes it. God will take care of the rest.

If he agrees never to see the adulteress again and return to his wife, skip to Chapter 7. This chapter explains what he must do next and details how you can prepare him and his wife for what they face.

IF HE REFUSES, HIS WIFE IS THE ANSWER

If he refuses to make the call, tell him that he cannot keep his affair a secret. God tells us to expose sin, and because you strive to live by God's word you must insist that he tells his wife. Your goal is to have him tell her so you can begin working with her to save their relationship.

If he refuses to phone the adulteress, it's an admission that his heart has begun to harden, and he appears to be beyond this initial level of help. He requires a stronger, sterner approach. Explain that you cannot help him keep his sin a secret. His wife must be told and by him before another tells her. Either he agrees to bring her or tell him you have to phone her and insist on seeing them together. Explain how it's much easier for her to learn from him and in your presence because your attendance keeps their emotions under better control

You may need to phone the wife and say you need to see her and her husband together – but <u>do not</u> say why. If she comes alone, send her home immediately, saying you must see them together, as her husband has something to share with her. You can be sure, she will either guess what it is or question him until he admits his affair.

If he refuses to end the affair or study God's word after your counsel, his wife remains the only hope of saving the marriage. But doing so requires her to take a strong position with him that, at first, she may not like. Your role now switches to helping her apply Biblical force to try and have him change.

She must love him and herself enough to ensure they both go to heaven, but it won't happen if she caves and accepts his straying as her fault or if she allows him to trample on her as she sits hoping his illicit relationship will just burn out by itself.

The wife must love him enough to confront him, demand that he stop his sinful ways, and refuse to accept any decision that fails to honor the Lord and her. According to Ezekiel, the wife needs to confront his sinful behavior. *"When I say to the wicked man, 'You will surely die, and **you do not warn him or***

speak out to dissuade him from his evil ways in order to save his life*, that wicked man will die for his sin, and **I will hold you accountable** for his blood. But if you do warn the wicked man and he does not turn from his wickedness or from his evil ways, he will die for his sin; but you will have saved yourself"* (3:18-19; 33:8-9; my emphasis).

YOU AS HER COUNSELOR. At this point, his wife has the best chance of saving the marriage and of him (and her) going to heaven. This requires you, as her counselor, to press her to act in ways that may cause her extreme discomfort. Serving and loving her husband as the Lord requires means confronting him, no matter her risks. She needs a lot of support from you to do this.

During your work with this couple, you will often feel you are riding an emotional roller coaster. Frequently, you will take three steps forward and two back. The only way to remain strong is to remember you still gained that one small step, and it was in the right direction. So keep pressing.

Chapter 5

INITIAL MEETING WITH THE WIFE

"*It's time for you take a stand and refuse mistreatment. You must set some boundaries, refuse to bend, and stop allowing him to manipulate and abuse you.*" These are difficult, but necessary, words that you as her counselor minister must say to a betrayed wife. Otherwise, her adulterous husband finds no reason to change. When she acts strong and determined, he has no choice but to alter the ways he interacts with her. Once she changes, the old pattern of tactics he uses to influence or gain control no longer work. He will be forced to make big readjustments

Your first meeting with the wife of an adulterous husband may come because he has agreed to stop his affair and wants your help to tell her before she learns through gossip. Or it may be that the wife knows about his affair because he flaunts it in her presence, and she still wants to save her marriage. Such was my call from Sally as described below. Regardless of what prompted this visit, your goal is to help her accept that she must behave differently. She has to refuse such treatment, and likely, she needs to stop believing any bad advice she may have received from others.

Sally's broken, quivering voice revealed how distraught she felt as she described, *"I need to make an appointment for marriage counseling. My husband is involved with another woman."*. But the day before her scheduled appointment, she cancelled. Two weeks later Sally again phoned. This time, she was crying hysterically, *"My husband is moving his girlfriend in with us, and he says I am to cook and do laundry for the other woman too. What am I doing wrong?"* She also cancelled this appointment, and I never heard from her again.

Sally's husband pushed her close to her breaking point, but each time she caved. It was easier to do as he demanded rather than stand up to him and face the consequences such actions would elicit. Likely, she convinced herself that she had no place to go, no one to help her escape, and it was easier to stay and be trampled, used, and abused. She put her life in her husband's hands rather than the Lord's. She had made her husband her idol, and earthly idols always disappoint.

Accepting such disrespect, shows that women like Sally will never have hope of a Christian marriage until they change.

To the type of man she finds attractive, she represents no more than a weak doormat, and he feels comfortable wiping his dirty feet on her. Even if Sally's husband tires of his new lover, he will not love Sally.

Men who are in typical marriages find this type woman and her tolerance of such abuse almost unbelievable, but it's how many who have no support, no job, and no education often choose to respond. I have watched these women linger in pain for years. In fact, I know a man who told his wife he was homosexual, and she continued to live with him and his male partner. Rather than leave, she chose to cook and clean for both men. Like Sally, this woman chose what she thought was the easier way to cope.

I firmly believe that few men love weak pushovers who accept their cruel treatment. Likely, her acceptance of such abuse contributes to his thinking he needs someone stronger, and her passivity makes it easy. Even if such a husband ends his adulterous relationship it does nothing to have him love a wife he doesn't respect. Few men love the women they abuse. They love the power they have over them. They ignore that the desire to have control is a trick Satan uses, the same one that will cost him heaven.

Few men love the women they abuse
They love the power they have over them

If you are required to counsel a woman like Sally, you need to help her realize that she doesn't have to take such abuse. Help her create options, such as seeking a restraining order, turning to supportive friends, finding a job, and showing how she can trust the Lord and know He cares and loves her.

REFUSE TO LET HER BLAME HERSELF.

Regardless of why the wife comes to you, your initial meeting must refuse to allow her to blame herself for his behavior. You must insist that it was his decision to be unfaithful, and no matter her concerns, she must not attempt to minimize his sin.

However, many will say, *"It's my defect. I've never really liked sex."* *"When we argue, I become emotional and scream and cry, and he hates that."* *"I have always rejected his sports and refused to go with him"* *"I know how unattractive he finds my weight, and I procrastinate going on a diet."* Her thinking, *"It's my fault because I did this wrong thing"* is a typical first reaction when a wife learns of her husband's adultery. She blames herself because she thinks she has failed her husband, and she probably has. But more importantly, his affair has her feeling second-rate as a desirable woman, and such negative thoughts drive such false thinking.

She thinks, *"If his straying is my fault, I know how to win him back"*. But even if she attempts to seduce him, refuses to show strong feelings while upset, tags along and pretends to enjoy his sports, and starves until she becomes a size two, it won't work. He gave his heart to another weeks ago. Smothering him in loving ways fails, because he no longer wants her emotional or sexual support. He uses another woman for that, and his adulteress is the one he currently prefers.

She thinks, "If his straying is my fault, I know how to win him back."

She ignores that she didn't suggest, ask, encourage, or force him to have an affair. He chose adultery instead of seeking professional help to resolve their problems. He will gladly lets her share the blame. It frees him of some guilt. Many men insist their adultery is 100% their spouse's fault.

Help her realize such comments show she clings to a marriage that no longer exists. She must accept the truth of what her relationship currently entails, not what she wishes it was like, or perhaps, as it once was. If she can excuse her husband and hold the woman entirely guilty, then she has little to forgive and thinks she can move forward in marriage, but she ignores how her husband has changed. Explain to her that you can never get back to what you had. You can only let the past cost you what you could have today and tomorrow. She must focus on what she wants, not what she once enjoyed.

You can never get back what you had
You can only let the past cost you
what you could have today and tomorrow

You may need to ask several questions that challenge her, such as the ones listed below.

Is he or is he not choosing a sexual involvement with another?

You say you wouldn't do this. Why not?

So is his being with another abusing you? Your children? The Lord?

Are you saying that a man who spends time and money on an adulteress is proving he wants a good marriage?

Does he give your kids enough time that he can spare more for another woman?

What if he gives you AIDS?

If he had asked you to go with him for marriage counseling to resolve differences instead of him turning to another woman, would you have gone?

Keep testing her with more questions until she accepts that his affair was entirely his doing. While she may be at fault for 10%, 50%, or even 90% of their marital problems, he is 100% at fault for committing adultery. Refuse to allow her to accept part of the blame for his unfaithfulness.

Protesting, she may attempt to excuse him and try to believe her marriage is better than it is. She may insist, *"He isn't that bad. He's good to me most of the time. We'd be fine if that woman would leave him alone."*

Hopefully, your questions will result in her accepting the reality that he currently chooses to ignore his vows to her and to the Lord. Until she admits how his heart has changed, she won't follow God's Biblical plan for winning him back. She must remember that he could stop and repent at any point.

Truth is difficult to accept when it goes counter to what she wants to believe, what she has been telling herself. It's why Jesus told people to let those with eyes see and ears hear. It's easier to believe things are the way we want, than to accept a differing truth that challenges all we thought about something or someone, especially when the truth causes the embarrassment of admitting we have been wrong. But she must accept that he is no longer the devoted, loving husband she wants to believe.

CHALLENGE ANY BAD ADVICE SHE RECEIVED

By the time you see the wounded wife, she has usually turned to girlfriends to ask what she could do to win back her husband. Remember, the majority of women want to salvage their marriages and tend to seek friends who will support them. Too often, the guidance these women receive works for couples in committed relationships, but such counsel does nothing to have her husband change or to resolve her hurt. In fact, it often lets him feel free to leave her. As her counselor, you may have to counter the recommendations she has received. Below are a few I have heard said to women that proved bad advice when the marriage was tainted with adultery.

Although some recommend it, she does not need the directive found in Colossians (3:18) where it tells women to submit to their husbands. Instead, she needs the latter half of that verse: *"as is fitting in the Lord."* God never wants a woman to submit to another's sinful ways. When she does, he takes advantage of her by having both his lover and his wife, and he digs deeper in sin. I've known some men who demanded that their wives participate with them in multiple, sinful activities like group sex or face divorce, and the wives believed they had to submit to his demands.

Some friends may refer her to Matthew (5:39) that says to turn the other cheek when wronged, but this Scripture means not to retaliate when insulted. It doesn't mean that she ignores or accepts his sinful adultery. She can still be polite and firm while rejecting his actions.

Friends may quote her, *"Love thy neighbor as yourself"* (Mt. 19:19), but this verse doesn't mean to lovingly accept him while he lives a sinful lifestyle and is hell-bound. Instead, the Scripture obligates her to love him in ways that encourage his changing so he desires heaven as strongly as she wants it for herself. We aren't loving anyone we willingly allow to go to hell.

We aren't loving anyone

we willingly allow to go to hell

Some insist she should apply Ephesians (4:32), by being kind and forgiving just as God has forgiven her. This advice ignores that God never forgives sinners while they remain unrepentant. God doesn't pardon the sinful person until he changes, and neither should she. Agreeing with, ignoring, forgiving, or trying to act especially nice is bad advice for a marriage partner who's trapped in on-going sexual betrayal. To "just forget it and act loving" gives him permission to continue his affair.

Others may insist if she will just stop complaining (Php.2:14) and ignore him that he will tire of the other woman. She's told to just wait it out. This ignores that she would still be passively granting him permission to have a sinful affair and that God tells us to confront one trapped in sin, not ignore it.

Such unwise counsel has her believing that with time his affair will pass and things will return to normal once the adulterous relationship ends. While many affairs do run their course and end in three months to two years, it doesn't stop because the wife accepts his affair. It ends because the adulterous couple finally see the other's faults, and/or the adulteress no longer makes him feel good about himself. Some feel guilt and shame and return to be right with the Lord. Others divorce their wives and marry their lovers, but these marriages also tend to end in divorce.

The advice many offered her ignores that his heart is hardening, and to attempt to love him differently tends to push him farther away emotionally. It allows him to leave her without feeling any regret. He tells himself that no man could respect or love such a passive, wimpy nothing of a woman.

SHE TREATS HIM LIKE GOD DID

She has to confront her husband and demand that he choose either her and their children or the adulteress. She tells him that he cannot have both.

Refuse to show any sympathy for her if she continues to cling to him being a good father and husband. She needs your support for being strong, instead of a victim having pity-parties. Help her accept the reality of their relationship and how he has changed. She can't do as the Lord says by feeling sorry for herself. As Paul told Timothy, God didn't give her a spirit of timidity, but a spirit of power, love and self-discipline (2 Ti. 1:7), and now she needs to use this strength to demand that he chose between her and the adulteress because both are not an option.

If she appears prepared to face her husband and tell him he must either end his relationship with the other woman or leave her and the children, because he can no longer have both, then skip the rest of this chapter and go to the following chapter, Chapter 6.

Many women fear their husbands will choose the other woman and need the added support of knowing how God dealt with continued sin and to know God expects her to take a strong stance against sin. If she wavers and appears unable to tell him that he must choose, explain the ways God dealt with sins of the Israelites.

GOD AND IDOLATRY. God is tough, and the wife has to model Him to have any hope of her husband changing. She may need the background of how God addressed such sin and how Jesus tells her to deal with it so she knows that what you ask her to do is Biblical. She must not allow sin to rule her home. Her husband has no reason to change if she attempts to excuse or minimize his sinful behavior. She must love him enough to insist he must change, just as God loved the Israelites enough to insist they had to change.

When addressing the Israelites sins, God used the word adultery to show their spiritual unfaithfulness. The people knew that God hated physical adultery so much that both the man and woman involved were to be stoned to death to purge the community of sin. Therefore, to use the word adultery showed the depth of God's anger and rejection of spiritual betrayal. He used a physical sin to communicate a spiritual truth.

The Bible calls sexual adultery idolatry (Col. 3:5) because adultery graphically portrays the sin of idolatry. The worship of man-made idols and sexual adultery both require forgetting the Lord and putting someone or something before God. Idolaters gradually fill their hearts and thoughts with longing for the idol until they believe it satisfies their needs better than the Lord. Eventually, the idol completely replaces all thought of the Lord and His commands. It's also how a sexual adulterer removes positive thoughts of his wife.

God anguished over the Israelites turning away from Him to worship idols, and He warned that, without change, He would allow their enemies to conquer them. God sent Jeremiah to explain, *"My inheritance has become to me like a lion in the forest. She roars at me;* **therefore, I hate her***"* (Jer. 12:8). Repeatedly, Judah's sin was likened to prostitution (3:1-2), a sin for which God ultimately divorced Israel: *"***I gave faithless Israel her certificate of divorce** *and sent her away because of all her adulteries"* (3:8, my emphasis).

When the Israelites worshipped idols at Gilgal, God described their behavior as sexual immorality. *"Their deeds do not permit them to return to their God. A spirit of prostitution is in their heart; they do not acknowledge the Lord. Israel's arrogance testifies against them"* (Hos. 5:4-5). The Lord explained, *"I hated them there because of their sinful deeds.* **I will drive them out of my house. I will no longer love them***"* (9:15). Again, God likened spiritual adultery to sexual adultery.

In his article, *Using Porn as Grounds for Divorce*, Luke Gilkerson explains that God divorced Judah because of hardness of heart (Jer. 4:4), and their heart condition let them commit all types of sin without any shame (3:3). Void of guilt, they continued to rebel (3:13), and their repentance proved no more than an artificial pretense of regret (3:10).

MULTIPLE CHANCES. Scripture says God drove Israel from His house just as an unfaithful spouse may be driven from his home. When the Israelites continued to rebel with no desire to change, God withdrew His love and divorced them. But He did not do this after a single instance of spiritual adultery, although He had reason on Mt. Sinai, in the wilderness, and during the reign of evil rulers. Instead, God waited patiently for them to transform their ways, but eventually He sent Israel into exile because of her continued, calloused rebellion.

When the Israelites continued to rebel with no desire to change, God withdrew His love and divorced them

God showed an undeniable hatred of sin. Just as Scriptures described God's feelings for the guilty Israelites, so are His feelings for us today if we participate in adultery, whether it's sexual, emotional, or spiritual. During the time we remain actively sinful, He agonizes over our sin, and likely, feels hate as He did with them. But with softened hearts that produce genuine repentance, He promised the Israelites (and us) forgiveness, and to remember the sin no more (Isa. 43:25). If

God hated such sin in the past, we can feel certain He disapproves of it today, nor will He accept it in the future.

When sinful people of the past worshipped man-made objects, or heterosexual or homosexual lovers, rather than idolizing the Creator of all, *"God gave them over to their sinful desires of their hearts to sexual impurity for the degrading of their bodies with one another"* (Ro. 1:24). He released them to live as they wanted.

When a person's heart hardens and he lives with no thought of glorifying God, Paul says he *"loses all sensitivity and gives himself over to sensuality so as to indulge in every kind of impurity with a continual lust for more"* (Eph. 4:19). *"For out of the heart come evil thoughts, murder, adultery, sexual immorality, theft, false testimony, slander. These are what make a man unclean"* (Mt. 15:19-20). But first God forced the sinful man out of His house (Hos. 9:15). He loved them too much to do otherwise. When the heart became so hardened that only unrepentant and constant rebellion was left, God turned away and let His people go pursue their desires.

God turned His back on them until they reformed to live as they should. As long as they continued to sin, they no longer reaped God's loving protection. Only by changing and adhering to God's laws did they regain His care. When those doing wrong continually refused to do what was right, God cut them off completely. God repeatedly showed that withdrawing support was required for changing people's behaviors.

God repeatedly showed that withdrawing support was required for changing people's behaviors

If the wife finds her straying husband packing and leaving for his adulteress, remember that God didn't win all those He loved. He just kept moving forward with those who proved worthy of His attentive love (Ro.11:4-5) and who will be welcomed into heaven. Recall that Jesus lost one of the 12 apostles because Judas trusted Satan's lie over Jesus' truth.

DETERMINING HARDNESS OF HIS HEART

Hardness of heart is a progressive turning away from the Lord which is why God gave them multiple chances to change. When God sent them messages of what would happen with their continued sin, sometimes, people showed immediate change; other times they clung to their own desires for years before changing, and others never changed. And God demonstrated how to address each.

Jesus explained in Matthew (18:15-17) how to determine the condition of an adulterer's heart. Jesus said, *"If your brother sins against you, go, and show him his fault, just between the two of you. If he listens to you, you have won your brother over.*" This confrontation tends to help change someone whose heart is still primarily soft and responsive. *But if he will not listen take one or two others along, so that every matter may be established by the testimony of two or three witnesses.* Jesus didn't want us giving up on someone who might still repent. The person's heart may be hardening, but with the added influence of others' help, the person may change and return to the Lord. His heart condition might still be salvageable. *If he refuses to listen to them, tell it to the church; and if he refuses to listen even to the church, treat him as you would a pagan or tax collector"* (18:15-17). Just as God treated the Israelites, Jesus provided the sinner multiple opportunities to repent through encouraging persuasion by an increasing number of different people. The Lord's goal is always to salvage the person's soul and relationship.

Jesus' confrontation model applies in cases of persistent sin. Rather than adultery being treated as a firm red line drawn in the sand, where if one crossed it, he is immediately exiled forever, Jesus offers multiple opportunities for change and restoration. Jesus' design provides the sinner several opportunities to reform, just as God had offered Judah.

SHE MUST CHANGE. Winning back a straying husband requires the wife to stop being a push-over. Although she feels like curling up in a corner and crying, she must cover the soles of her shoes with gorilla glue and stand her ground. She must follow Jesus' command for addressing her husband's sin. She has to believe that Jesus knows best, no matter how she feels.

While the husband's heart may belong predominately to another, most men still possess a deep attachment to the things he shares with his wife and children. But he will only miss them if she stops being readily available. He has to respect his wife, and that requires her to change, act tough, and prove that she will no longer tolerate his seeing another. She has to give him no other option. She must respond as God did when He rejected the unfaithful Israelites. Specific actions that support such a stance are explained in the following chapter.

TELL HER TO SEE A PHYSICIAN. Her immediate task must be to see her family physician for AIDS and STD testing. Her husband will likely insist that his lover has never been with another, but why risk the word of a man who, for the past months, has been lying to her? This proves humiliating, but it is less painful than learning she is infected after it's too late.

Chapter 6

CONSEQUENCES OF HIS SIN (Mt. 18:5)

"*Consider, therefore, the kindness and sternness of God: sternness to those who fell, but kindness to you, provided that you continue in his kindness.* **Otherwise you also will be cut off**" (Ro. 11:22, my emphasis). The wounded wife needs to put this Scripture into practice. She must apply godly sternness and reserve kindness for when her husband fully repents, just as God does. She must adopt the tough love approach taught in Scripture, stand firm, and cut off her husband completely in every possible way: emotionally, sexually, intellectually, and spiritually unless he changes. She prays that he hungers for her as a newly changed woman, one who refuses to allow sin to reign in her house.

She leaves no doubt that she rejects his adultery and does this by having as little interaction with him as possible, while he continues in his willful sin. As Ephesians teaches, "**Have nothing to do with the fruitless deeds of darkness**, *but rather expose them*" (5:11; my emphasis). Help her to prepare to do as Scripture teaches in Matthew (18:15) "*If your brother sins against you, go and show him his fault, just between the two of you.*" If his heart fails to soften along the way, she must follow through on all three steps Jesus provided (15-17).

SHE MUST REVEAL HER TRUE FEELINGS. It's time for her to demonstrate how deeply she loathes his mistreatment, hates his being with another woman, resents his lying, and abhors how he thinks his sin is acceptable. It's time for her to practice step one of Jesus' redemption plan as outlined in Matthew (18:15). *"If your brother sins against you, go, and show him his fault, just between the two of you. If he listens to you, you have won your brother over."*

As the one counseling her, refuse to allow her to waver. How convincing she remains will contribute more than anything else to her husband returning to the Lord and to her. Prepare to press her as hard as you dare so she does what's required. A part of being faithful and loving one's mate is confronting the spouse when he does something sinful in hope he will change. Below are ways she takes a stand against his continued sin.

She demands that he immediately ends the affair or moves out of the house
If he refuses to do either, she recruits prayer partners to keep her strong
She shuns him:
    Moves his things from their shared bedroom
    No longer cooks, washes his clothes, or does tasks that are exclusively for him
    Refuses to talk with him or answer when he speaks
    Definitely refuses sex
    Does fun things with the kids so he can't participate
    Attends worship without him or sits in other places
Prepares for possible rude attacks

SHE DEMANDS THAT HE ENDS THE AFFAIR. Her first and most difficult task requires her to confront her husband's sinful behavior (Mt. 18:15). She must insist that he stop the affair immediately. She demands that he phones the other woman and ends the adulterous relationship – and does it now.

She needs to require him to tell the other woman four things and use words and a tone that convinces his adulteress he means it -- and do it as she stands at his side listening. He needs to say:

    Our relationship is sinful
    We are finished and will never again meet or talk
    I am telling my wife everything
    Don't ever contact me or my family

PREPARE HER BY ROLE PLAYING. Prepare her to stare him in the eyes and give him an unquestionable ultimatum: *"Telephone the adulteress right now and tell her it is over, or move out today and find another place to live. I will not live, sleep, or eat with an adulterer. It's what God teaches."* She is not kicking him out but leaving the decision to him. Ending the affair or losing his family remains his choice. *"For you to be emotionally and/or sexually involved with another woman proves you are not committed to me or our family. So the choice is yours to make: us or the adulteress. You cannot have both."*

Role play with her by pretending you are her husband and have her say to you what she must say to him. Repeat doing this several times until she convinces you that she can speak with the firmest of confidence, and her ultimatum shows she will no longer tolerate his adultery. Her husband will only miss her if she acts worthy of being missed, and no man misses a pathetic pushover. She must act and speak with a powerful, unquestionable conviction. The straying husband must believe the only option for keeping his family is to end the affair.

Write the words he needs to say to the adulteress on a note for her to take home and hold in front of him as he phones his adulteress. That way she cannot forget what he must say or let him add any additional comments that could trigger his emotional connection to the adulteress.

HAVE HER RECRUIT PRAYER PARTNERS. If her husband refuses to phone the adulteress and refuses to leave their home, it shows, that for now, the other woman comes first, but he still wants to occasionally use his wife -- on his terms. Encourage her to immediately increase the number of prayers going to heaven for their relationship. She should ask one or two people whom she sees as being devoted to God to pray for them. She asks them to tell no other and pray for her marriage. She needs prayer partners who show they care about her struggle.

Calling on others for support has her applying the Scripture that Jesus gave immediately after He explained the three steps involved for confronting a sinner to encourage his change: *"Again, I tell you that if two of you on earth agree about anything you ask for, it will be done for you by my Father in heaven. For where two or three come together in my name, there am I with them"* (Mt. 18:19-20).

NO FELLOWSHIP WITH DARKNESS (2 Co. 6:14)

Keep assuring the wife that discontinuing fellowship with her husband is Biblical. Paul, in his letter to the Corinthians, wrote, **"You must not associate with anyone who calls himself a brother but is sexually immoral**, *or greedy, an idolater, or a slander, a drunkard or a swindler.* **With such a man do not even eat**" (1Co. 5:11, my emphasis). Too many well meaning friends ignore that this command is applicable for a betrayed spouse because if both are Christians, they are brothers and sisters in Christ, as well as, husband and wife. They share a double union, and this command applies to her. If he isn't a believer, it may be the only thing that shocks him into changing.

If her husband will neither phone the adulteress to end their illicit relationship nor leave the home, she waits until he leaves the house and removes all of his things from their bedroom. She confiscates every item that identifies the bedroom as a shared space and installs a new lock on the door (and uses it). If they do not have a spare room, she can leave a pillow and blanket on the sofa and his clothes stacked neatly in a corner in a box. She removes all semblance of him from what has now become her personal, private bedroom.

However, she should not shred, destroy, or damage any of his possessions. She must do nothing wrong herself but strive to remain right with the Lord. She needs God's help now more than ever and assurance that God hears her numerous prayers each day.

If the husband should find a way to sneak his clothing back into the bedroom, then she can remove her things and sleep elsewhere. This proves to him that he cannot sleep with her while he sexually involved with another.

Effective immediately, there should be no communication between the two of them, except what is absolutely mandatory regarding the children's health. He should receive such a silent, cold shoulder that it makes him painfully uncomfortable. Hereafter, just as hell is not a pleasurable place, neither is home. She rejects him as sternly as the Lord will on judgment day unless he repents. Home becomes a place that's receptive only to repentance and change, or else it feels like a lonely, hotbed in a fiery dungeon ruled by an angry, nonverbal fire-breathing dragon.

She refuses to answer when he speaks and there should never be physical contact of any kind, and that definitely means no sex. If he attempts to touch her, she jerks away and ignores him without speaking. She treats him as if he is dead – just as he has been treating their marriage. The goal is to leave him feeling abandoned, as God will do at the end of time unless he repents.

She no longer washes his clothes, cooks his meals, or does any chores she typically did exclusively for him. She can eat with the children before he comes home and freeze any leftovers. He is now in full self-maintenance for all his desires.

She plans outings with the children, and arranges them so he cannot participate. She chooses activities the kids enjoy and when they return home, she laughs and talks with the kids about what fun they had, while ignoring him completely. She wants him to miss being a part of family fun, especially things he liked doing with the children.

If he attends worship, she and the children can leave early and go in separate cars. Or they can ride with a friend if there's only one car, or leave before he dresses and go without him. Currently. his going is hypocritical, and Jesus was most critical of hypocrites.

She may argue he needs to attend worship in hope that you, as the counseling minister, will say something to soften his heart and have him change. This argument ignores that he has been attending for weeks without it having any effect. He has pretended to love the Lord, but his heart remained absent during worship, and then later met with his lover. He mocks the Lord by attending. He isn't committed to the Lord any more than he is to his wife or his adultery would not be occurring. If he does attend, she and the children can find a new area to sit without him.

He isn't committed to the Lord any more than he is to his wife, or his adultery would not be occurring

PREPARE THE KIDS. Neither of them should move into one of children's rooms. At this stage, his adultery stays between them. If there's the possibility of his changing, the children have no reason to know everything. However, they do need some explanation or they might form worse ideas inside their thoughts. They can be told that mommy and daddy are having a problem and trying to resolve things. Meanwhile, as long as daddy is not treating mommy as God says he should, he will be sleeping in another room. If the children are very young, they would understand her saying, *"Daddy's in time-out."*

PREPARE HER FOR HIS ATTACKS

If he hasn't phoned or left, he will likely begin making defensive verbal attacks, hoping it will cause her pain, and in some way reduce his guilt. He will say things like *"I never loved you. I just felt trapped into marrying you."* Or, *"I will divorce you, take the kids, all our money, and put you out on the street."* Or, *"All my buddies told me I shouldn't marry you. Wish I had listened."* He is angry, wants to hurt back, and hopes to make what he did seem less terrible.

PRE-PLAN A RESPONSE. Help her develop an answer to his intentionally hurtful comments. It's essential that her rebuttal shows she refuses to back down, and they have no relationship as long as he refuses to phone and end the relationship with his adulterous partner.

By now, she knows his mean side well. Advance preparation helps soften the blow when it comes. Help her develop a long list of cruel things he may say to hurt her. Then help her develop a response that defends herself, no matter the hurt he intends to inflict. Doing this keeps her focused on the man she currently dislikes, instead of yearning for the man she used to enjoy loving.

EXAMPLE. When Susan's husband threatened divorce, her friend Debbie gave her a good response. Debbie said, *"Why do you care? He's never been supportive of you. He's never there when you need him. What could you miss?"* After that, Susan responded to her husband's attacks with words similar to Debbie's. She asked, *"Why should I care? You're continuing to support the other woman, not me. Until you stop being with that sinful slut, there's nothing about you that I would miss."* Or she said, *"I don't love you today. I loved the way you used to treat me and the kids but not how you are today. Until you stop your sinful affair and act loveable only to us, we have nothing to discuss!"* Susan barked her response and quickly walked away so if he replied to her snippet, she couldn't hear it.

This disarmed her husband and showed she would no longer allow him to mistreat her. His words that intended to inflict pain no longer left a raw sting, and gave Susan a huge sense of self-control and self-protection.

DON'T LET HER BACK DOWN

Counsel her that no matter what her husband says, she must not share how destroyed she feels or beg him to change. She must remain strong and refuse to crumble. If she caves and pleads for him to change, he will believe she will eventually return to normal. He has to accept that their old normal is finished forever. His adultery ruined that.

She should ignore him in every way possible and work to make him hunger for her and all that made them a family. He needs to miss what they once shared. Yet she leaves the door open for his change. Remind her that until he repents, her creating distance follows God's example of how she should respond to one who breaks his vow. She must put her full trust in the Lord.

PREAPRE HER FOR POSSIBLE OUTCOMES

Requiring him to phone the adulteress or move out will prove extremely difficult for her because she fears he will choose to leave and file for divorce. But that's unlikely. He has no place to go unless he rented a place for his sexual escapades, something few have done. If the adulteress is married, he can't move to her place. Instead, he would be homeless on the street or in a motel that he probably can't afford for long.

But if he does grab a few things and leave, she knows the condition of his heart, and she no longer holds first place in it. It shows that his heart has left her, and at this point, he has no regrets. Her only hope of his returning to her is his missing what he once enjoyed as a family.

If he should leave and file for divorce, it stops her from dragging out the inevitable, and it avoids the daily on-going pain that locks her in a continual emotional upheaval. But rarely does a man leave. Rather he usually barks, *"This is my house too! Who do you think you are to tell me to get out?"* If for no other reason, his pride will resist being pushed out.

TIME LINE

If after being spurned by the wife for a week, two at the very most, he still refuses to end the affair or leave, skip to Chapter 14, and complete the necessary work as Jesus commanded for addressing a sinner's unrepentant condition. She must now take two or three witnesses with her to confront his sinful condition.

If he phones the adulteress and ends the affair, the following chapter explains what is required to begin the couple's healing. The requirement details a painful and difficult process but one that begins to put the marriage back on track as God wants.

Chapter 7

IF HE ENDS THE AFFAIR

"*How can I ever trust him again?*" is the most frequently asked question by a betrayed spouse. Without trust, there can never be love because fear of further betrayals overrides all positive emotions. Even if they stay together, the wounded spouse may question every action of his that she can't explain. Her thoughts frequently flood with ideas that he is again seeing the adulteress. Until every detail is exposed, they will argue more and more about trivia, but not about what's really bothering them and the fears they avoid expressing.

To be invited back into the family's life, the affair must have ended. He and the adulteress must have no further contact. He must promise never to see or phone the adulteress under any circumstance nor accept any calls from her. The same commitment holds true for his avoiding girlfriends from his past, or an ex-wife if he was previously married. To prove his loyalty, he must keep his vow of forsaking all others, especially from those he once shared an emotional and/or sexual closeness. He can't leave his wife wondering who he is speaking with on the phone or see him lingering to visit with any other woman. Faithfulness demands exclusion of all other women. He cannot risk making his wife jealous again or their marriage is finished.

Dr. David Clarke in a presentation for the American Association of Christian Counselors emphasized the importance of having a permanent separation by having the adulterer imagine the other woman being in a serious automobile accident and pretending he is the first to arrive on the scene. The man has to promise not to stop to check on her. Instead, he phones the police as he drives away and leaves without looking back. Nor does he phone later to see if she was hurt. That's what it means to sever all contact. Complete severance of all connection requires him to agree that there is no condition in which he allows himself to be drawn to her, not even in a life and death situation. That's what is required for keeping the promise of forsaking all others.

If the adulteress phones him, he must commit to immediately hang up without saying a word. If they accidently pass and she speaks, he does not answer or nod. He ignores her presence as if he does not see her. Anything less does nothing to rebuild trust with his wife and risks his emotional reconnection with the adulteress.

TELL HIM IT'S CONFESSION TIME

Explain to the adulterous husband that he must be totally transparent and tell his spouse every detail about the illicit relationship. He must share every fact of the affair in a written letter that he will then read aloud to his wife. There can be no more secrets for the marriage to survive.

EXCEPTION. It should be noted that if the wife was the unfaithful party her husband may not want to hear details of her affair. Many men can compartmentalize a wife's wrong and never want to hear another detail. Instead, they want her to promise she will never mention it again. However, women cannot do this when their husbands stray. A woman can only stop dwelling on her husband's betrayal when she feels she knows every detail, and that he loves only her. If the wife was the adulteress and her husband does not want to hear the details, but wants to save the marriage skip to Chapter 10.

As Dr. Susan Heitler explains in Psychology Today in her article *Recovery From an Affair*, the deceiver needs to get past defensiveness and shame enough to be able to offer full transparency and answer the spouse's questions, even when she asks the same question multiple times. Full accounting helps a betrayed wife feel that trust will again be possible.

He needs to write a history of the affair, beginning with the day they met and a step-by-step story of how their relationship developed up to today. It needs to include the list below and any other details that supported their continuing to see each other:

Who the woman was. Until she knows the woman's name, every woman in his world remains suspect. The wife deserves to be able to focus on one woman, not every woman he knows.

How they met

How often they talked face to face, by phone, email, text, mailed letters

The types of things they discussed that bonded them to each other and where they had each conversation

When they first met alone and where

The types of personal/family/spouse information they shared with each other

Private details he shared about his wife and their relationship

Where they typically met

When and where they first had physical contact and touched

When and where they first kissed

Where they first had sex He does not describe the various ways they had sex because knowing this would put vivid images in his wife's thoughts she can never erase.

How often they tended to meet and have sex

Where they usually had sex

Public places they met where others could have seen them. If a friend says she saw him with a woman at a restaurant, the wife better already know about this meeting.

Who else knows of the affair and how he knows that this person(s) knows

How much money (approximately) he has spent on her and to be with her If his wife later finds a receipt for something he bought his lover, but he failed to share in the letter, it takes her back to square one with her believing she can't trust him.
Gifts and cards he bought her
Gifts and cards she gave him
Pet names they may have called each other
Their last meeting/talk
How it ended
A sincere apology
All other types of sexual sin he has participated in since marrying, such as pornography, dirty magazines, one-night stands, dirty sex jokes, intentional flirtations, etc.

If the wife later finds a girly magazine that she had no idea he viewed, she will feel betrayed again and is likely to leave permanently, thinking she faces nothing but an on-going continuation of a long list of different sinful involvements

He needs to recall their affair by describing how one thing led to another. Explaining the circumstances that escalated his attraction to the adulteress helps him understand how the affair progressed until their relationship spiraled out of control. If he does not address what caused his decisions, he risks repeating them. He must confront why he allowed himself to do something that threatened the marriage, and he must learn what is lacking in the marital relationship that let an affair appear appealing. Identifying the progressive steps will let him know how to recognize and stop any future attractions before they progress too far. Otherwise, he remains easy prey for another illicit involvement.

Do not let him protest that to know all the facts will do more damage to their marriage. The truth is that wife finds it easier to hear everything from him in one painful session than to learn it piece by piece and with some details possibly coming from others. Until it is all available for her examination and questioning, her mind envisions it as possibly worse than at times it was. Still, hearing such information proves an excruciatingly, gut-wrenching experience that produces a variety of reactions, none of which are pleasant.

She needs assurance there's no more secrets that might arise later, and only his letter can provide that. If he hesitates to reveal a particular detail, he needs to fear her finding out. It might just be the unreported secret that kills the marriage. Right now, their relationship is extremely fragile and cannot tolerate an omission of facts.

Peggy Vaughn, author of *The Monogamy Myth*, interviewed 1,083 couples and discovered that rebuilding trust after an affair is possible, provided the adulterous relationship is thoroughly and completely discussed. Only by intentionally focusing on what happened can they talk openly and recover. Both must commit to complete honesty and this includes ongoing, truthful communication beginning immediately after the adulterer commits to ending the illicit affair.

Multiple researchers and therapist insist that sharing every detail is all that works for rebuilding trust, provided his letter to his wife convinces her that he accepts 100% responsibility for his sinful decisions. He cannot attempt to trivialize or minimize what happened. He betrayed his wife in the most serious of sinful ways. She will not feel secure with him until he admits his sin, shows a willingness to talk openly, and proves he is committed never to straying again. Plus, the magnitude of sin he admits helps to increase his guilt and shame, which boosts the likelihood of total repentance.

EXPECT HIS PROTEST. However, you can expect many men to protest. They will insist that hearing the details of his affair will cause his wife more pain. He insists because this is what he would want if the situation were reversed. He forgets she is an emotional being and heals by talking about every detail. Plus, she wants him to understand her horrific pain.

His willingness to be totally vulnerable and share every aspect of the affair helps his wife recover. He may feel tremendous remorse and guilt, and want to sweep it under the rug, and insist, *"It's over. So let's forget it and move on."* As explained in my book, *Women Talk Men Walk*, most men want to walk away from emotional issues, but women will not recover without thoroughly discussing what happened. She cannot recover emotionally with so much unknown. Her negative feelings do not disappear until lingering questions are addressed. He must come prepared to answer every question she asks with complete openness. She can't spend the rest of her life wondering what she might find out next.

Men want to walk away from emotional issues, but women must talk about them

Keeping things secret and her not knowing exactly what happened is what fuels her agony. It is easier for a woman to face the shock of such a harrowing experience once, than to face a series of on-going, small mini-shocks that cause her pain to last twice as long. Any attempt to drag out the details a little at a time continually reopens her wounded heart. Each new finding feels like another betrayal, and many wives become so overloaded they can take no more and leave.

If he protests telling his wife everything, remind him that Scripture tells us what is required to be forgiven (Col. 3:12-13). James tells us, *"Confess your sins to each other and pray for each other so that you may be healed"* (5:16). Humbling himself and confessing fully, he can learn to love the Lord for His promise of total forgiveness (Lk. 7:47).

Hopefully, their discussing the affair will create a brokenness in him that allows the Lord to soften his heart and bring him home spiritually and relationally. He may resist and become defensive, but he must exercise strong self-control no matter his wife's reactions or how bitter a comment she might make. He has committed a gigantic marital sin, and he must be repentant and keep repeating, *"I'm so very sorry. I wronged you. I want to save our marriage and earn your trust again because I love you."* For the next weeks, he cannot say this enough.

The advantage of having written specifies is it allows the spouse to keep the letter and form lingering questions that when answered let her stop worrying about unknown fears.

In your next counseling session, the husband will be required to read the letter aloud as his wife listens. Your presence is to help better manage the emotional fallout. Ensure you tell the wife that she should not be peeking over his shoulder this week as he writes. They do not share anything until they are in your office.

I instruct the adulterer to write the most thorough account of the affair that he can produce. He uses his calendar and receipts to put things in the order in which they occurred. In essence he is reliving the affair from day one to the last time he and the adulteress spoke. He includes the conversations they had and where they were as they discussed each topic. The more details, the better. He must not ignore certain facts, no matter how insignificant it may have seemed at the time. If in doubt, he includes it.

He includes, with the same degree of specificity any other affair and inappropriate relationship he has had during the course of their marriage. And yes, brief flirtations or bouts of using pornography are included. He needs to know that anything he omits is his continuing to lie and be unfaithful to his wife.

He is to bring the letter to your office and read it to his wife in your presence .After the reading, he hands it to his wife. She'll keep it and has permission to ask questions based on it for as long as she needs to. This might be weeks or in some cases even months.

Satan wants the adultery to end the marriage, but he'll settle for the husband staying with his wife and yearning to again be with his mistress. The emotional tie between the adulterous partners must be broken. His written letter can help break their bond. Seeing the impact hearing his sinful secrets has on his spouse will have him regretting his straying and feeling shame. Writing and reading his letter may be the most difficult thing he has ever been required to do.

EXPLAIN THE NECESSITY OF THE HOMEWORK
The written letter should be completed by the next session and it doesn't matter if it takes 50 or 5000 pages, because every element must be exposed. He may complain he doesn't have time, but that's part of his challenge of putting his wife's needs

first. He can stay up all night, or call in sick, which is true, because their marital relationship and his spiritual relationship with the Lord are both very sick. He can offer no acceptable excuse. The sooner his wife hears the details, the sooner they begin to heal.

Remind him what the Bible says about honest and open confessions, *"He who conceals his sins does not prosper, but whoever confesses and renounces them finds mercy* (Pr. 28:13). *"If we confess our sins, He is faithful and just and will forgive us our sins and purify us from all unrighteousness"* (1 Jn. 1:9). The trust – the whole truth – gains freedom from Satan's control. And it initiates the spouse's understanding so she can forgive.

WHILE HE WRITES, SEE THE WIFE ALONE

Ask the wounded spouse to give the adulterer uninterrupted time to complete this task, because such thoroughness requires hours. She should not see what he writes until they return together to your office. Suggest that she visit with you while he spends time writing.

She needs help preparing for what she may hear her husband say. Address every possibility you can thing of so she won't feel completely overwhelmed when it happens. Below are some ideas.

If her husband told the other woman that he loved her, explain that it was not because he loved her, but because she had something he wanted. He wanted her respect, her admiration, and sex with a new body. He was selfish and liked someone finding him appealing. He is emotionally addicted to this woman, but he does not love her. His addiction is sinful and not godly love. He doesn't know her well enough to love her. He has no idea what she would be like if he had to fight with her to go fishing with the guys, or have her spend his weekly salary on a new pair of shoes. He has no conception of what daily living is like with her, and that's required to love someone. They shared a secret, illicit life, not a public one that's blessed with friend's approval.

If he shared secrets with the adulteress, it was to gain her emotional trust, and he likely never considered what he told her as betraying his wife. Many men see the sexual act as sinful, but not talks of personal details. Few men think on emotional levels like a woman, and it likely never dawned on him that sharing personal information hurts his wife as deeply, and possibly more, than their sexual encounters.

I've seen a man share with a large group how much his wife weighed, and he had no idea that he had committed an unforgivable betrayal in her eyes. Sadly, many men do not think about the emotional impact many of their actions have.

If he told the other woman he was leaving his wife, it was Satan's way of helping him convince the adulteress to continue the affair. Such phony lines are just that: phony. He used his wife as an excuse for not being with the adulteress full time. If he had been serious, he would have left his wife and told the adulteress after the fact. He just wanted to have her and have his family too.

HELP HER KEEP GOD FIRST

During your meeting with the wounded spouse make it your goal to help her keep God first. She, too, made mistakes in the marriage, and therefore, she should not be too determined to condemn his weaknesses and sin. Ensure that she doesn't acquire an arrogant attitude of *"I'd never do such a thing to him."* Placed in the right situation, at an opportune time, Satan could grab her or anyone, including you and me. No one is free of Satan's temptation.

Religious people make bad decisions and violate their morals, and believing in God does not make anyone exempt. Because we believe in God is why Satan attacks us. Satan attacks believers because unbelievers already belong to him.

Satan attacks believers

because unbelievers already belong to him

As gently as possible, explain that just because his sin differs from hers, it doesn't mean God views it as worse. To the Lord, all sin is evil. All sin is wrong. All sin, no matter how minor and insignificant we might consider it, pains God deeply and insults His holiness.. No matter her sin or his, or how major or trivial she sees them, both break God's law, and therefore, both are guilty of lawlessness (1 Jn. 3:4).

ASSIGN HER SCRIPTURES TO READ. At this stage, she needs to give all hurt to God for His healing. Suggest she choose Scriptures and put her husband's name into each one as she prays. *"Father, let me forgive John, as you forgive me when I do wrong."* Or read the Scriptural definition of love (1 Co. 13:4-8), inserting his name. *"Love is patient." Because I love the Lord, I will be patient when John doesn't do as I want. "Love is kind." Because it will honor the Lord, I will treat John with kindness no matter how angry or hurt I feel.*

She must take her mind off her husband and lay his sins at Jesus' cross for her healing and forgiveness. She must not make her husband or their marriage her idol and place it above her relationship with the Lord. First place belongs exclusively to the Lord, and being right with God must remain her primary priority. She needs to confess all of her sins and learn to talk with God continually and ask Him to remove all thoughts of revenge. She can't immediately forgive all the anguish and grief his affair has caused her. She needs God's help. Her intense sadness, anger, and disillusionment are justified, but she must never use those feelings as an excuse to sin herself. She does this by daily reminding herself of her husband's absolute best qualities, not his failures.

REMIND THAT SHE MODELS FOR HER KIDS. She needs to know that unless she forgives they will likely divorce, and she risks passing the divorce curse onto their children and, perhaps, even her grandchildren may be impacted. It's why God says in Malachi that He hates divorce. For their children's sake, she must practice giving every negative feeling to the Lord and teach their children how to do the same for their own spiritual development. Right now, she proves the best role model they have, and she must use this opportunity to show how to allow God to handle relationships when they encounter serious struggles.

Ask her is to pray for her husband. She should plead for God to stop Satan's control of him. Remind her each time you see her that it was Satan who stole her husband. Her task is to ask God to stop Satan and return her husband's heart home.

Reassure her that most men who cheat despise themselves after the fact. Remind her that he, too, is now an aching person making big adjustments with bouts of anger, fear, sadness, and loneliness. While he may not miss the adulteress, he definitely misses how good she made him feel about himself and how she boosted his ego. He will feel a lonely emptiness for quite a while.

If every interaction has her fearing the pain will last forever, remind her that such times are when God listens to our hearts and refuels our souls, provided she immediately prays the very second such thoughts arrive. Satan wants her doubting their restoration, but God wants to heal her and their marriage. Encourage her to let Him. If she focuses on all she fears, the fear will become her reality. If she focuses on instantly praying, God's peace will calm her emotions.

Give her a list of Scriptures to read and memorize, such as how the Lord condemns complaining and arguing (Php. 2:14), and how we will account for every word we speak. She can use these to reassurance herself that God will take control of her marriage provided she behaves as He commands. Remind her that 23rd Psalm begins with *'The Lord is my Shepherd'* and that requires her to agree to let Him lead her, just as David did when he lived in fear and anxiety about his future.

Ask how she wants tomorrow to be better, and what she can do to move it in that direction. Stress the importance of her staying future focused so they don't fall into same old routines that tore them apart.

INSIST SHE GUARDS HER TONGUE

It is imperative that she not talk badly about her spouse to others. If her parents learn he is involved in an affair, they may never forgive him. Strife could remain in the family forever. They may even insist that she divorce him. If his parents discover he is having an affair, they may recall every mistake she has made and blame her. At this point, she needs to work at keeping the family distanced from their personal problems.

Family members can know they are seeking counseling and are determined to work out their differences. She can even ask the parents to pray for them, but she should refuse to share what their issues are. Keeping their personal matters private is part of God's commandment to leave parents and become one with the spouse. Because he is committed to changing and making the marriage work, there's no need for them to know any details.

Keeping their personal matters private is part of God's command
to leave parents and become one with the spouse

Meeting alone with the wife provides a way for you to know how things are progressing at home, and it lets you better prepare for their next emotionally heavy joint session.

If he returns prepared to read his letter, it will be one of the most demanding, stressful counseling sessions you will likely ever experience, and it will prove the couple's most difficult and challenging. You need to plan on this session lasting two or three times longer than usual. Be sure and purchase several boxes of tissue.

Chapter 8

THEIR TURNING-POINT

"*I just didn't have time to write the letter, and I don't think she will ever forgive me no matter what I say. So why should I risk adding more fuel to the fire?*" Refuse to accept any excuse the adulterous husband may attempt to use. His writing the letter is mandatory for her healing.

If he refuses to write the letter or shows up with one or two short paragraphs, he proves he hasn't changed. His heart still treasures how he feels when he is with the other woman. Give him one more chance to do it correctly. After that, if he still refuses, you are wasting your time until he wants to do what's right.

For his own reasons, he doesn't want to accept responsibility for his willful sin of adultery. He is either continuing to contact the adulteress or he wants his wife to pretend it didn't happen, and that's something she cannot do.

Either way, he hopes to fool you and is only feigning regret for his affair. He acts similar to how Judah treated the Lord, and God rejected her because *"Judah did not return to me with all her heart, but only in pretense"* (Jer. 3:10).

Accept your limits, and set boundaries you will keep. His problem is a sin problem, and the battle is not yours. It's the Lord's. Such people have yet to learn to let Jesus act as their counselor and physician, and sadly, you can't force them. If he refuses to complete the written assignment, refuse to see him again.

It's time for his wife to move to Step Two that Jesus provided in Matthew (18:16). She now takes two or three others with her to confront his sinful behavior, as described in Chapter 14.

IF HE COMPLETED THE LETTER. If he has completed the detailed homework, have him read aloud his written account of the affair, with an understanding that the wife can interrupt at any time to ask for a more thorough explanation. This will prove a heartbreaking session for all concerned, but without hearing all the facts, the wife will create more painful scenarios inside her thoughts. Only when everything is exposed and he genuinely repents, will healing begin.

FIRM EXCEPTIONS. She needs to receive counsel, and in his presence, that there are two exceptions to his openness which she is not to violate. First, she does not ask him to compare her body with his lover's body. He does makes no comment about the adulteress' body. Society puts such emphasis on how a woman looks that if the wife feels less, her feelings of inferiority can control her thoughts for years. Second, she does not ask him to describe specific details of the various ways he and the adulteress had sex. Hearing this would leave vivid mental images in her thoughts that are impossible to erase. Such questions remain off limits.

This is also a good time to ask both to commit never to saying the word divorce again. Threatening to divorce is one of Satan's evil attacks, and the Lord hates even the mention of divorce (Mal. 2:16).

THEIR DEFINING MOMENT

His reading the letter to his wife begins their recovery. Sharing full details with total openness creates the way for God to begin healing the wife so forgiveness can begin, and it highlights the husband's guilt, shame, and regret so she sees that he is genuinely repentant. Likely, her tears and hurt will overwhelm him, as he finally realizes how ravaged her heart is and know it's all his fault. He will remember forever that insufferable look on her face and see her tearful anguish. For a first time in a long time, he will connect with her on a deep emotional level, as he admits the truth of how he treated the one he promised to love and remain forever faithful. He cannot avoid knowing the undeniable devastation she experiences.

Only with such realization can full recovery begin for both of them. Only then does he feel the full weight of the devastation he did to their relationship and genuinely regret his actions. Only then does he again desire to live on the right side of a moral boundary and have no more secrets from his wife.

Seeing his wife in such torment also serves as painful punishment for him. Pain proves a powerful deterrent to repeating a wrong. This session becomes a defining time for them as a couple, relationally and spiritually.

Pain proves a powerful deterrent to repeating a wrong

Remind them how King David suffered with the death of his and Bathsheba's son, and how the depth of his hurt created a spiritual turning point in David. Pain that's deep enough creates a positive change in one's heart and then in one's actions.

Recall how the prodigal son felt no need to return home until he was completely broken, financially, physically, emotionally, and spiritually. Only after he admitted that his bad choices and behaviors had degraded to such a low level was he prepared to change. At that point, he wanted to come home, but he knew he didn't deserve to be allowed to return. He admitted how deeply he had hurt God, and he was now willing to work as a servant because of the shame his actions had brought on his father. Because he was broken, he accepted that he deserved nothing better.

To save his marriage, the adulterer has to experience a similar realization. He must want to come home and know that, after all the destruction he has caused for his wife, he doesn't deserve to be allowed. He must be willing to pay whatever price his wife demands to regain full entrance as her husband.

NO MENTION OF HER FLAWS. The adulterer needs to know that, at this point, he has no right to mention any mistakes or failures his wife contributed to their marriage. The wife's positive emotions are dead and must be revived before any marital problems can be discussed or corrected. He has put her through overwhelming trauma, and it's going to take several weeks for her to want to discuss issues they had before his affair. His entire focus must remain on having her trust him again. Without trust, any prior marriage problems won't matter.

Encourage the adulterer to meet with the church elders and ask them to pray for him. He does not need to share details, just to acknowledge that he has been unfaithful to the Lord, hurt his wife and children, and needs prayful support. He doesn't need to share any more information. The more people supporting his change, the more solid and permanent it is likely to be. Part of the earlier problem was that there was no one he answered to for his actions, and at this stage of change, the wayward spouse requires a lot of accountable support to ensure he remains committed.

ELIMINATE ALL CONTACT WITH ADULTERESS

Explain that it's time to clean house of everything related to the affair, and they should do it immediately. Removing all memory of the adulteress and ensuring there can be no accidental contact helps reduce the wife's doubts and worry, and it provides him on-going support for remaining faithful. Just knowing he is being held accountable to keep his word provides him added strength.

He must be willing to remove anything and everything that can remind him and his wife of the adulteress. This will likely require him to make some very difficult changes, some that may cause him serious loss. He does it because it is required to ensure the affair had no chance of reigniting. Remember, he remains emotionally addicted to this woman and any contact, even if accidental, can enflame his feelings for her. His focus now must be on increasing his wife's trust and belief that he really does want to remain faithful to her and only her.

Emphasize that from this moment forward, he must treat his wife with consistency and caring. He must not make any agreement that he won't keep, or their marriage is doomed. Although it will make him extremely uncomfortable, he must agree to answer all his wife's questions, and give his wife permission to destroy everything that might remind either of them of the adulteress. He has to give his wife full control of deciding what things must go or be changed, and he needs to know that, for months, she will continually be checking on him and monitoring his every move.

He must continually demonstrate that she has no more reason to fear his being with another woman, not just the adulteress but with any woman. This is mandatory for earning his wife's forgiveness, trust, and respect.

Such changes require them to trust that the Lord will provide for all their needs. They must give their concerns to Him and learn the real meaning of being fully dependent on the Lord. Below are some things, people, and places that may require changing or completely eliminating for their full restoration as loyal marriage partners.

Eliminate all possible written and verbal contact with the adulteress
He may have to change jobs.
They may need to sell their house and relocate.
Some family or friends may have to be avoided
They may need to find another church
He needs to avoid all places he took the adulteress
Let his wife decide what to do with all gifts the adulteress gave him
He relinquishes all right to privacy for several weeks
He acts especially guarded in public places and social settings

ALL WRITTEN AND VERBAL CONTACT. Ask him to hand his phone to his wife, and tell her to delete every message and picture that offends her. This way she knows it's all removed. Then have him phone his provider and have his phone number changed. If they have a home phone, she has the number changed and posted as unlisted. If he has a private postal box, they go together and cancel it.

Once home, he must give her all computer passwords so she can wipe his computer clean. Or she can format the hard drive and eliminate everything. Afterwards, he agrees to no longer having private passwords or private email accounts. He allows her to change their shared passwords and email addresses at often as necessary for her to feel satisfied there's no contact between him and the adulteress.

One woman smashed her husband's computer to pieces. Another woman moved his computer to a kitchen cabinet and told him it better never be turned on again unless she is in the room. She daily checked the history stored on the computer, scrutinized every flash drive in the house, and even burned one.

If he and the adulteress spoke on a regular schedule, for the next couple of weeks, he agrees to phone his wife at these times. He fills the void of his prior illicit emotional chats with time talking with his wife – and he better not miss a day or call at the wrong time. He remains under constant scrutiny and must pass the test or his wife's trust will never be earned, and earning it is mandatory.

CHANGE JOBS. If he needs to change jobs to avoid seeing the adulteress, it will be one of the most painful requirements he has to make because many men are more fused with their jobs than with their families. But to save his marriage, if he and the adulteress see each other regularly at work, he needs to update his resume, because he needs to find other employment and do so quickly. He cannot continue seeing the adulteress on a regular basis and break their emotional bond. Nor will his wife ever believe they aren't talking and possibly being together during lunch breaks or company meetings.

If he and the adulteress work in different buildings or on different floors, the wife decides if she feels comfortable with him remaining at his job. If so and he stays, he must commit never to going into the break room or getting on an elevator if the adulteress is present. If he sees her in passing, and she speaks, he acts as if he doesn't know her, and then he tells his wife. His staying or leaving immediately should be the wife's call, but my finding is that safety is best guaranteed with an immediate job change.

He may protest that he expects a promotion in the next few months, however, if his resigning causes him to miss the opportunity it's the cost of his sin. He must prove to his wife that she and their marriage mean more to him than a job where he might again become trapped in a sinful relationship. I have seen a reconnection at the work place happen too many times, and if he and the adulteress begin seeing each other again, it guarantees the end of the marriage.

One man who seemed genuinely committed to stopping the affair, failed to consider that his lover might not feel the same. When Jim told Mandy that they were not going to see each other again, she didn't believe he meant it. At least, she didn't mean it. She would go the floor where Jim worked and leave notes atop his desk that reminded him of things they had shared. If she saw him in the breakroom, she would grab a chair and pull up beside him. At the end of each work day, Mandy followed Jim to his car. If he refused to talk with her and tried to brush her aside to get into his car, she would begin to raise her voice to call attention to them. Her pursuit of him became so uncontrollable, Jim resigned from his job without his wife's suggestion.

An adulterer cannot pray to stop doing wrong with the left hand while tightly gripping sin with the right one and expect God's protection. He has to put all effort into keeping his word.

MOVE AND LIST THE HOUSE. If the adulteress is a close neighbor it always proves better for their marriage if they move and list the house to sell. They can live elsewhere until the house sells, without a need to return to that neighborhood.

Seeing this neighbor can trigger his old feelings, and it definitely intensifies the pain and rage in the wife.

Their children will adjust to a new school faster than the wounded spouse recovers from her husband's affair. It's better for the kids to make new friends than to permanently lose one parent.

It's better for the kids to make new friends than to permanently lose one parent

One couple carried on their affair in the man's house while his wife was at work. The first thing the wife did after hearing him read his letter was to go home, drag their mattress and sheets to the back yard, sprinkle them with gasoline, and burn them. She then moved her and children's clothes to an apartment and gave him the option of moving with them or remaining behind. She was more upset over where they had sex than over his attraction of the other woman.

Learning her husband and his lover had sex in the family car, without telling her husband, another woman traded it the next day for a new one. When he complained about how much her trade costs, she assured him that her other options were to set it afire or let it roll off a tall bridge because her children were never going to sit inside that 'contaminated' car again.

He must be prepared for the possibility for such immediate anger. Such a woman will calm and focus on healing, but an immediate desire to destroy every semblance of the other woman often grabs a wife's immediate thoughts.

AVOID SOME FAMILY/ FRIENDS. If the adulteress is a family member, they can decline all family gatherings. Other members they want to see can be invited to visit in their home. He should never place himself or his wife in the presence of the adulteress, regardless of whom the other woman is. If his adulteress was a close relative, the wife's hurt runs even deeper because his behavior causes her to lose a family member she once valued.

> **If his adulteress was a close relative, the wife's hurt runs even deeper because his behavior causes her to lose a family member she once valued**

However, the wife must not be allowed to react as so many betrayed wives do and shift all blame to the other woman. It took two for an affair. He and his lover are equally guilty. The wife needs to remember that he is capable of saying no and ignoring someone when he wants, just like he had being doing her and the children since his affair began. God holds both parties equally sinful, and she needs to view them the same.

A NEW CHURCH. If the adulterous couple sees each other at church, the marital couple needs to immediately find another place to worship and never again visit their former congregation. They do not need to explain why they are changing. Saying, "*I miss you guys, but we need to make new friends*" is an honest reply, and it shares enough.

They may need to establish an entirely new network of friendships. This will prove difficult, and they will grieve the loss of many people they love, but it's necessary for saving their relationship and moving forward with a new and better marriage.

AVOIDS ALL PLACES THEY MET. If he and the adulterous ate together at certain restaurants, he must commit never to eat there, or even drive by these restaurants. Not only is he ensuring there's never an accidental contact, he also avoids repeated memories. Above all, he never suggests to his wife that he will take her to these places.

SHE CAN DESTROY ALL GIFTS. He needs to give his wife all gifts he received from the adulteress, and let her decide what to do them. One man who received an expensive watch from his lover had allowed his wife to think it was a gift from his supervisor for completing a special project. He had bragged about it to many of his friends. The wife was furious when she learned the truth. She laid the watch on the floor, banged it with a hammer until it was flattened into several pieces and then dumped them in the garbage disposal. Turning on the water, she let the disposal grind until it would no longer run. She said the watch represented garbage like their relationship had been for months, and the broken disposal showed the condition of their marriage and how they needed a new and different one. She told him that she had solid reasons to feel this angry, and he needed to remember it or she was done with their marriage.

NO MORE PRIVACY FOR HIM. He needs to expect his wife to unexpectedly drop by his gym or work place. He must phone her if he will be 10 minutes late, no matter where he is or whom he is with. Without such calls, her mind envisions him with the adulteress.

If she wants a key to his briefcase, he needs to be prepared to let her rummage through it and to check his phone regularly. If he must take a business trip, he needs to invite her to go with him or expect that she will occasionally surprise him with visits in his motel room.

He gives her permission to go home, check phone records, search through his drawers, and create a chart for weekly monitoring of his car mileage. She is going to do this, so he might as well tell her it is okay. If he complains, ask why he would mind if he is no longer doing anything wrong. He must not think of it as losing his right of privacy but as her right to know he is genuinely trustworthy. To be able to forgive, the wounded spouse must know, without any doubt, that there is no further contact between him and the other woman. Trust isn't re-established quickly.

While the adulterer may not appreciate it at this stage, his spouse's checking on him helps him remain honest and faithful. The more evidence the wife finds, the more of his sinful activity is exposed, and the increased brokenness he begins to feel. The more broken he feels, the more he realizes his need to change, and the more he wants to save their marriage.

Have him read how Joseph challenged his brothers before he trusted them again (Ge. 42-44). Scriptures teach that after a betrayal, trust has to be tested in multiple ways. The betrayer's actions must prove trustworthy before he's allowed back in the victim's life.

Scriptures teach that after a betrayal, trust has to be tested in multiple ways

TELL HIM TO GUARD HIMSELF SOCIALLY. In public places, he needs to guard how he acts with other women. If she thinks he gives additional attention to a particular woman, any gain in trust they have gained to this point is challenged. To ensure there's no grounds for suspicion, when they are with others, he keeps his arm locked around his wife's waist. He can limit the time he talks to other women and the type of topics they discuss. He can boast of his wife to these women to ensure she remains the center of his attention.

He can expect many of his behaviors and comments that his wife ignored in the past to no longer be tolerated because she has proof they are risky and cannot be trusted. Never again will she assume that things which used to make her slightly uncomfortable are now okay. Nor will she accept that she may be overreacting. He must be willing to stop any and all mannerisms that can possibly create distrust. He does this by keeping his wife in the forefront of his thoughts at all times when another woman is around and while talking on the phone.

For months, she needs continued reassurance of his faithfulness. He lives in a constant test. To save his marriage, he better pass with an A+. One minor slip will cause a dangerous set-back or even a permanent one.

Prepare him for what the next few months will be like. He should expect his wife to react with loaded drama and emotional pressure, and he must remain compassionate and supportive no matter how difficult it proves.

Chapter 9

HOME BECOMES ON-GOING DRAMA

"*Is she never going to forgive me and stop bringing up what I did?*" When he asks this question, your answer is, "*Not for a long time. Not until your answers completely empty the boundless pit of pain and resentment you created in her heart. Remember she has a serious reason to feel hurt and angry. God made a woman an emotional being and when her heart and soul have been ripped apart, it takes a long time to heal. But know it will heal, and her questions will stop.*"

The worst reply the husband can offer is *"I've answered that a dozen times. Will you never be satisfied and stop asking?"* Or, *"I refuse to talk about it anymore."* The point is, he has yet to convince her that he has changed and genuinely loves her more than any other, and such responses hurt her more. Suggesting that she needs to get over his adultery reveals an arrogant attitude of entitlement, a right that even God says he doesn't deserve without full repentance. He must realize that such remarks sound to her like he wants to pretend he is the victim rather than accepting responsibility for the hurt he caused.

Many men want to return home and act as if nothing is wrong and think the relationship should pick up as it was before his affair. If things were reversed, some men would want just that. But that denies a woman healing. She requires a very different process to recover and forgive. She views any curt responses as an attempt to avoid responsibility for the damage he caused. The marriage cannot be saved unless the man takes full ownership of the harm he did, and he must do it in ways that convince her that he is truly repentant. He made the choices that got him into this mess, and only he can choose to do what it takes to get out of it. This is time for him to respond as a woman needs. It's going to prove distressing for him but not nearly as heart-rending as what she experiences.

She fears any hesitation or refusal to answer prove he may still be seeing the other woman or at least thinking about her. Beneath her anger, she lives wondering if he will see this woman again, or be with another. She needs ongoing reassurance to calm her worries, not words that cut her short. His replies must reaffirm her of his love. Otherwise, she will never trust him.

To the wife, nothing justifies what he did. He chose to sin. Even if the other woman was the aggressor, he chose not to stop it. You may need to remind him that unless he changes and helps her heal, she has a Biblical right to permanently leave him.

Dr. Susan Heitler's research found that insufficient empathy from a betrayer invites a wounded spouse's ever increasing resentment. The number one indicator of whether a relationship survived infidelity was how much empathy the unfaithful spouse showed for the wounded spouse's pain, especially during the times she became emotional and was obsessed with crying, screaming, and asking for specific details.

The number one indicator of whether a relationship survives infidelity is how much empathy the unfaithful spouse shows for the wounded spouse's pain

Explain to him that rarely is an adulterer's confession a one-time event, and he can never say, "*I am sorry. It's you I want to spend the rest of my life with. I want to save our marriage because I love you,*" enough times. To save the marriage, he must be completely open, honest, accountable, and allow her to emotionally show how deeply she hurts. He must patiently answer her many questions.

For several weeks, usually months, his wife will likely experience times of uncontrollable crying or even fits of yelling angrily because something has reminded her of the affair. It might be the way he says something, a song on the radio, or a place they pass. While she remains hypervigilant and her behavior erratic, he must tolerate her reactions without becoming defensive or the marriage is doomed. His ability to show empathy when she reacts with drama is something he can learn to do and control. He must answer her questions, even if she asks the same one several times. Betrayal is so offensive, it takes multiple moments of positive reinforcement for a woman to fully accept that her husband's promise is sincere.

Help him understand that she seeks reassurance of his faithfulness, and she wants him to realize the gut-wrenching pain his adultery caused her. This drama will continue until she heals, and only the Lord knows the future. It's not unusual for things to calm and appear significantly better, and then without notice, the upheaval begins again. However, each new episode tends to be shorter than prior ones. Infidelity creates the profoundest of heartache, and healing comes in separated spurts of peace with times of turmoil sandwiched in between.

If she wakes at 3:00 a.m. and has a question about his affair, counsel him that he must agree to sit up in bed and answer her right then. A truly repentant sinner remains ready at all times to give needed responses to assure another of his faithfulness.

If she calls the adulteress horrible names, he must not disagree. He must let her vent without any doubt that he accepts and understands her opinion. His reaction must leave her knowing he takes her side, and is not defending or caring for the other woman. She must never again feel she competes with another woman and loses. Ranking second with her husband is something no woman can handle.

Ranking second with her husband is something no woman can handle

Prepare him to realize that she will continue to ask questions until she feels loved, emotionally protected, and first in his life. Meanwhile, he needs to know that she will experience periods of multiple emotions such as helplessness, hopelessness, shame, guilt, fear, loneliness, and fury. A part of her wants to punish him, a chastisement he justly deserves. But if he responds and answers completely and honestly, her desire to penalize him will pass quickly, and she soon will only be testing his loyalty and love. The difference will show in how fury is replaced by slow, streaming tears.

Assure him that her on-going emotional out-bursts will end. Meanwhile, it's the price he pays for sinning against her and the Lord, a consequence an adulterer should expect. Her continued need to discuss his affair is necessary for her to fully process what happened, to heal, and trust him.

Tell him that intense emotional ups and downs are normal for couples trying to recover from betrayal. But also promise that these episodes will become fewer and farther between and with more frequent stable periods of calmness.

FACE WHAT'S DREADED

Keep reminding him that for a long time, his wife needs on-going guarantees that he isn't contacting the adulteress. She can't be certain without his telling her, and few men tell their wives without being asked. They fear mentioning it will lead to another heated attack, something they prefer avoiding.

I challenged one man to face what he feared. I asked that he stop and pray each evening before entering the house, seeking God's help to confront whatever mood of his wife he faced. Trying it, he learned he could avoid a lot of drama by informing his wife before she asked. As soon as he walked in the house, he immediately hugged his wife and said, "*I had no contact with that woman today. There's nothing to fear because I promised God I will never betray you again. What I did was sinful. I love you, and only you, and I will keep my promise.*"

Then one day, the worst happened. The woman phoned him at work, but he used her call to continue building trust with his wife. When he returned home, he immediately shared, "*that woman called, and I hung up on her without saying a word."* After giving his wife daily reports for several weeks, she began to believe him. Her trust in him grew by knowing he would do what he said and hide nothing from her, no matter how difficult it was for him to admit all.

A man not telling his wife if the adulteress phones continues their secrecy, which initially helped fuel the affair. If the adulteress phones more than once, he needs to get a restraining order to stop her contacting him. An order of protection would definitely reassure his wife that he never again wants any interaction with the woman.

SHOW HIM HOW TO SURVIVE

Show him how to struggle through such a lengthy, distressing period. It's now that you can teach him how to keep a right and tight relationship with God, and it must remain his top priority. By now he wants to learn – and to daily put it into practice.

His goal must focus on speaking to his wife as Jesus would, and that requires his words to sound gentle, kind, and void of any annoyance. The more he shows compassion for the pain his betrayal causes his wife, the faster she heals because it helps her believe that he understands the depth of her injury. She knows he can't go back in time and erase his affair, but he can move forward proving how much he regrets the pain he inflicted.

Each time he thinks of the adulteress (and he occasionally will for a while, but it must become less and less), explain that he should immediately turn to God and ask forgiveness for having sinful thoughts. As Peter explains, "O*ne must be clear-minded and have self-control so he can pray*" (1 Pe. 4:7). After seeking the Lord's forgiveness, he can plead for help to stay focused on his wife's good qualities and for strength to answer the same painful questions.

The Lord commands that he **must** love her. He responds lovingly because of his desire to remain obedient to the Lord (Eph. 5:33). His obedience to God does not depend on how his wife expresses her pain.

His obedience to God does not depend on how his wife expresses her pain

With continued prayer, he will avoid a need to argue, complain, or have a selfish pity-party. With the Lord's help he can endure his wife's challenges and develop a covenant love for her. Regardless, of the heavy drama, he must remain loving, and he can only do this by keeping all his words and actions directed at pleasing the Lord, more than trying to please his wife.

SHOW HE UNDERSTANDS HER EMOTIONS. He has to man-up and accept her negativity, just as she has to learn to accept what he did. If he works to describe how she feels with each outburst, it can help her recover quicker. Just his saying, *"I understand that you are still hurting and angry. I am sorry I caused you such pain, and I will tell you all you want to know and as many times as you need to hear it,"* contributes to her healing. A willing attitude does more healing than hearing the actual facts.

A willing attitude does more healing than hearing the actual facts

To many women, a man's willingness to share every detail of the affair is a way he can betray the other woman and return his loyalty to her. Remember she cares much more about his emotional tie to the other woman than the sexual part and wants him being emotionally bonded only with her.

He needs to learn to identify the emotions behind her words and use it to show he is trying to understand the pain she experiences. Let him practice with you, by identifying the feelings that prompted her questions, and repeat doing this until he feels comfortable and sounds believable.

For example, pretend you are the wife and say something that she may say, *"Is that why you refused to go with me for counseling early in our marriage?"* Have him try to identify the feelings that would have her asking this question. Below are others.

"What did you plan to do if some of our friends saw you together at that restaurant?" What feelings could cause a wife concern about friends knowing about his affair before her?

He could reply, *"I know what I did causes you great embarrassment with those who know, and I..."*

"What did I do to cause you to turn to another woman?" What self-doubts might have her asking such a question?

He might say, *"My sin had nothing to with you. Don't blame yourself. It was me, and I..."*

"Was she better in bed than I am?" What fear would cause her to ask this question?

He should begin each response with an identification of the pain that has her asking the question and then answer directly and briefly. *"I understand your hurt makes you want to know more, but my sin had nothing to do with how you are in bed. I love sex with you. Sex with you leaves me feeling loved and valued, and I cherish your responsiveness."*

TELL HIM WHAT SHE SEEKS. The greatest need for every wife is to know she ranks number one in her husband's heart. She can't stop wanting to understand why she lost that position until she believes he loves her completely – and loves only her. A wife can't tolerate competition for her husband's heart where she loses. Losing rips her very core, tearing her soul.

Explain to him that his betrayal demonstrated she was of lesser importance to him, and now he has to prove he is putting her back in her rightly deserved, God-given place. His words and actions must continually prove he wants to keep her first, above all others, and do so until he convinces her. It takes hundreds, maybe thousands, of positive reinforcing moments for her to believe that he regrets his affair, and remains fully committed to her and only her. Only after he genuinely convinces her, will she stop pounding him with questions.

His betrayal demonstrated she was of lesser importance to him, and now he has to prove he is putting her back in her rightly deserved, God-given place

SUGGEST SHE KEEPS A JOURNAL

Likewise, she needs counseling to lean heavily on the Lord every time she thinks about his affair. Doing so, allows God to remove her painful thoughts and replace them with forgiveness and love. Remind her that God judges our thoughts, and He wants her to turn to Him with all feelings that inflict pain. She must not continue seeing herself as a victim, but realize the Lord will care for her every need.

After each prayer, she needs to think of one positive trait she values about her husband and tell him. He needs to know she likes him enough for him to endure the emotional ordeal he faces. She has to remember that one reason he strayed is how the adulteress made him feel good about himself. *"A gentle tongue can break a bone"* (Pr. 25:15).

In addition to praying, many women find comfort in writing in a journal, expressing their many feelings and describing which of her husband's comments help and which hurt. Writing helps many women grieve and detach from what's happened. Ask her to keep a record of the ways her husband is trying to prove his love. This helps her focus on his words and actions and shows he wants to behave positive, predictable ways.

At some point, her deciding to read parts of the journal to him can create another opportunity for their emotional bonding. Counsel him that if she offers to share her journal entries with him, he must force himself to listen. He needs to look for the feelings that caused her to write such words. To refuse to listen to her journal entries is to reject the deepest, most private part of her.

Hearing her journal entries can serve as a growth experience for him, because it helps him monitor how he is doing at restoring their emotional connection. He should view it as a teaching-learning tool, not an attack or manipulation. She is sharing intimate thoughts that she shares only with the Lord and now with him. He should be thankful she wants to reveal such personal privacy, because such sharing proves they are slowly re-connecting.

Both must place their relationship fully in the Lord's control. By praying immediately with every damaging thought, they will both learn what it means to pray without ceasing and to depend on the Lord for supplying every care. Giving their relationship to the Lord puts their marriage on a path where He can control their recovery, and it rids them of Satan's influence.

HELP HER CONTROL HER EMOTIONS

It is advisable to schedule a visit alone with the wife. She will need on-going support for several weeks. Women make decisions by talking, and she needs someone she trusts fully, and right now, you are the most trustworthy person she has.

Expect her to express various emotional reactions, from hurt, to arguing, to anger, and even resentment. Your goal is to ensure revenge doesn't grab hold of her thoughts, as Satan will surely work to make happen. You may have to ask frequently, *"How would doing that make things better for you or the children?"* Or, *"How would doing that improve or help save your marriage?"* Or, *"What would the Lord thinks about that idea?"* And you may need to remind her that any form of revenge is sinful and never serves to improve things.

You will likely have to work with her on the reasons revenge is wrong. Retaliation is a sinful attempt to make one's self feel better. Sin is sin, and all disobedience pains the Lord.

Your goal must be to ensure she isn't completely obsessed with the affair, but rather that she focuses on their recovery. Ask questions that have her wanting to move their relationship forward. Otherwise, she will become bitter, and once bitter she will never forgive.

Retaliation is a sinful attempt to make one's self feel better

Explain to her how men respond more as a woman wants by softening her emotional comments. She needs to gradually be able to describe her feelings rather than act them out by screaming with anger. Saying, *"I am feeling unbearable hurt right now"* proves more effective than yelling. Crying is easier for a man to handle than her throwing things. Asking with a whisper, *"How could you do this?"* receives a kinder reply from a man than shouting the same question. Any revengeful punishing words or actions only serve to retard her own healing.

Listen carefully for her comments that intend to punish or attack, or words with a tone that appears overly critical. Explain how these hinder her from receiving the compassion she needs from her spouse.

All of us sin, we just sin differently. The sin the Lord hates the most is a proud, arrogant, haughty heart because such an attitude keeps one from repenting. In this family, the husband repents of his adultery; the wife of any desire for revenge. *"Do not offer any part of yourself to sin as an instrument of wickedness, but rather offer yourselves to God as those who have been brought from death to life; and offer every part of yourself to Him as an instrument of righteousness"* (Ro. 6:13).

This wife is entitled to her anger. She has been betrayed, but she must not allow her feelings to give her permission to sin. The only way to avoid this is to turn all negative feelings over for the Lord's care. She tells God when she feels angry and asks for help to let such emotions pass.

She must pray, and pray often, because her fight is with Satan, not her husband, and only God can defeat Satan. Ask her to memorize Ephesians 6:10-12 and repeat these Scriptures when she feels down or upset. Any weakness in her spiritual or marital relationship risks her being exploited by Satan, the enemy of her soul. She strengthens her stand against Satan's attacks by repeating Scriptures each time she feels overly upset. They help her to stop playing the victim and find her significance in the Lord, not her husband. Explain that her job is to learn to forgive as God has forgiven her.

REQUEST TRUSTWORTHY ACTIONS. Some wives benefit by making a list of actions they want their husband doing that to her prove he is acting trustworthy. This serves two purposes: it shows him what she needs, and it has her watching for trustworthy behaviors, actions she cannot deny. A woman's heart is like a 1000-piece puzzle; some pieces fit easily and neatly into her heart while others require diligent effort on his part. He cannot be passive while their relationship remains weak and expect her to trust him.

You can tell when she begins to forgive him by the reduction of drama in her speech. The pain will be there for a long time, but the heavy emotional display will soften.

QUESTIONS TO CHALLENGE THEIR BEHAVIORS

Below are three questions that can be used with either of them. You may decide to use them as you work with one of them individually or in a joint session.

1. What are you currently doing that defeats the hope of tomorrow being better?
2. What could you do so your spouse believes you want to remain together forever?
3. What should you do so your actions promise a better future for both of you as a couple?

"You have searched me, Lord, and you know me. You know when I sit and when I rise; you perceive my thoughts from afar. You discern my going out and my lying down; you are familiar with all my ways. Before a word is on my tongue you know it completely, O Lord" (Ps. 139-1-4).

Chapter 10

GRADUAL RECONNECTION

Becoming one spiritually, emotionally, sexually, recreationally, and financially with one's spouse remains the highest priority of a couple's earthly relationships. Obviously, one or more aspects were neglected that made a partner vulnerable for an affair. It is now time to focus on healing and strengthening the couple's susceptible areas so an affair is no longer desired.

According to extensive Biblical study by Carl Brecheen and Paul Faulkner of Abilene Christian University, the marriage partner comes directly after one's relationship with the Lord. God is to remain first, spouse second, minor children take third place, jobs fourth, elderly/widowed parents fifth, adult children next, and lastly others. The only person Scripture says we are to become one with is the spouse, and God would not tell a couple to become one unless it was to remain their primary goal.

Intimacy is infrequent for a couple plagued with adultery, and their attempts usually occur in brief, superficial ways. The affair simply masked the couples disconnect. They likely stopped investing their time, attention, and money in their marital relationship. Many report thinking that as long as they shared regular family time and had the basic necessities things were fine. The majority of resources went to places other than fostering their relationship. Eventually, they began treating their sexual life with similar benign neglect and this created temptation for an affair. The adulteress came along, provided special attention to the hungering spouse, and offered what was missing in the relationship.

Rarely do these couples know the real person with whom they live, and it's time they did. They need to learn what the spouse thinks and feels, because knowing the spouse this well is mandatory for becoming one and knowing they are loved.

CHALLENGING FOR MEN. Sharing on an intimate level, in any way other than sexual intimacy, is often demanding for men. Men don't discuss feeling with other men like women do with women. In fact, women tend to share about every type of emotion with their best friend, and the more negative feelings they reveal, the closer they bond. Few men discuss how they feel about anything. Men can talk hours about sports, the weather, or politics, but they seldom tell how they feel about them. Most women focus on how they are impacted inwardly; while men highlight things external to themselves. Men discuss more rationally; women emotionally.

EXAMPLE: Sarah sought counseling to stop her attraction for another man before it turned sinful. Her attraction for this man began when he told her in passing that she looked pretty. Most women when paid a compliment brush it aside with a quick, "Thanks" or they discount the comment with, "This old thing," or "My hair's a mess." and then forget it. But instead of the man's words being treated as a trivial comment, Sarah froze and began to cry. She was so emotionally starved for positive attention she lost control.

Later, the man phoned to apologize, and asked what he had said that was wrong. His compliment and desire to apologize laid the foundation for a relationship to blossom. Sarah was so starved emotionally that one positive comment drew her to this man.

Admitting the attraction, Sarah drug her husband for counseling and during the first session she revealed that they had been married 14 years and she had never seen her husband, or any man, naked. A man who cannot be sexually intimate, hides from his wife, and can't look at her naked will not be emotionally intimate in ways a woman yearns to connect.

Sarah explained that on their honeymoon, each time her husband changed clothes, he went into the bathroom and shut the door, something Sarah never entered marriage expecting. Finally, she attempted to help them be closer by suggesting they shower together. When her husband refused, Sarah asked if he was hiding from her, and he responded with fury. He grabbed the motel TV, tossed it on the bed, and bounced the lamp onto the floor. He raced to the closet and yanked all of her clothes off hangers, flung them onto the floor, and stomped on them. He tore open her new luggage and ripped out the lining before tossing the suitcase into the air. Then letting out a howling scream, he turned and bolted from the motel. He was gone hours as she sat terrified and crying. Sarah was so overwhelmed with fear of how he behaved that she never again mentioned his avoidance until this first counseling session 14 years later.

During these years, they infrequently had sex in the dark, with each ending with him saying, *"Don't look at me."* The husband continued changing clothes in the bathroom with the door shut. Three children later, Sarah convinced her husband to come with her for counseling, but her reason was because of how deeply she was attracted to the man who had complimented her. She had lived without emotional support so long that she interpreted the other man's non-personal compliment as deeply and intimately personal.

After their second counseling session, Sarah's husband refused to return. He did stop changing in the bathroom, but he still had no interest in learning to create intimacy in their marriage, something his wife deeply needed. He simply found it too challenging and told her, *I'm unwilling to pay the price this would require. I don't want that kind of marriage."*

Several ideas to help a couple reconnect are provided below.

Take time to be alone
Learn what was lacking in the marriage
Identify the positive
Resume sexual activity
Offer an emotional intimacy task
Pray together

INSIST THEY MAKE TIME TO BE ALONE

Encourage your couple to spend 10-30 minutes each day discussing how their day went, not just the day's activities, but how they felt about each activities. Intimacy isn't developed by only sharing what happened but by how what happened impacted them. Intimacy is sharing, *'how I privately felt about what occurred.'* It is sharing how upset you felt when your manger made a curt remark or how you felt in the present moment when your spouse surprised you with an unusual comment. It's the part you are unlikely to share with anyone else.

Suggest they meet for lunch or put the children to bed at a specific time and turn off the TV so there's no distractions. At least once a week, they need to take time to go alone for coffee or walk around the block without the kids, and discuss dreams, fears, disappointments, and wishes. Ensuring they discuss positive topics, keep them from being completely overwhelmed with talk of the affair.

Every couple needs to reserve time alone without the children or friends, and a couple who has experienced adultery needs more private time than others. Their creating special times for each other is also for the sake of their children. The way to rear healthy children is for the children to feel their home is secure and safe, and any possible fears of disruption eliminated by watching how their parents like being with each other.

Insist that they place their marriage as a higher priority than requests from others. They should plan couple time in advance so his and her calendars are marked as time for themselves, and refuse to let others bump or alter their set dates. *"Sorry, but we already have a firm commitment that day"* is enough explanation. Help them both learn to say no and understand they are obeying the Lord by striving to become one. For several months, they need to reconnect as a couple more than they need to share as a family.

They must place their marriage as a higher priority than requests from others

Recommend that they take turns planning an enjoyable activity to share on the weekends, an event that is unlikely to create tension or friction. Watching humorous movies in the evenings can create a better mood for reconnecting. They need to find common interests and pursue them together. Some of the closest bonding comes by mutually tackling pleasurable tasks. It's not enough to attend their child's little league games or music recitals. They need shared adult activities.

LEARN WHAT WAS LACKING IN THE MARRIAGE

Help them process the dynamics that created the opportunity for an affair. This couple does not understand the different gender responses to disappointments and need to learn.

When a wife becomes disappointed and dissatisfied with their relationship, she tends to tell him. It is her way of improving things. After she tells him, she often loves him more than before, because she fills with positive hope that things will improve. She believes that telling him will have him wanting to please her. But if things don't change, she assumes he no longer loves her. She convinces herself that he knows what she needs and obviously doesn't care.

However, he may have heard her words as complaints and put downs, rather than as requests. He doesn't tell himself, *"She's unhappy and I will do whatever I can to help her feel better."* Instead, of moving closer he tends to withdraw thinking either *"She must think something's wrong with me."* Or, *"I can never do anything right to please her."* Feeling shame, he pulls away.

When he withdraws, she tends to become even more pushy and unpleasant as she attempts to force him to care, but this behavior has him moving away even farther. If another woman comes along to tell him how good or smart, or wonderful he is, he may move towards that woman's warm comments, and increasingly withdraw more from his wife.

Or the wife eventually tires of trying to have him move closer, and she withdraws. As she distances herself, he enjoys the peace but fails to realize that her detachment means she has become vulnerable to responding to another man's kind, supportive words.

PROCESS WHAT HAPPENED. They need you to help them process what made their relationship susceptible to adultery. By understanding what happened, they can better ensure it isn't repeated by either of them. Insist that they stop blaming each other, but now blame their relationship. How they interact and withhold from each other is the root of the problem.

How they interact and withhold from each other is the root of the problem

IDENTIFY THE POSITIVE. An affair focuses on the positive aspects of both parties, while a marriage ensures they eventually sees the partner's every flaw. In an affair, most men say they like the person they became while with the adulteress. Because many hear little praise for the things they think they contribute to the marriage, an affair often becomes a type of revenge for feeling ignored and lonely. The goal of your questioning is to free the adulterer to be himself at home, and this frees his wife to more easily express herself.

Explain that all people want appreciation, attention, and acceptance. Keep reminding that the goal is never to place blame but to make their relationship stronger.

Help the adulterer identify what he found pleasurable in an affair and how, as a couple, they can revive happiness together. Just ensure you ask questions in a way that does not let him say something negative about his wife. For example, ask questions similar to those below.

What did you like about yourself in the other relationship? How were you different? What do you tell yourself to stop from being that way at home?

What made you comfortable in that relationship? What do you tell yourself to stop you from acting the same in your marriage? What would you have to think to behave that way at home?

What were you able to say/do in that relationship that you would like to do or say with your wife? What do you tell yourself that stops you from being/saying the same with your wife? How do you hold yourself back?

What were the positive aspects of the affair that you can now bring to your marriage?

What about you makes it difficult to discuss issues that you find uncomfortable in your marriage?

Why do you not talk about them? What part of this needs to change? How will you work to change?

What should you now do differently?"

The wife needs to list the ways she contributed to their emotional disconnect. Ensure she includes 1. What she thinks the other woman found desirable in him; 2. How she can make him feel desired in similar ways; and 3. Times she failed to give enough of these, and how it may have made it easier for him to excuse his decision.

EXAMPLE. As we ate breakfast in the motel eating area, I hung my purse on the back of the chair. After we finished, we returned to our room, and as soon as we shut the door, I realized I didn't have my purse. I raced back to the breakfast area, and my purse was gone. We phoned the police who insisted we needed to leave the motel because the thief now had my car keys and would likely take our car during the night. We spent the next couple of hours cancelling credit cards, packing, and calling our bank. I was not responsible for the thief stealing my purse, but my actions made it easy for the crook. This is what the wife needs to realize about her husband's affair. Choosing to have his needs met in an affair was 100% his choice, but some of her actions made it easy and contributed to the aftermath being so painful.

Choosing to have his needs met in an affair was 100% his choice, but some of her behaviors made it easy

He must be willing to admit what he liked during the affair and to behave with his wife in similar ways so his wife wants to respond lovingly to him. Likewise, she must be willing to agree to meet his needs and ask for her own. Ask them to do something each day to make the other feel good. Perhaps, making a list called *'these are things that make me feel good when you do them'* would solicit ideas and promote positive responses.

Expect both spouses to feel guilt over how they have treated each other in the past, and realize some things have to change. Foremost, they must stop criticizing each other, and accept that what makes one feel good may do nothing for the other. According to the Lord they are to *"Do everything without complaining or arguing"* (Php. 2:14). Refuse to accept any response of, "Yes, but. . ." A spouse's words carry tremendous power to hurt or to help the other feel good. Only when blame and critical comments stop can relationship healing occur. When God says 'do everything without complaining', He means it.

Let each ask what they need from the other. It should include what they want more and what they want less. Their list may look similar to this:

Her	Him
Sit and talk with me every day about us	Stay on budget and allow for some fun
Help with the kids' housework	More sexual response
Refuse to let others speak negative about me	Tell me what I do good
Support me when I take a stand with the kids	Time on weekends for myself
	Help with lawn work

Each request needs negotiation and ongoing discussion. Both need more positive attention, and both hunger for praise, so help them decide how they can give more.

DISCUSS THEIR RESUMING SEXUAL ACTIVITY

The time for resuming sexual activity differs for every couple. Some women want to immediately reconnect because it helps her feel femininely desirable, and reassures they are not going to lose each other. Other couples wait several weeks. Typically, the wounded spouse makes the decision. Some wives need to wait until they feel they can trust him, and others resume sexual activity immediately as a way to start their relationship fresh and anew.

Some couples allow shame, anger, or a lack of forgiveness to hold them back and you must help them discuss and resolve these concerns. It's not unusual for both spouses to vacillate between a strong desire to again win their spouse's love and an intense desire for space and freedom. They can accept that resuming sexual activity does not mean things are totally forgotten or that all hurt has stopped. Instead, it can mean, "*I love you and want to learn to love you more.*" Or, "*I am committed to us staying together, and this is proof of my commitment.*" They are married, and it's appropriate to resume sexual activity when both want to, provided both have veto power.

Suggest they do more touching because it tends to soften the idea of being sexually active. They can give foot massages, back rubs, hold hands, and hug more often. Explain, that they need to touch for the pleasure that touch brings, not just so it leads to the bedroom. Touch is a powerful tie that promotes closeness. Once they are comfortable with the added touching, sex seems to come naturally. Many couples, especially the women, need to feel emotionally connected as friends again and prefer to cuddle and hold each other in bed for several weeks with assurance there's no intent of intercourse. For many women this works wonders. Once they feel bonded, their desire for sex will come naturally.

Once they feel bonded, their desire for sex will come naturally

The sexual experience is going to carry a different meaning for each of them, but hopefully, this time it won't just be sexual relief but carry a feeling of genuine love and giving and caring. Hopefully, they now realize the need to discuss any sexual concerns, such as lack of desire, what best increases arousal, or inability to climax. Knowing each other better gives sex a deeper meaning. Leading them in a discussion of their likes and dislikes elicits talks of what was missing for them in the past.

OFFER THEM AN EMOTIONAL INTIMACY TASK

To help them begin sharing in intimate ways, 98 questions are provided in Appendix C that requires them to share how they feel about certain things. Their responses have them relating the ways they are often emotionally impacted which helps them better understand the likes and dislikes of their mate. They are to answer these together when they are in a quiet undisturbed place.

They may want to occasionally add questions they would like the spouse to answer. It might be something like, *"When I think about our children marrying and moving far away, I feel. . ."* Or *"When you criticize my driving, I feel. . "Our current level of closeness makes me feel. . .?"*

Many couples find answering the questions in writing works best. Writing slows the thinking and helps raise consciousness about how one genuinely feels. The point is not how it's done as much as ensuring they talk openly and know the other listens. Knowing themselves better helps to remove the fear of 'if you knew the real me, you might not love me.'

SHOW PRAYING TOGETHER IS MOST INTIMATE

Once they are connecting recreationally, emotionally, and sexually, they need to learn to bond spiritually. Encourage them to begin praying together and out of the children's presence. This is not intended to discourage or replace a family prayer time but be additive.

As part of their prayer time, recommend that they list their own faults and weaknesses and seek mutual forgiveness. They need to remove the plank from their own eyes before trying to help their spouse. Never underestimate how praying softens their hearts and allows the Lord to return them to Him and to each other. Once a sin is forgiven, God forgets it and it is not to be mentioned again. They are to pray about their present wrongs, not those committed in the past, provided they were previously confessed.

MODEL FOR THEM. At first, praying together may make them extremely uncomfortable, so ask them to initiate such praying in your office today. Make the prayer a threesome. Model what you expect of them by opening the prayer with a confession of one of your today's regrets, especially a thought you wish had not entered your mind.

They need to learn the joy of being able to give every problem to God as they struggle as marriage partners because every couple has differences. To strengthen their faith, they need to learn to tell themselves, *"Yes, this happened, but God will. . ."* *"Yes, it hurt, but God cares that I. . ."* *"At least, God knows and will. . ."* Satan has them thinking issues must be resolved immediately, but faith provides assurance that God knows the required time for complete healing. A daily connection with God is crucial. Remind them how submission to God ensures His care and control, and that God hears all their prayers because the Holy Spirit and Jesus intercede to ensure their prayers rise to heaven worded perfectly for addressing the care they need (Ro. 8:27, 35).

BONDING EXERCISE

Read Matthew 19: 4-6 aloud to the couple as a reminder that because God says a couple is to become one, He wants them working towards that goal. The exercise is designed to increase their oneness and willingness to change in ways that benefit their marriage and family.

Explain they are to evaluate how they are working together and see if they discover other ways that would strengthen their bond. Have them answer the questions in writing, and finish writing answers to each question before you ask the next one. At the end, they share their answers aloud. Begin with spiritual involvement.

Spiritually
1. What do you currently contribute to your marriage so, as a couple, you grow closer to the Lord?
2. What could you do so your relationship would be closer to the Lord?
3. What should you do to have your marriage closer to the Lord?
4. How could you teach your children to depend more on the Lord and less on you?
5. What should you do so your children depend more on the Lord and less on you?

Moving from - what do you - to what could you - to what should you - forces them to realize their own shortcoming and to identify ways they can change and do what's right for their relationship. Having a goal and knowing what they can do to achieve it continues building hope that things can and will improve. After they have finished, ask them to share what implementing each should would contribute to their marriage and family.

Emotionally

1. What do you currently contribute emotionally to your marriage so your partner feels good about himself/herself?
2. How could you contribute more emotionally to make your spouse feel better?
3. What should you do to help your spouse feel good about self so your marriage is emotionally strong?

Recreationally

1. What do you currently do that is fun for both you and your spouse?
2. What could you contribute that would be more fun and make your marriage better?
3. What should you do to make your relationship stronger and more enjoyable for both of you?

Financially

1. How do you currently contribute financially to your marriage?
2. How could you contribute financially that would make your marriage more financially sound?
3. What should you do to make your marriage stronger financially?

Sexually

1. How do you currently contribute sexually to your marriage?
2. What could you contribute sexually to make your marriage better?
3. What should you contribute so your relationship is strongly bonded sexually?

If a couple continues in counseling this long, they appear to have the motivation to make the marriage succeed. As they begin to know each other in deeper ways, trust gradually develops, and they are ready to resolve marital issues that have weakened their connection. Resolving differences bonds them closer. Remember, Solomon told his son that if he is intoxicated with love and desire at home, he has no reason to look outside the marriage.

Couples who work to rebuild intimacy after an affair deserve a lot of respect for the painful, yet rewarding, work they do to heal their relationship and their closeness with the Lord. With God's help, they have the ability to recover and make their marriage blossom stronger than ever.

And you, as their counseling minister helped them cover a multitude of sins. God is surely watching and blessing you from heaven.

Chapter 11

GOD'S COMMAND FOR MARITAL SUCCESS

God is demanding. He wants us to have successful, fulfilled lives, and He knows what it requires. God expresses His goodness through commandments of how we should live. When we respond in ways worthy of Him, we have great marriages. For example, in Ephesians (5:33) God tells a man that he **must** love his wife because men are not naturally good at showing their love, especially not in ways a woman desires. Still, loving his wife is an effort God expects him to apply so he does his part in making their marriage successful. The Lord instructed women that they **must** respect their husbands. Giving respect is what women are required to develop in a marriage because without respect, her husband lives constantly dissatisfied with their relationship. God requires her to learn how. God says

must because He loves us and knows our obedience proves good for our relationships.

Love and respect are felt when our basic needs are met: Being noticed and listened to, protected and feeling secure (usually more valued by women), valued for what we do and how we are, and included to feel a part of something larger ourselves (tends to be more valued by men). When these needs are satisfied, we feel loved and respected. Some virtues are easier for a woman to provide; others come easier for a man. God expects us to admit and correct the areas where we fail or are weak, and marriage seems to be our training ground. Unfortunately, we often make them battle grounds.

Providing an explanation of the different desires of each gender can help prepare your couple to resolve lingering issues that have threatened their relationship. The information below is to prepare them so they realize why some issues about their behaviors may bother their mate.

EXPLAIN WHAT'S MORE NATURAL

Most man are naturally respectful. Watch how he talks with other men, even with men he dislikes, he speaks respectfully. They don't interrupt or discount what the other says. They wait until asked to give advice. They can even share lunch with a man who just hurt their feelings and talk about trivia matters in respectful ways, something a woman could never do. The problem is that few know how to have their wives feel loved. For most men, caring and nurturing is not an innate trait. So God requires that men **must** learn to love as their wives need.

Women are naturally more loving. For them, caring for others comes easier. If a friend is ill, they respond with food for the family or offer to care for the children. They can cry just hearing another describe her pain because they stay attuned to other's emotions, especially their negative ones. But women are not always respectful. They can speak bluntly and catty and think little of interrupting if they think the speaker is mistaken. And they remember forever the ways another hurts them and keep these relationships at a comfortable distance. They never go out to eat with someone who just hurt their feelings or threatened them. God told women that they **must** treat their men respectfully because men desperately crave respect, and few women know how.

Obviously, both can learn to supply enough of what their mate needs. Otherwise, the Lord would not demand they do it. And they can learn to depend on the Lord to complete all the needs their mates can't.

DISCUSS WHAT LOVE IS FOR A WOMAN

If a man never told his wife that he loved her, or did special things to show her, it's unlikely she would have married him. If the most romantic thing he ever said was, "I like you. I like you a lot," she would not wear his engagement ring, let alone a wedding band. To her, such words hold no more value than his saying he likes hamburgers or baseball a lot. She craves romance and intimacy and these demand that he must do some things differently, even if they hold a lesser value for him. In fact, he may consider such ideas a waste of time. But it's what he must do to be right with the Lord – and with her.

A wife wants to feel that her husband holds her closer to his heart than he does anyone else in the whole world. After God, a wife must know she ranks first with her husband, and she measures his love by observing how he treats her compared to how he treats others, especially other women. She can only tolerate competing with another if she wins, and that includes his mother, the children, his co-workers, and even his job or recreation. His actions are what prove to her that his words of loving her are genuine. If he spends more money on his mother for Christmas, his actions show that his mom ranks higher. If he takes the side of one of the children against her, he has not only shown bad parenting, but he has weakened trust in their relationship. If he shows too much attention to another woman, she floods with jealousy. She wants to be the one he gives the majority of his time, attention, and loving actions.

A wife wants to feel that her husband holds her closer to his heart than he does anyone else in the whole world

Feeling she ranks less or is insignificant in her husband's heart crushes a wife's spirit. She needs his love more than she needs oxygen to breath, or at least as much, and once married she depends predominately on him and the Lord for her emotional survival. She may have one or two girlfriends with whom she shares secrets, but her primary source always remains her husband and her private prayers.

A wife wants to crawl inside her husband's head and learn what he likes and dislikes about every aspect of his life. Each evening when he returns home, she wants to hear every detail of his day and to share hers. For her, explaining such events is how she emotionally reconnects after their time apart. She likes his arm around her or holding hands in public and hearing him tell others positive things she has done. She likes him assuming a household chore without her needing to remind him and hearing him say she looks nice.

A wife likes flowers, long talks, mushy cards, his remembering special events and holidays, unexpected gifts for no reason, going places where they dress especially nice, holding hands in public, and walks on a beach. It's the same beach where he would prefer playing volley ball or scuba diving. For her, their togetherness and talking helps her feel loved; for him, their sharing ball and diving activities has him thinking she values sharing his interests.

She craves him writing her love notes. I know a woman who framed her husband's hand-written love letter and kept it setting beside her bed for 40 years. A young man I counseled pleaded for something he could immediately do to improve his struggling marriage, and I suggested that he write his wife a love letter. He was to explain what he loved about her and how he valued the ways she cared for him and their children. When I saw him again, you would have thought I had sprinkled his wife with magical fairy dust because of how she responded and their relationship improved. It made the three hours it took him to write the letter worth every second. Wise men write long love notes to their wives.

Women need to be listened to and to feel protected. In fact, she needs these so strongly that even if she must yell to get her husband's attention to tell him, she will. When he fails to listen until she has to insist, she feels rejected and abandoned and that creates unbearable pain for her. Because of her pain, she fails to realize how disrespectful her demands appear to him.

A woman needs to know her man will protect her from people she considers immoral or ones she thinks intrude on her marriage. It's as though she keeps an invisible bubble around the two of them, and she won't risk letting another close enough to puncture it. She holds many things close to her heart, like her weight, her fears, and secrets. She wants to share these with her husband and to know he will do whatever is necessary to protect her privacy of these.

SHARE HOW MEN CRAVE RESPECT

Because feeling loved is so very important to a woman, she often fails to understand that hearing, "I love you" carries less impact for a man. He craves respect, more than soft, romantic whispers.

POWER OF COMPLIMENTS. Husbands spell love differently. They spell love r-e-s-p-e-c-t. He hears that she respects him with words that praise how he helps her, how hard he works, and how she appreciates all he does. He feels loved – not by what she does for him – but by how she shows appreciation for all he does for her. He would rather hear, *"I really value that you did it for me. . ."* than, *"I love you."* He welcomes hearing, *"I really like that you listen when I need to gripe . . ."* and *"Thank you so much for protecting me when . . ."* Once she learns the power of her compliments, she will receive an ample supply of love and attention.

> **He feels loved**
> **- not by what she does for him -**
> **but by how she shows appreciation for**
> **all he docs for her**

She can change his annoying habits with compliments by praising him when he does what she likes. For example, perhaps he watches hours of football, but after 30 minutes of watching her movie, he no longer hides his displeasure. As he sits tolerating her movie, she can shower him with praise, give him a pillow, make him hot cocoa, and ask him questions about what one of actors might have meant and tease about his knowing more about men that she may never understand. Her asking gets him involved in the movie and shows she respects his trying to watch what she enjoys. Then she can be especially responsive sexually as she says, *"This is to thank you for watching my movie with me. It makes me love you so much, and I want you to know how you doing special things for me makes me love you even more."*

Praise is a way to show him what she wants, rather than complaining about what she doesn't want. Nagging about an overdose of football creates negative distance emotionally. Praise for the times, no matter how seldom or infrequent he does what she likes, reaps her positive attention.

He needs to know that she appreciates the mundane, boring, on-going tasks he does for her and their family, like his mowing the lawn and feeding the dog. He wants her to notice when he shields her from other's un-Christian behaviors, such as their use of profanity in her presence and she needs to thank him. Or that she notices when he has a bad day and gives him have some quiet time to unwind.

A man experiences serious emotional pain when his wife says something that leaves him feeling shame as a provider, protector, or lover. He carves appreciation for what he does and how he is. When he thinks he has failed her in one of these ways, he withdraws inside a private mental shell to hide his hurt. He aches so deeply, he can't talk about it.

He feels guilt for what he has done or failed to do that displeases her. Then he feels shame which has him questioning his ability and worth and value as a husband. Once guilt turns to shame, he cannot talk about it. She must guard her comments so he doesn't feel a failure or he begins to doubt his ability to do better.

He cannot stand being compared with other men if he loses or even if they tie in these areas. He needs praise and to know she values him for striving to do his best.

He feels respected when his wife responds to his sexual advances and knows she considers him a prized lover. Being disrespected with a series of 'No, not tonight," crushes a husband's very being, as deeply as a wife hurts if he flirts or puts another woman before her.

A husband may hate his job, but he still wants his wife to know that he is working so he can care for her. Feeling he accomplishes something by working is one way he feels a part of something larger than himself. He takes being financial responsibility extremely serious. He wishes he could give her everything her heart desires.

He wants her to recognize how he strives to give her everything she wants and likes. He likes knowing she appreciates his decision-making that's intended for making her life better. Knowing it pleases her, leads a man to take her to her favorite places to eat, or suggest they watch her kind of TV shows. It's why he buys her the lamp she doesn't need or her sixth pair of black shoes. He has learned she likes them and knows it will make her happy.

A husband will die for his wife if it becomes necessary. Think how our military is predominately men and how they wear their uniform with great pride because it shows their commitment to protecting family and country. To a man, protecting his wife is a badge of honor. He wishes he could defend her against everything she fears and every person she finds offensive.

To keep her man happy, a woman needs to learn how to give him some freedom and have times without her. Men appear to need more time for recreation with other men than she does with other women. She may talk hours on the phone, but he appears to need time in other men's presence. They may golf, or fish, or bowl, but for him it's the competition and companionship with the other men he craves and that can't be done by email or text messages.

DESIRES CONTIRUBTE TO DISAGREEMENTS

God wired the brains of men and women differently. Remember Eve came from Adam's rib, and surely, it was one near Adam's heart because of how important emotions are to a woman. It's certain that Eve did not come from Adam's brain because they rarely think alike. As you counsel couples, you will find that she focuses on distressing emotional aspects of how a problem impacts her, while he tends to provide a more logical, factual framework for consideration of each issue.

During counseling, the topic a couple first describes is rarely the root of their arguments. A wife evaluates her husband's actions by them leaving her feeling loved or unloved, while he considers if her ideas and behaviors show him respect. Feeling unloved, she feels devalued and less as a woman as if 'something significant is missing in me. With disrespect, he feels shame, fully unworthy, and then unloved and unappreciated as 'a man having little to no value with the one he craves to hold the highest esteem.

A wife evaluates her husband's actions by them leaving her feeling loved or unloved, while he considers if her ideas and behaviors show him respect

FORCEFUL ARGUING FAILS. Often, an unhappy spouse attacks the mate in an effort to force the spouse to respond as the unhappy one wants. The dissatisfied mate thinks, *"I want you to love/respect me, but I don't feel you do, so I'm going to force you by arguing how wrong you are to behave this way."* Talk about illogical thinking. But when either hurts because of feeling unloved or disrespected, they make the worst of decisions.

Arguing never has the spouse wanting to respond the way we want. Instead the mate attacks back, and both lose. We humans behave the craziest of ways to try and obtain the love and respect we so desperately crave. But regardless of how much we try, we never argue another into liking or valuing us. We only make our partner defensive and want to self-protect.

Couples may say they fight about money or sex or in-laws, but these only become problems when the partner's words or actions cause the mate to feel unloved or disrespected. Once they resolve differences regarding money and sex in a way that leaves the partner feeling valued, appreciated, and understood, the issues are no longer problematic.

EXPLAIN HOW ASSUMPTIONS SUBSTITUTE FOR SHARED FEELINGS

As their counselor, you can help couples recognize their errors and the marital problems that are created when one spouse insists she knows why her spouse behaved as he did.

You will find that marital partners rarely share how they feel or explain what causes them hurt. Disappointed, they convince themselves that it was the mate's actions that caused the pain. They see themselves as victims and judge the spouse as doing wrong. Yet, it's often the hurting partner who failed by not asking for what was wanted, and in a way that would reinforce feeling loved or respected. .

Instead of asking for what we want, we tend to think our mate should just know. We question, *"Can't he see how many chores I have to do?"* Or, *"Doesn't she see how worried I am about money?"* We think our spouse should not only know but should want to fix things for us. *"He/she should want to help. I shouldn't have to ask."* We live out the blame game and develop expectations that say, "If he loved me he'd..." "She doesn't respect me. If she did, she would. . . "

Our insisting that we know why our spouses acted as they did helps to explain why God says we will be judged as we judge others. For example, when a woman judges her mate as intending something hurtful and thinks it's because he doesn't love her, she reacts with words like, *"Why did you do that? You knew I didn't want that. You never listen to me. You care about others more than my feelings."* He tends to respond by judging her in return. He wants to defend himself and replies with, *"You can be so mean in how you speak. You don't care how you treat people. Why do you accuse me of such stupid things?"* Judging begets judging (Mt. 7:1).

You need to help your couple learn to share the interpretation they assign to their spouses actions and words that leave them hurt or annoyed. What they tell themselves inside their private thoughts leaves them hurting far more than what the spouse has done. Rarely, if ever, is the meaning they assign to their partner's behavior what the spouse intended. Perhaps, this helps explain why God says, *"We will be judged as we judge others. For in the same way you judge others, you will be judged, and with the measure you use, it will be measured to you"* (Mt. 7:1-2).

Certainly, when we judge our mates as intending something they never meant, we use a defensive tone and hurtful words that have the mate responding by judging us for having judged them wrongly." Instead, show the couple how to be honest and say, *"When this happened, I told myself you meant to. . . Is that what you intended?"* And insist that they accept their mate's s honest explanation. Help them realize that what the spouse did/ said had nothing to do with loving or not loving nor of respecting or not respect them. We tend to be so quick to self-protect that we put wrong interpretations on other's behaviors.

It is easier to blame each other and avoid the responsibility of identifying and expressing our feelings and desires. Rarely, do we share the interpretation we assign to other's actions. The more negative assignment we use, the less likely we are to admit what it is that we think their actions mean. But doing that causes us more hurt than what our partner did. Truthful honesty is what sets us free of such agony. . .

Attacking our mate with criticism for not understanding our sensitive areas may have our spouse extinguishing their behavior, but it ensures they will hurt us again in other situations. While it's easier to say, *"If you would do X or stop doing Y, there would be no problem,"* that type of problem-solving offers no understanding of why X or Y created a problem. Without identifying the unmet need, the same desire will create pain again and again with other issues. Once we can identify the desires of our mate, and understand the vulnerable areas, we can work together to find a way to relieve any discomfort or pain.

By sharing our private interpretation that we assign to our mate's actions, we learn to connect emotionally. This lets us understand each other's pain and know how to handle our partner with gentleness. It has us wanting to satisfy our spouse's most wanted desires. But our mates cannot please us if they don't know what these desires are, and they know only if we tell them. Otherwise, they are left guessing and usually guessing wrong.

We feel loved and respected when our mates value and prize us. But, no one can treat us positively all the time. There's no perfect spouse or parent. At times, their own needs block their ability to give as we want.

IMPORTANCE OF FUNCTION, BEING, WILL FOR SUCCESS

Successful marriage counseling consists of addressing three aspects of the couple's behaviors as they seek solutions to their problems. These are Function, Being, and Will.

FUNCTION. This is what we do, the behaviors and actions we take during daily living. How we Function is how others judge us, because it's the actions others observe as we work, play, and relax. How we Function reveals the purposes we are pursuing and what we hope to achieve or avoid.

BEING. Our Being reveals character traits and qualities. It is often described as our attitude. Paul prayed for the Ephesians to be strengthened with *power through Jesus' Spirit in* **their inner being** (3:16, emphasis mine). *"In my inner being I delight in God's law"* (Ro. 7:22). A positive Being is observed in those who act as good Samaritans, who go the second mile, or who sacrifice for others' good no matter how they feel. Scripture says, *"Your attitude should be the same as that of Christ Jesus"* (Php. 2:5).

However, our Being can also be shameful. We can do all the right things (Function) and have such a poor attitude

(Being) that others wish we weren't around. It's a negative Being that lets a mate know we'd rather not help as needed. Being is noticed in a two-year-old who has a melt-down (Function) because he can't have his way (selfish Being), and some adults still experience similar reactions when something's said or done they don't like. Scriptures are filled with the types of Being we need to change to live right with the Lord, such as stop being selfish, dishonest, lying etc.

WILL. Our Will determines how much energy and commitment we put into each task (Function). It shows the level of motivation we apply. An example is seen in the motivation of a quarterback playing to win the super bowl vs his playing with his sons in the backyard. The different levels of will he applies is observed in how he Functions.

Another example is the college student who goes without sleep and fun times to study (Function) and ensure his grades are acceptable for admission to a desired graduate program. This student demonstrates a strong will (Motivation) to fulfill the goal. However, if this student is cranky, and difficult to be around, the attitude (Being) may keep friends away.

We can have an attitude that's cheerful and pleasant (Being) but work so slowly that we drag out a fix (Function) until it's too late to be of any value, because we lack the motivation (Will) to do what's necessary. Or we can display a Will that's determined to do things our way (negative Being) regardless of how it displeases others. Consider the strong-willed child in a grocery store who's determined to have the piece of candy that mother says no to his having. He will grab for it (Function), and when she takes it away and places it back on the shelf, he reaches for it again. The mother has to hold his hand to stop him. Then when she turns away to address the cashier, the child snatches the candy and sticks it in his mouth still covered with paper. The child has a highly motived Will to succeed, albeit, with a negative, disobedient, controlling Being that's focused on Functioning opposite of what his mother says. Too often how our rebellious Being and Will treat the Lord is similar.

Failure to keep our Will focused on the Functioning that God requires is the result of having a Being that desires self-control, not God-control. It is how Satan acted, and it cost him heaven.

Our failure to keep our Will focused on the Functioning that God requires is the result of having a Being that desires self-control, not God-control

FAILURE OF BEING. Most often, our failure to live up to another's expectation (and the Lord's) is the result of a flaw in our Being. It's our bad habits. We want to control things our way, have them when we want them, and exactly as we want them. James says it best: *What causes fights and quarrels among you? Don't they come from your desires that battle within you? You want something but don't get it. You kill and covet, but you cannot have what you want. You quarrel and fight. You do not have, because you do not ask God. When you ask, you do not receive, because you ask with wrong motives, that you may spend what you get on your pleasures* (4:1-3). When our heart is selfish and we want what we want, regardless of the cost to our mate, it reveals a tainted Being. The challenge is to keep the Will motivated for achieving the right Function while our Being holds an obedient, servant attitude so *"the power of Jesus' spirit works in our being"* (Eph. 3:16).

Consider giving this couple a copy of the 15 requirements for teammates having a Being that encourages one's Will to Function as agreed for resolving their problems. Below is a list of traits necessary to resolve conflicting issues in their marriage:

- The goal must be to stop the mate's pain that is caused by the problem.
- Both are accountable to share relationship power.
- Staying connected must be more valued than having control.
- Both accept responsibility for the impact their actions and words have on their mate.
- Both must give the other the special treatment that's wanted for self.

- It one forgets, the mate that's hurt has to remind the other of the agreement and stop being a rescuer and refuse to take over and do it.
- Withdrawing is as destructive as attacking, and both displease the Lord and must stop.
- Both must do what's right and complete what's hard, not just what's easiest.
- Sacrificial love often requires suffering for the other's good.
- Sacrificing for each other must be done freely, without coercion, manipulation or with an attitude of drudgery, or it's not sacrificing.
- Both are accountable to the Lord to do what's required so the other feels loved and respected, no matter the cost to self.
- Both must behave as if Jesus stands beside them helping as they give the Holy Spirit room to work in their hearts.
- Both must be willing to hear the truth about oneself, and remember they are never abandoned, alone, lacking enough respect, or love because Jesus promised we would never be without Him.
- Repeat of the same misconduct once or twice is wrong. Three times it's a pattern of sin.
- I must change me, not you.
- *"Submit to one another out of reverence for Christ"* (Eph. 5:21).

Have both agree to the necessity of keeping their Functioning, Being, and Will aligned as you tackle issues that continue to create their relationship problems.

RESOLVING DIFFERENCES CREATES HOPE

You next challenge is to counsel the couple to resolve irritating differences that have kept one or both unhappy. Resolving marital problems offers a couple hope that their relationship will succeed. Hope consists of two parts: a plan for obtaining what you want and the motivation and ability to complete the plan. The more hope a couple has of achieving what's important to them, the better satisfied they are with their marriage. Identifying things that one partner does that annoys the other and finding acceptable ways to resolve the irritants creates hope in that their marriage is finally going to provide them the love and respect they want.

Expect to find one partner unaware of how displeasing his behavior is to the spouse. He knows the partner's annoyed, but because he does not understand why, he tends to believe the partner's frustration is unjustified. It's rare for offending partners to intentionally cause their mate pain. He just puts a different interpretation on the situation and is trying to achieve a different goal.

Chapter 12

YOUR INVOLVEMENT AS THEY PROBLEM-SOLVE

As their minister-counselor, the shift to resolving marital problems places a different demand on you. Adultery counseling had you working to convince the illicit person to change, commit to faithfulness to the Lord and the spouse, and to have the injured spouse forgive. You prayed for him and with him, you read Scriptures to him, or you refused to counsel him until he stopped his adulterous relationship. You coached his wife on how to better relate with him and worked to keep her from desiring revenge.

However, during reconciliation of specific marital problems, you do not take sides or push for a particular outcome, no matter how strongly you feel about an issue they work to resolve. You must keep a poker face, and refuse to allow your body language to reveal your feelings. Without your input, they must decide together how to handle their differences and resolve problems together. It's their marriage, and it's their responsibility to determine outcomes that will hold themselves accountable.

Your role is to watch how they interact as they discuss problems and ensure both have equal say and both express what it will take to feel loved and respected. Ask them to avoid taboo topics. If there is an issue that creates heated, painful feelings in either party, they can agree to accept it, and live peacefully without resolving it. Research finds that most long-term, happily married couples have three issues they have not revolved. They work around the matter and have long since quit trying to discuss it, and they have refused to allow it to influence the positive parts of their relationship.

PROVIDE A LIST OF TROUBLESOME ISSUES

Provide the couple with a short list of typical issues that often create disagreements among married couples. Doing this can help your couple realize that their concerns are normal problems that all marriages face. Knowing that other couples struggle with the same problems is a major step for resolving them because it keeps them from exaggerating how bad and unique their own troubles are.

Giving them a list is preferred to asking them to create their own problem list because the recall of troublesome issues tends to begin the session with negative thoughts focused exclusively in the past. This is especially true of women.

Research shows that when a woman remembers a past situation that caused her pain, her thoughts inflame with the same degree of negative emotion she felt when the event actually occurred. This happens even if the event occurred 20 years earlier. So, prepare them a list of topics.

Research shows that when a woman remembers a past situation that caused her pain, her thoughts inflame with the same degree of negative emotion she felt when the event actually occurred

Below is a possible list for your use, and do add others. You will have them rank each topic by the amount of annoyance or discomfort they experience because of the way they currently handle the concern.

Bible study	Budgeting/money	Careers
Children	Church attendance	Forgiveness
Cleanliness (house, self, kids)		Driving
Communication	Future dreams/goals	In-laws
Hobbies/ sports	Holidays	Jealous
Money	Politics	Sex
Praise/ put downs in front of others		Time alone
Time together		

When they are drowning in pain, you need to remind this couple it is the great Physician who walks on water and can rescue them. If both partners submit to the Lord's control, their marriage can become better than ever. They can and will find ways to relieve the hurt. The cure that brings relief is for the spouse who contributes the pain to Function differently and hold a Being that show caring. Once they truly understand the pain their way of behaving (Functioning) causes their mate, they tend to be motived (Will) to change and their attitude (Being) shows they do it out of love.

Let both spouses individually rank each item on your list of typical marital issues using a scale of 1-10 in the order of personal importance. Ten means it's very important to the person. Hopefully, some items on the list have not been a problem, and it will receive a zero and never need discussing. Expect the husband's and the wife's rankings to differ.

Next, ask them to rank their top three problems by how painful it is for them, using the same 1-10 scale. Ten implies that their current way of addressing the issue leaves them with extreme anguish and discomfort.

Ask their advice about which issue to address first. Expect one or both of them to begin problem-solving with a mind-set of what would be an acceptable solution and unreceptive to other options. Also expect that one partner may be unaware of why such actions are displeasing and to think the partner's frustration is unjustified. However, you will also learn that it's rare for an offending spouse to intentionally cause the mate pain.

HOW TO DETERMINE WHO HAS FINAL SAY

Explain they don't have to agree, but they must be willing to support what means the most to their partner. Both will be required to sacrifice for the spouse just as Jesus sacrificed for the church. To make their marriage great, it requires that they work as a team, not competitors. Remind that according to the Lord, whoever wants to become great must act as a servant (Mt. 18:7). Sacrificing to reduce the mate's pain is often required for couples to increase their oneness.

Sacrificing to reduce the mate's pain is often required for couples to increase their oneness

Give them firm ground rules that are nonnegotiable: no speaking rudely, no withdrawing if things aren't going your way, no name calling, no blaming or attacking each other. If any negative response happens, stand up, and call a time out. Stop all discussion, and insist they each quietly pray and seek the Lord's forgiveness and continued help. Afterwards, resume again. Remember the goal is to move all issues near the bottom of the problem list, close enough that the aching spouse feels comfortably valued. Also expect the wife to have a longer list than her husband. While men tend to brush aside many concerns, women dwell extensively on problems.

PROBLEM: HIS SPENDING--HER SELF-DENIAL

How he views the issue: He spends without telling her and when she finds out, she explodes, thinking he spends more than they can afford. This leaves her thinking she can't spend on herself.

He lists this money problem as an 8 and ranks the discomfort he feels when it happens a 9. He is the one drowning in pain, so he initiates the negotiation and has final say of a workable solution.

<u>You ask him</u>: What would it take so this was no longer a problem for you?
<u>Him:</u> I need a set amount that I can spend and never have to tell her I spent it, or at least not tell her how I spent it. I need to feel free to spend without her blowing up and leaving me feeling I've done something wrong or am a bad, selfish person.
<u>You ask her</u>: How do you feel knowing he thinks you view him as bad and selfish?
<u>Her</u>: I don't make him feel that way. I just worry about money.
<u>You ask her</u>: He says he feels like the bad guy. How does his feeling that way affect you?
<u>Her</u>: I don't want him feeling like a bad guy. He's not bad, he just spends too much without letting me know. I guess I think it's sad that he feels bad. He isn't selfish. He just seems to want to have this separate life, and unless I understand where we stand financially, I can't plan for my needs or that of the kids.
<u>You ask her</u>: How do you feel when you learn he has spent money for his pleasure?
<u>Her</u>: Hurt. Used. Cheated out of having something I might want. Like I can't have anything. Like he gets it all.
<u>You ask him</u>: How does her reaction make you feel?

Him: I'm not sure. Angry, I guess. Like I work hard to make the money and should be able to spend some without asking permission. Cheated I guess. I just don't understand her being upset. I don't overspend. It's not like I do this all the time. (defensive)

You ask him: As a child, were you ever criticized for spending too much?

Him: No, but once my allowance was spent, I knew better than to ask for more. I rarely had enough to buy the things I really wanted. I always got plastic toys, not wooden or metal ones. I never felt I could have nice things like the other kids. I guess in some ways I still feel poor and now buy something nice because having nice things means so much to me. I don't want to buy cheap things all my life. (cheated, less important, devalued)

You ask her: Does knowing he never felt he had nice things, change how you feel about his spending?

Her: I want him to have nice things, but he always buys them without telling me, and then I worry about us not having enough left for what the kids want or I might need. I feel left out of what should be an important part of us working together as a family. And most of the time, it's just for his toys, not necessities. (feels neglected and at times discounted)

You ask her: How do you feel about using money for pleasurable things?

Her: I feel cheated. He overspends and that means the kids and I can't also have such things. I just want us working together so we all share equally.

You ask her: Do you think money is wasted if you use it for pleasurable things?

Her: Not if everyone in the family can do the same.

You ask him: Be specific. What is it you want? How much would you need to feel okay doing this?

Him: I would like to spend $100 without telling her that I did. I balance the books and there's no reason I should have to ask her permission as if she's my parent. *(Feeling disrespected)*

You ask her: Could you agree that he can spend $100 without telling you?
Her: Only if I can also have $100 to spend when I want something that he might not like or think I don't need. (*If he loved me, I'd have the same amount as he spends*)
You ask him: Can you afford for both of you to spend an additional $100 a week? If not, how much could you both have so she felt loved by thinking she had an equal share of your income?
Him: No. Two hundred a week would prove too big a splurge. That would be $800 a month, and we can't afford that. But maybe we could afford somewhere between $10 and $15 a week and save the money until it was enough to buy what we wanted. I never say anything about what she spends, so why would she not feel loved? (*surprised, questions if she's criticizing him*)
Ask her to explain why she thinks she can't have an equal share.
Her: When I hear how much you spend on your toys, I fear if I get something for myself, we won't have enough left for the things the children need. So I always do without. I tell myself that if you loved me, you'd want me to have nice things too.
Him: I do want you to have nice things. I never knew you worried about spending on yourself. What is it you want? What are you doing without? Tell me and I will get it for you today. (*fears being disrespected but wants to prove her wrong and without a reason*)
Her: It's nothing in particular. It's just that when I am shopping and see something I'd love to have, I always tell myself we can't afford it, and then I think your overspending is why we can't. I think if you loved me, you'd see that I had spending money too.
Him: I do not understand this. I love you and all money is our money. It's yours to spend too. I don't want you doing without. I have never said anything about what you buy. (*feels attacked*)

Her: It's because I never buy anything for myself. I live a life of self-denial. I know you don't tell me to do that, but it's what I do. I am not blaming you, but it is the thought process I use to deny myself things. I want to be able to stop thinking this way. *(She realizes how she blames him for how she thinks/acts and uses her thinking to tell herself that he is not loving her in order to justify her reasoning)*

You ask her: Are you aware of how you blame him for your private thoughts and how he had no idea you thought this way?

Her: Yes, I admit it. I make myself upset, and I want to stop.

You ask her: Could you agree with $10 to $15 a week, and if it's not enough to purchase something you want then wait until you save your weekly amount until you have enough?

Her: Yes, provided he promises to save and wait until he has saved enough before buying things that cost more too. *(isn't feeling completely loved/trustful)*

Him: I can do that. I promise. How about each Friday when I stop at the bank that I withdraw $15 for you and $15 for me, no also $15 for you to spend on the kids. If that proves too much, I will cut it back to all of us having $10. You can spend it all immediately or put it away and save until it's enough to get whatever it is you really want or the kid's want, and I will do the same. Let's try it for a month and then see what our checkbook shows. If needed, we will readjust. But do you promise not to care when I spend my share on something I want, and do it without giving you advance notice? Do you promise not to be upset and complain?

Her: Yes, just as long as I know you saved for it until you had enough and didn't withdraw more to get it.

Him: You have my word on that.

Date, document the problem and their solution, and have them sign it. Give both of them a copy of their agreed upon solution and put one in your file. Then insist they do something special to celebrate.

PROBLEM: HE FLIRTS WITH WAITRESSES

The issue is he doesn't think he flirts. He calls it being friendly. For him this issue rates a zero on both rankings. For her this is a 10 for concern, and she ranks it a 10 on hurt. She is drowning in pain, so she begins the negotiation and has final say on a solution.

<u>You ask her</u>: Describe how you feel about the way he treats the waitress.
<u>Her</u>: It makes me angry, jealous, and abandoned. I can't think of enough words. I only know I hate it.
<u>You ask her</u>: What is it you would like him to do differently so you felt comfortable around other women.
<u>Her</u>: I want him to act professional and not keep chatting and teasing with other women.
<u>You</u>: Be specific what is it you want him doing?
<u>Her</u>: I want him to only speak to waitresses to give them our order or ask for our check. He can do that nicely and stop there. I want all other words directed at me. We are there to eat and enjoy time together, not to make new friends with people we might not even like if we did know them. *(Feeling unloved, in second place instead of first).*
<u>You ask him</u>: Can you agree to direct all your talking to your wife and limit what you say to waitresses?
<u>Him</u>: I guess I could, but I would sure feel gagged. I like chatting with strangers and getting to know them. I'm a real extrovert. *(feeling disrespected /controlled)*
<u>You ask her</u>: Are you agreeing to only talk about your order and your check with waitresses and direct all other conversation to your wife?
<u>Him</u>: If have to. *(feeling disrespected)*
<u>You ask her</u>: Is this satisfactory?
<u>Her</u>: Not really, because his hesitation tells me that he prefers flirting with them to talking with me. *(feels unloved)*
<u>You ask her</u>: Explain why this is important to you.

Her: Because it makes me feel like I tagged along just to watch my husband put on a sexy flirt show. They even subtlety hint at inappropriate things right in front of me. Or she leans on his shoulder, and he laughs at her every word. I want to be first in his life, not a tag along who ranks at the bottom. *(Feeling unloved and ranking lower than a waitress)*
You: Read aloud the Scripture where God says a man leaves his parents and becomes one with his wife. Ask him: How does attention to a waitress help you create oneness with your wife?
Him: It doesn't, but I don't mean anything when I talk with other women. I sure have no personal interest in them? I'm just a friendly guy.(tries to justify his actions)
Ask him: How would you feel if I told you that your wife was seriously interested in another man?
Him: I'd be jealous and probably angry. I guess I'd resent it.
Ask him: What part of her relationship with another man would upset you?
Him: I'd resent the time she spent with the man, their talking about personal things, and how close they were. If it was sexual, I'd be furious. But that's different. I have no personal interest in any waitress. I just enjoy joking and kidding.
Ask him: But now that you know she takes it as a personal insult, is joking and kidding worth leaving your wife hurt?
Him: Well, no, but it shouldn't hurt her. It's all in fun.
Ask him: What if she begins a serious relationship with a man and says it began as just kidding and having fun. Would that be okay?
Him: No, not if it turned serious, but I have no intent of this turning serious.
Ask him: But what if it did with your wife, and she told you that she now cares deeply for the man?
Him: I'd be angry and probably hurt and jealous.
Ask her: Is the time he spends talking with another woman the part that makes you hurt and jealous too?

Her: You bet it is. I feel betrayed every time it happens. Sometimes, I laugh or force a smile to hide my hurt, but I hate every minute of it. Inside I am crying.

Ask him: Can you now understand her hurt and agree to stop all unnecessary talk with other women and direct all attention to your wife who hungers for it?

Him: Since you put it that way, I can.

You ask her: Can you accept that as a solution.

Her: Only if he promises and assures me he will stop all flirting and give me all the attention he has been giving other women.

Him: I said I could, and I will.

Her: Then yes, it is a workable solution. It's what I've wanted for a long time and can't wait to go to our regular restaurant now that I know I will be the one having your attention. I will enjoy seeing that same waitress, whom I have always resented, learn she can't hang around our table and have your attention. I want to show her that it's our time for us, not her time with you. I want her to know she can no longer linger and flirt with you. Thanks. I've needed this for a long time. I love you and want to be the one you attend to.

Him: Okay. I never knew it bothered you this much.

You ask him: So, you admit you did know it bothered her some?

Him: Yes, but because I knew I meant nothing by it, I guess I thought it didn't matter.

You ask him: Now you know that each time she felt less important and lacked the oneness God commands, how do you feel about your actions?

Him: Well, since you put it that way, I guess, not so good.

You explain: When you are one with your wife, you never attend to another woman if it leaves your wife feeling badly. You don't buy other women gifts, send them cards, or give them attention that your wife needs. God takes being one as a couple very serious. God leaves no room for a threesome, not even briefly or occasionally no matter how innocent you think it is. It could always lead to something more serious on the other woman's part. The waitress may not consider it just teasing, as you say you do. The bottom line is: Your pleasure should never cause your mate pain. If it isn't pleasurable for both, you don't do it.

Him: I never thought about it that way. Yes, I can go to that restaurant and stop chatting with the waitress, or any other place and do the same. I apologize. I really didn't think about how it made you feel.

Ask Him: How will you act differently next time so the waitress gets the message that you are no longer going to chat and tease with her?

Him: How about I give her our orders without looking at her. I won't make eye contact no matter what she says and does.

Ask Her: Would that be enough?

Her: Probably, most of the time. But if she still lingers or says something personal it may require more.

You ask her: What else do think might be required of him?

Her: He may need to look at her and say, "Sorry, to interrupt, but we would really like to be alone, please.

You ask him: Could you verbally cut her off if your body language didn't send a strong enough message?

Him: I could. Yes. But know it would make me very uncomfortable.

You tell him: But not nearly as uncomfortable as your flirty attention has caused your wife, and how displeasing it was to the Lord.

Him: Then yes. If necessary, I will say it.

You ask her: Is this a workable solution for you?

Her: Yes. I just want to be first with him, not compete and lose to some waitress. I want to feel he is loyal to me and only me.

Document the problem and solution. Have them sign it and date it. Suggest they celebrate by eating at the restaurant tonight where the flirtiest waitress works. Prepare him for the waitress lingering to chat because it's what he has trained her to do.

He will be required to give her a cold shoulder and keep a poker face when she attempts to joke and tease. He has agreed to ignore her by refusing to make eye contact and responding to her with dead silence, until she learns it's time that she left them alone and behaved like a professional waitress.

Two additional problem-solving examples are provided in Appendix D. They discuss her wanting more help with cleanliness/household chores and a mother-in-law who sets up competition with her daughter-in-law.

ASSIGN THEM HOMEWORK. A couple's agreed solutions only prove successful if both parties' Will (how motivated they are to do as agreed) and Being (how they are as they do it) are aligned as they attempt to implement their solutions (Function). Ultimately, these three qualities determine if their solutions are successful. New ways to Function succeed only when Being and Will support their decisions.

New ways to Function, succeed only when the Being and Will support their decisions

Assign them the reading of specific Scriptures before they see you again. God's word provides many Scriptures for correcting attitudes and behaviors. This couple has been through a turbulent relationship period and need a deeper study and constant reminder of how God can work in their lives, provided they strive to live in ways that please Him.

Below are some suggestions for studying Being and Will verses. Give them copies and ask them to discuss how each might apply to their life. Tell them to come prepared to discuss the Scriptures in their next counseling session before they tackle another problem. Add others that you know this particular couple needs.

TABLE 1

SELFISH	UNDISCIPLINED
■ argumentative ■ blaming others ■ boastful ■ controlling ■ complains/grumbles ■ disrespectful ■ envious ■ greedy ■ ignores partner's needs ■ insensitive ■ manipulative ■ must always be right ■ rude ■ self-seeking SCRIPTURE READINGS: 1 Jn. 2:16-17; Js. 1:26, 3:6-12, 14, 4:1, 5:9-10; Phil. 2:3-4, 14-15, ; Titus 3:9-11; 2 Tim. 2:14, 23-24; Eph. 4:29-30, 5:21; 2 Co. 10:5-6, 7	■ anger uncontrolled ■ dishonest ■ disobedient ■ disorganized ■ disruptive ■ impatient ■ lies ■ loses temper ■ uncontrolled anger ■ undependable ■ unruly ■ untruthful ■ yelling/profanity SCRIPTURE READINGS: Col. 3:8; Rom 12:17-19; 2 Tim. 1:7; Eph. 4:1-3, 5:4-6; Tit.1:6,8, 16; Ac. 5:4; Pr. 10:18-20,15:18, 28:25; I Pe. 4:7; Lk. 19:10; Ps. 39:1
UNRELIABLE ■ broken promises ■ incomplete tasks	**UNFORGIVING** ■ bitter

■ lazy ■ passive ■ procrastinates ■ stubborn ■ untruthful ■ undependable ■ withdraws SCRIPTURE READINGS: Js. 4:17; Jn. 8:44; Pr. 6:6-11; Eph. 5:15-16, 119:113; 1 Thes. 4:11-12	■ critical ■ envious ■ gossip ■ judgmental ■ resentful ■ retaliating ■ revengeful ■ speaking badly of SCRIPTURE READINGS: Js. 2:13, 3:14-16; Ti. 3:3-8; Js. 4:11-12; Mt. 6:14; Lk. 11:4;Co. 3:13; Mt. 6:12-15; Col.3:12-14; Heb. 12:14-15; Pro.15:21
LACK OF FAITH ■ anxious ■ afraid to trust ■ feels helpless/hopeless ■ prayer-less ■ insecure ■ negative ■ untrusting ■ worrisome SCRIPTURE READINGS: Heb. 3:6, 10:19-25; 1 Pe. 5:7; Mk. 9:24; 1 Pe. 1:1-9; 1 Jn. 5:9-13,4:15-16, Ro. 5:1-11; Phil. 4:6; 1 Co. 4:17, 28:20	**OTHERS THEY NEED TO READ**

Chapter 13

ASSESS THEIR PROGRESS

Begin this session by reviewing the definition of Function, Being, and Will with God's first and most important commandment.

Love the Lord
 is how we are commanded to **Function**. It's what we do in an attempt to please God. It's the activities we do that show we love Him: studying His Word, obeying His commands, continually praying. Keeping the Lord the focus of all we do shows our faith.

With all
 Will is the degree of motivation and determination we apply to Function as commanded. With all we do, whether at work or play, or relaxing, we are determined to use our time, money, attention as a sacrifice for worship of God

Your heart, soul, mind and strength
 is how we are to **Be** as we do as He asks. He wants our entire **Being.** With complete surrender to Him and sacrifice of our entire life to keep Him first, while holding an attitude like Christ's.

HOMEWORK REVIEW. Ask what they learned about themselves by reading the homework Scriptures and how they applied to their relationship. Ask how things progressed with their agreed solutions. Hopefully, both kept their commitments, but if not, do not let either attack or bully the other as they describe what happened.

DISCUSS THEIR REACTIONS TO DISAPPOINTMENT

Remember, working together to resolve relationship concerns is new to them. Expect them to face struggles. Discuss how they handled each problem they worked to resolve during the previous counseling session. If one partner feels disappointed, use the following ideas to discuss what occurred.

<u>Ask the disappointed spouse</u>: When your spouse did not abide by your agreed solution (Function as agreed), how did you respond (Being)? What did you say and do? After the spouse's explanation, ask the uncooperative spouse to add anything that seems appropriate to the disappointed spouse's description. (Example: She not only did all she said, but she also threw the paper she was holding).

<u>Ask the one who failed to keep the agreement</u>: When you failed to keep your part of the resolution (Function as agreed), how did you respond to your mate's disappointment and frustration? Not what your spouse did, but how you reacted. Then ask the disappointed spouse to add anything to the uncooperative mate's description. (Example: When he walked away like he said, he also said a few choice words that weren't nice).

Take out Table 1 of Being (attitude) traits and character qualities with Scriptures they were to read as homework. Ask them to circle the traits on the list that each think applies to themselves personally. She circles behaviors that apply to her; him to his behaviors. They do not describe their mate, but circle only the ones that describes self.

NO LONGER REMAIN NEUTRAL

At this point, you no longer stay neutral. If one spouse is unwilling to examine self, for you to remain quiet about how the person behaved or failed to keep their commitment would imply you agree even if it was sinful. Failure to respond would support this mate without regard to the impact it had on the other.

Remind them that their solutions are meaningless unless they back them with a change in how they Function, their actions. If one spouse failed to do as agreed. It likely was because of a weak or flawed Being.

If one spouse failed to do as agreed, it likely was because of a weak or flawed Being

Ask if you may circle the traits and qualities you think describes each of them. Once you have their approval, circle the ones you think are applicable. If he is controlling, circle it (under selfish). If she has tantrums, circle it (under undisciplined). Use one color for his circles and a different color for her. Using different colors lets them compare themselves with how they appear to someone other than the spouse. Circle all you have observed. Share your list. Then compare all three lists.

Ask if they are prepared to change the Being traits that cause them relationship problems. Explain that motivation (Will) to do (Function) as agreed is hindered by these negative character traits (Being). Remind that these are the sinful qualities damaging their relationship, and the ones God expects them to change. *"Rebuke a wise man and he will love you"* (Pr. 9:8).

Stress that the irresponsible party must develop a cooperative, participative mentality. And the disappointed spouse must remain respectful/loving regardless of their mate's actions. They now know the Being qualities they need to correct.

TEACH HOW TO REWIRE THOUGHTS TO CHANGE BEHAVIOR

If they reacted rudely (Being) to each other or if they failed to do as promised (Function) ask both spouses the following questions:

1. Is your reaction similar to how you typically act when disappointed –and/or -- when you let your mate down? See if both agree on the other's answer.

2. How did you feel when your mate acted this way? What did you immediately tell yourself? What was the interpretation you put on your spouse's actions? (How the mate Functioned)
   (Expect such comments as, He knew it would hurt me, and he didn't care. Or I felt unloved, hurt, disappointed, and angry. Or I wanted her to prove she had changed, but she failed, etc.).

3. What is the truth of the situation? Such thoughts are inaccurate because they only reflect negative feelings and such negativity is never accurate truth. What truth needs to replace your immediate negative thought? (NEGATIVE THOUGHT: He doesn't love me; She isn't respecting me; I have reason to feel angry/be upset — REPLACE WITH: We do love and respect each other, but often disappoint each other. We become lazy, selfish, etc., and let that hinder our need to show love to each other).

4. What did you fail to do that would have helped? (Discuss behaving politely; asking for another chance; praying before responding)

5. How might things have ended differently if you had prayed at the very moment you felt a strong negative emotion taking hold of your hearts and thoughts? The truth of every situation is that God's Spirit lives inside your hearts and wants to help. You only need to ask.

6. What will you do differently next time your spouse lets you down so you stay connected and feel close? Because we are human, we often disappoint each other. Disappointment in a marriage is normal. How we handle it determines if we recover quickly, or if we stay angry for days, or we let enough issues accumulate until we decide we can take no more.

What should you do next time so you stay close when you or your spouse forgets to immediately pray and reacts as usual?

Insist they state very specific behaviors they will do differently the next time they feel negative, and fearful of being unloved, uncared for, or disrespected?

Suggest they do the following: "I will take three deep breaths and ask myself, 'What am I telling myself about what he/she did that could be inaccurate?" Or "Tell myself that I will put my arms around her and say, 'I love you." Or "I will remind, 'We are both wanting the same thing here, so let's act like it."

If one pretends not to know what to do differently, ask the wounded spouses what behavior is wanted from the mate.

Explain that saying aloud what you will do differently, helps you remember to do it. Staying closely connected with your spouse keeps your feelings of love and respect alive. Remember that Jesus' Holy Spirit lives inside your core Being and is wanting to help, but He does need an invitation.

REPEAT SAYING THE NEW BEHAVIOR ALOUD. Ask each spouse to repeat aloud two or three times what they will do differently the next time the spouse disappoints or fails to do as agreed. If they hesitate or stumble, say their desired behavior aloud for them and let them repeat after you. Or do like Virginia Satir is described in Steve Andres' book, *Virginia Satir: The Patterns of Her Magic:*

> Virginia frequently pointed out that people tend to stay in, or return to, a behavior that is familiar. Actively trying out a new behavior is one way to make it familiar. Virginia often suggested to people what to say and how to say it. She would sometimes even say it for them, demonstrating exactly what she wanted them to do. (pp. 12)

Hearing them repeat the words creates new pathways in their brains, and it helps to prepare them to remain calmer in future incidents. Give them a brief overview of why repeating a new, desired behavior to yourself works.

WHY REPETITION WORKS. We know through the use of MRIs that the human brain can reorganize itself by experiencing changes in the environment, changes in our thoughts, and changes in our emotions. The brain is more plastic and moldable during our younger years, but neuroplasticity (reshaping/flexibility) occurs throughout one's lifetime. This plasticity lets people recover from strokes and other disabilities by rewiring their brains to learn new ways of Functioning differently.

When you deliberately try to change how you think, chemicals are released in the brain that create new pathways so you think differently. The harder you try to think and act differently, the more the brain changes.

The more times you repeat what you want to do, how you want to respond differently during negative times, the more your old, typical connections are changed to include the new way you want to Be (Being). This lets your brain predict what will happen next time and how you prefer to respond.

Rewiring the brain is what you do as you learn to replace a wrong note with a correct one while playing a musical instrument. You repeatedly hit the correct note until it becomes an automatic response. It's how you learn a second language and to type correctly.

The brain changes by mentally rehearsing something a new way. The change becomes permanent when the outcome is important to you. The brain records your good attempts and progressively improves. As you get better at doing as you want and keep repeating what you want to do, the old neuron connections weaken because you use them less and less.

FACE EACH OTHER & REPEAT A NEW WAY. Before they leave your office, try having them stand, face each other, and say the new behavior to the other. "I will speak in a softer tone and be polite." Or, "I will pause and remind that I want you to still feel loved." Remember it's to the partner that they want to learn to speak this way.

Ask both of them to daily say aloud multiple times the new behavior they want to learn. Suggest they say it aloud while showering or when alone in the car. Research shows that it takes repeating a new way of thinking and acting differently for two months to adapt consistently by the change. So, two months and 'you are a new you' and behaving in ways that please the Lord, regardless of how your spouse acts because you have mastered self-regulation.

SELF-CONTROL. The way to create intimacy and a better marriage is to first learn to self-regulate and develop the type of Being God expects. God uses marriage as a discipleship tool for teaching and developing the type of person He approves.

Repeating aloud the new ways to react let them eventually realize that their prior behaviors often invited or encouraged the mate to respond as he did. With a new Being, the Will tends to naturally be motivated to Function in ways that please the other.

With a new Being, the Will tends to naturally be motivated to Function in ways that please the other

MARITAL COUNSELING SUCCESS

According to research by UCA psychologists, Lisa Benson, Megan McGinn, and Andrew Christensen, 97% of families and couples who received therapy reported receiving the help they needed. The sooner the couples sought help, the greater their success. Waiting too long, often found one partner had given up and had no interest in making things better.

After marriage counseling, 93% of the couples said they had more effective tools for dealing with their problems. If one partner refused to participate, the spouse attending alone often changed the dynamics of the relationship enough to make it successful. However, when both partners attended therapy, it required a third fewer sessions to produce the desired outcome.

While approximately 38% of the couples who received marriage counseling were divorced within four years of completing counseling, that meant 62% of the marriages moved from weak and struggling to stronger and successful. Those who reported a fruitful change, credited both partners modifying their dysfunctional behaviors that caused their mate pain. This decreased their emotional avoidance, improved the ways they communicated, and acknowledged both partner's strengths.

When counseling included helping the couple understand and reorganize their emotional responses, they showed the most success. When they committed to changing their needed Being traits, they showed significant improvement because this development fostered a healthy attachment in emotional and spiritual ways.

As their minister counselor, you won't always end counseling with the marriage intact. Some couples will divorce. But such a decision is theirs and has no reflection on you. Leave them for the Lord to change, and keep praying for them to learn to hate sin.

Focus on couples who, through your guidance, say their relationship is better than they ever hoped. Take joy in the fact that these couple are more likely to spend eternity with the Lord.

And use the same techniques to keep your own marriage strong. When you have a genuinely strong marriage yourself, you model what the Lord wants of couples. So keep praying and keep working to help others, and God will bless you beyond measure.

Chapter 14

IF HE REFUSED TO END THE AFFAIR

"*My husband refuses to end his affair. I treated him so cold that he should have ice cycles hanging from his teeth, but he refused to leave the house, and he will not call and tell the woman their affair is finished. He tries to act as if sleeping on the sofa doesn't bother him. So what am I to do now?*" You can only imagine the agony this woman suffers.

When a man leaves your counsel and remains committed to seeing their adulterous partner, as his minister and counselor, Scripture says you still have work to do. As much as you likely wish you were, you are not finished. You are obligated to try and have him return to the Lord. As a worker for the Lord, you need to complete the steps provided in Matthew (18: 15-17).

If after one week, two weeks at the very most, of the wife's shunning and excluding her adulterous husband from all involvements with her and the children, he still hasn't telephoned the adulteress to end the affair, it's time to take step two. The wife is to follow Jesus' command in Matthews 18:16: *"Take one or two others along, so that every matter may be established by the testimony of two or three witnesses."* Intervention that describes ultimatums and follow through is required.

Her adulterous husband has shown that he isn't ashamed of his behavior, and he needs to hear strong disapproval from more people. *For it is shameful even to mention what the disobedient do in secret. But everything exposed by the light becomes visible."* (Eph. 5:13-14).

WHAT'S REQUIRED FOR CONFRONTATION

Confronting sin may be one of the most difficult commandments in the Bible, but knowing about a fellow believer's sin and ignoring it, or appearing supportive or sympathetic, entangles all in the sin. Silence implies approval. And any approval of sin will surely be addressed by God.

Silence implies approval

You hope confronting him will create such a significant impact that he crashes emotionally, feels the heaviest of shame and guilt, and wants to correct his behavior. Without confrontation that elicits enough guilt and embarrassment to shock him into reality, he's likely to dig deeper in sin.

EXPLAIN TO HER WHY IT'S NEEDED. Confrontation is very uncomfortable, but at times it's required, and it's what Jesus modeled. Jesus wasn't always politically polite. He confronted those who chose sin rather than obedience. Jesus spoke boldly to those whose sins were self-destructive and influenced others. He called Peter Satan (Mt. 16:23), and the scribes and Pharisees hypocrites, snakes, and vipers (Mt. 23:13–25). Paul, filled with the Holy Spirit, called Elymas, the magician, a child of the devil, an enemy of all that's right, and then struck him blind (Ac. 13:10). James in his letter to the 12 tribes called them adulterous people (4:4). In front of others, Paul opposed Peter for his hypocrisy of refusing to eat with Gentiles (Gal. 2:11-13). Such confrontations shocked those entrenched in sin with the truth of their behavior.

There's a time for a gentle, comforting, accepting kind of love, but now's not that time. The adulterer needs a firm, truthful, disciplining love that uses words the adulterer will dislike hearing. Genuine love in this situation requires discipline that strives to stop wrongdoing. Soft love that's coupled with firm discipline, when it's needed, keeps relationships perfectly balanced. Both types of caring are necessary for anyone to know with certainty they are loved. I explain with, 'Love me enough to refuse to let me go to hell no matter what you must say that hurts.' Such confrontation requires a balanced spirit of sternness and gentleness.

Love me enough to refuse to let me go to hell no matter what you must say that hurts

If adultery is ignored, it tells the community that the church tolerates sinful behavior, and outsiders have no respect for the church. Allowing such negative influence to spread disrespects the Lord. People are needed who will confront the adulterer's sin to save his soul. And people are needed who care deeply about protecting the health and unity of the Lord's church.

"The Lord disciplines those he loves, and he punishes everyone he accepts as a son. . . God disciplines us for our good that we may share in his holiness. No discipline seems pleasant at the time, but painful. Later on, however, it produces a harvest of righteousness and peace for those who have been trained by it" (Heb. 12:6-11). Stern discipline is what Paul insisted the Corinthians had to employ to change the sexually sinful man in their congregation (1 Cor. 5:1-5).

Tough love requires strong strength of character and a genuine caring about the adulterer's soul, enough to try and shock the adulterer from his sinful sleep so he realizes how deadly serious God considers sin. It requires loving the person too deeply to ignore where he's currently headed to spend eternity. It's why Paul confronted the sin in the Corinthian church.

CHOOSE HELPERS CAREFULLY

The wife must be very selective who she asks to help confront her husband. Or she may be too devastated to even consider who should confront him. In that case, she might ask the elders to take the lead. Or they may have already contacted her saying they know of his adultery, and they need to confront him. Or, perhaps, you, as her minister, could help her by laying out the qualifications she should want in such a person(s).

First, she should seek people who love the adulterer too much to ignore the consequences of his not changing. They must genuinely fear God's punishment for him and care that he's self-destructing. Preferred are people who have been directly affected by his adultery so they can attest to the harmful effects it has on them. *"A truthful witness saves lives"* (Pr. 14:25).

Secondly, the selected people must not be so angry about his behavior that they possess a desire to punish him. Confrontation requires people who love him enough to hurt him with God's truth and call him to repentance, not ones who drive him further away because they think he doesn't deserve forgiveness. Their attitude must reflect belief that if God treated every one as they deserved, He would have destroyed every believer long ago. But God's forgiving grace has no limits. He forgives individual sins and with repentance restores the most damaged relationships. The wife's helpers must believe this. *"Better is open rebuke than hidden love. Wounds from a friend can be trusted, but an enemy multiplies kisses"* (Pr. 27:5-6).

Thirdly, she must choose people who will keep the confrontation a secret, at least for now. Added gossip is the last thing the wife and children need. They hurt enough without his sin being broadcast more, especially while she clings to hope he will change. The goal must always remain to bring him home, home with the Lord, and hopefully, home with his family.

Provided they disapprove of his adultery and aren't overly upset, his adult child or his parent, best Christian friend, you or an elder might be good choices for confronting him. Only the wife knows for sure who can touch his heart.

ENSURE AGREEMENT ON DIVORCE- REMARRIAGE

The wife needs to know those doing the confrontation accept the scriptural reasons God provides for divorce and remarriage because remarriage remains one of the most controversial issues today. The group's beliefs around this issue will determine what they say to her husband, and she needs to know in advance that it's Scriptural. How they handle the issue of divorce and remarriage can prove the difference in his being restored to his wife and the Lord or his feeling he has found support for divorce.

First and foremost, the group must believe adultery is a serious concern to the Lord. If he divorces his wife and marries his lover, Jesus says he is living in adultery (Mt. 5:32). I find no place in Scripture that says there's a time line when a Christian's living with someone who was his former adulteress counts no more or that all is forgotten. Confession and change are required. When he accepted the Lord and showed his faith by being baptized to wash away his sins, he became accountable to a higher standard.

When he accepted the Lord and showed his faith by being baptized to wash away his sins, he became accountable to a higher standard

Jesus explained how to handle a sinful attraction, and it wasn't with divorce. Jesus said, *"If your right eye causes you to sin, gouge it out and throw it away. It is better for you to lose one part of your body than for your whole body to be thrown into hell. And if your right hand causes you to sin, cut it off and throw it away. It is better for you to lose one part of your body than for your whole body to go into hell"* (Mt. 5:29-30). Jesus was saying to let go of the illicit partner, and cut her completely from his life.

However, there are three situations under which divorce and remarriage appears scripturally acceptable. If divorce is valid by God's standard, then remarriage must also be acceptable.

First, if the divorce and remarriage happened before the person accepted Jesus' plan of salvation by being baptized then this is forgiven. God's promise in 2 Corinthians 5:17 appears to apply: *"Therefore, if anyone is in Christ, he is a new creation; the old has gone, the new has come."* After listing the many sins they used to be guilty of doing, Paul tells the Corinthians (6:11) *"But you were washed, you were sanctified, you were justified in the name of the Lord Jesus Christ and by the Spirit of our God."* Prior sins were no longer held against them. They rise from the water a new, clean, and fully forgiven person.

The second situation is when the spouse is guilty of sexual immorality, unwilling to repent, and refuses to return to live faithfully to his marital mate. Jesus said in Matthew 19:9, *"Moses permitted you to divorce your wives because your hearts were hard. But it was not this way from the beginning. I tell you that anyone who divorces his wife, expect for marital unfaithfulness, and marries another woman commits adultery."* Jesus message in Matthew provides the way to know if the adulterer's heart had hardened or if he would change (18:15-17).

Finally, divorce is approved when an unbelieving mate chooses to permanently abandon a believing partner, the believing partner is no longer bound (1 Co. 7:15). Again, Jesus told us how to determine if there is hope of saving the relationship and reviving the former commitment (Mt. 18:15-17).

ADVANCED PREPARATION FOR EVERYONE

The selected group needs to meet together in advance of confronting him to discuss what they will say, who will say it, how they will say it, and which order each will speak. They need to ensure he realizes how those confronting him ache at the thought of his possibly facing an eternal hell. The speaker(s) words and actions need to convince him that they love him, and he's breaking their hearts with his adultery and detachment from the Lord. They must be prepared to give him examples of how it upsets them. They need to prepare a short statement of how his sin causes each of them hurt and use 'I' statements. *"When you canceled our meeting to meet with the adulteress, I was devastated that you made our time together of no importance. It was to share a special event for me, only to be crushed because I realized I was unimportant to you."*

They need to use Scriptures to reinforce his need to fear God while he disobeys. He probably knows all of these verses, but he needs reminding and to hear it said in a way that shows the speakers' genuine concern. They need to agree on the Scriptures they will use. The Bible provides many that are appropriate, but do ensure they include a summary of Malachi

2:10-16, and stress the impact his behavior may have on his children's long-term faithfulness and their salvation. The goal of the group is to serve as a wake-call that demands he realize the devastation of his current choice. For too long, he has been telling himself that he can compartmentalize the illicit relationship and keep it in a proper place. He needs to face the reality that this never works.

Prior to confronting him, some of the group members may want to read Proverb (5-7) that provides an excellent understanding of how someone becomes entangled in adultery. Those who have never experienced sexual temptation don't realize how alluring it is to have someone show special interest in you, and how Satan ensures no thought is given to long-range consequences. Adulterers never considers the costs of their affairs: *"A man who commits adultery lacks judgment; whoever does so destroys himself . . . And his shame will never be wiped away"* (6: 32-33b). His condition is *"Leading down to the chamber of death" (7:27).*

The day of the confrontation, the lead person explains why they are meeting, *"We are here because we all know about your affair and are very concerned about you. We aren't here to judge you or condemn you, but to help you regain your life back. We want to help you avoid losing your family. We want to help ensure heaven's your eternal home."*

Satan has the adulterer locked in sin, and he cannot defeat Satan by himself. The group needs to understand how desperately he needs them. When tempted, Jesus quoted Scripture to defeat Satan's attacks, and as Jesus prayed in the Garden, he told his disciples to pray so Satan would not overtake them with his temptation (Lk. 22:40). Defeating Satan is God's role, but God requires the adulterer to ask for help (Jas. 4:2). Humbling himself and drawing close to God is what will free him of Satan's control (Jas. 4:7-10), and it's the group's job to help him realize it. He must examine the sin in his heart, humbly ask God to forgive him, and supply the necessary strength to say no to Satan's temptation of the other woman. Otherwise, *"The cords of his sin hold him fast. He will die for lack of discipline, led astray by his own great folly"* (Pr. 5:22-23).

Chapter 15

HIS REACTION TO CONFRONTATION

"*I can't help how I feel. God wants us to feel loved, and I don't with my wife,*" is a common response of an adulterer. The group should prepare for his many possible reactions. His human nature will have him react defensively because Satan still controls.

He needs people who are willing to act as God's spokesperson, because he's so deeply entrenched in sin, he can no longer change his spiritual condition alone. Satan controls his thoughts and heart and exerts a greater force than he can handle by himself. The group's challenge is to allow the Lord to use them to carry His message. The adulterer needs to hear four things:

How God treats unrepentant adulterers (briefly, because he already knows this and just needs reminding);

How deeply those who confront him care about him and his spiritual condition, that they love him with a love that covers a multitude of sins (1 Pe. 4:8);

The impact his affair is having on his wife, children, and on those doing the confrontation; and

How God forgives and forgets with repentance.

Those confronting him needs to prepare for the multiple ways he might react. He may attempt to cover up his sins with excuses, as King David tried by having Bathsheba's husband murdered in hope of concealing his rape of her and her resulting pregnancy. He may attribute his behavior to flaws in his marriage, but running from marital problems only ensures that troubles multiply.

Expect to hear him justify his actions with how he only wants to be happy. That requires him to focus on his feelings today, not how he will feel if the adulteress later betrays him, or his children reject him, and how he feels each time he thinks about facing the Lord on judgment day. If he thinks it might work, he may even deny the affair is sexual and, therefore, not wrong.

LIKELY, HE'LL CRY IT'S LOVE. Those confronting him may hear a long list of justifications and claims that he's helplessly trapped with no way to escape because of how he loves this woman. It's what he tells himself to make his actions acceptable. The worst of all lies is the one we tell ourselves, because it's the most difficult to admit. But statistics of those who divorce their spouses and marry their lovers prove that few love the adulteress because the vast majority eventually divorce the adulteress too. He's infatuated with her. He's emotionally addicted to how he feels while with her, but it's not love.

The worst of all lies is the one we tell ourselves, because it's the most difficult to admit

When he's with her, he likely feels excited and experiences happy, emotional sensations that perhaps, he hasn't felt in years. But his relationship with her has little to do with loving another for whom and how she is.

Love is not a feeling. Love is choosing to sacrifice for another and following the head when it disagrees with the emotions and God's word. He can feel elated and/or miserable and still choose to do what's right.

It's unlikely that he knows the adulteress well enough to love her. In fact, few trapped in adultery know each other at all. They have lived in a fantasy world they created that's free of normal daily living events like intruding in-laws, the drudgery of burying the family pet, or almost losing a child to cancer. He knows none of this woman's serious faults and bad habits. They haven't openly dated to see how each behaves in the presence of others. They haven't argued and fought over money. Instead of it being love, he's become emotionally dependent on her for making him feel good about himself. Love never requires destroying others to make oneself feel good.

Love never requires destroying others to make oneself feel good

For him to lose all feelings for the adulteress, their emotional connection must be completely severed. This tends to take three months to two years with them experiencing total separation with no contact of any kind. How dependent they were on each other influences how long it takes. But separated long enough, he can and will realize it wasn't love.

HIS SIN IS MORE THAN ADULTERY

An affair is similar to tossing a stone into a lake. The concentric rings that result when the rock disturbs the water are the affairs aftereffects. Never is it just the pebble and one isolated spot of water that's impacted. Just as the stone's ripple effect expands outward disrupting a large area of water, so does an affair create anxiety and discomfort in the lives of many others.

The group needs to help him understand that his adultery is not a single, stand-alone, disconnected sin. His sin goes much deeper than emotional and/or sexual unfaithfulness. He has broken his vow of loyalty to both his wife and God, lied, left his spouse and children depressed and embarrassed, used family money wrongly, stolen time from his family, set a wrong standard and model for his children, embarrassed extended family and any church members who know, caused others to no longer trust him, lost support from close friends as they struggle with their relationship, ruined his reputation, given reason for unnecessary gossip among the weak, etc. The list goes on and on. He needs to confess and repent of all sins. The more he realizes the depth of his wrongs, the more aware he becomes of how far from the Lord he has strayed, and the more he realizes how great his punishment remains without confession and repentance.

He must rid himself of his arrogant attitude because God judges both attitude and private thoughts (Heb. 4:12-13). Thinking he could handle things on his own shows the influence of Satan and has resulted in his self-reliant smugness that entrapped him in an adulterous situation. Remind him of strong Biblical characters who yielded to such temptation and their ultimate fate (Pr. 7:27), and how pride goes before destruction (Pr. 16:18).

HAVE EACH SHARE THEIR CONCERNS

If there is someone whom he deeply respects, that person may be able to discuss the defects of his character that led to his affair, such as selfishness, anger, resentment, fear, etc. It must be said in a loving way, not condemning, *"I can understand feeling angry when you go long periods thinking your needs are not met. It makes you want to behave selfishly and ask when is it time for me, but. . ."*

Even brief comments like, *"It must be lonely not to be able to discuss/reveal a relationship publicly,"* or *"You seem tired and angry a lot,"* can be beneficial when said at the right moment and with the right tone. *"I am begging you to get help and make your marriage work. I love you, but if you don't, I can't continue our friendship any longer, and the thought of losing you breaks my heart."* The group must refuse to argue or get defensive, no matter what he says in return. *"The hearts of the wise make their mouths prudent, and their lips promote instruction"* (Pr. 16:23).

Every person in the room needs to take turns stating care and concern, providing evidence, discussing consequences, and offering help. The adulterer needs to interpret what's said as being gentle and kind, but firm. *"Stern discipline awaits him who leaves the path; he who hates correction will die"* (Pr. 15:10).

USE HIS KIDS TO TOUCH HIM EMOTIONALLY

Malachi (2:16) clearly says that God hates divorce because He wants believing children. The adulterer knows his affair is wrong, but I have known several who did not know those exact words were written in Scripture. Opening a Bible and showing it to the adulterer serves to reinforce what they've always been taught. Seeing it in writing, makes it almost impossible to argue.

After briefly covering the Scriptures that show how God hates adultery and its consequences, and the impact his behavior is having on those confronting him, the group should focus on the impact his sinful lifestyle has on his spouse and children (Mal. 2:13-16). Likely, he has ignored the impact he is having on them.

God hates divorce because He knows the negative impression it leaves on the involved children. For anyone to change, they must be touched emotionally, and usually, concern about his children grab him the most. Facts alone change no one. This will, likely, prove an emotional period.

For anyone to change,

they must be touched emotionally

Facts alone change no one

I wish I had noted the number of children who told me during counseling, "If mom and dad had not divorced, I don't believe I would have either." Their parents' behavior taught that instead of keeping God first in their lives and working to resolve marital differences, fleeing was more valued. Such couples chose what they believed was the easier way without giving thought to what it demonstrated to their children.

I also wish I knew how many children stopped attending worship after their parent's divorced. The children felt betrayed by their parents – because they were. And it was worse for the kids who prayed for God to save their parent's marriages, because when the parents chose to disobey and divorce, the kids felt betrayed by their parents and by the Lord. The children were too immature in their spiritual walk to understand that God forces no one to obey. God pleads, begs, cries, but He never overpowers anyone or forces them to do what's right.

God pleads, begs, cries, nudges, but He never overpowers anyone or forces them to do what's right

If he insists that his adultery won't leave a negative impact on his children, remind him what happened to David's children after he sinned with Bathsheba. One son raped his half-sister and another son killed the rapist for what he had done. The murderer fled, and David mourned for the loss of his son every day. David's children hated each other, and one wanted to kill him to replace him as king. David wept over the state of his children (2 Sa. 15:30, 18:33). And this man will too.

The adulterer needs to answer: *"If you knew a marital breakup would cause your children to go to hell, would you be willing to learn how to be happy with your wife and create a secure home for your kids?"* *"If it meant that they were far more likely to have failed marriages themselves, would that be reason enough for you to create a healthy family?"* Ask. *"Would you be willing to die if doing so would save the soul of one of your children?"* Emphasize, *"You need to die to this woman who's taking you away from them – and away from God."*

Although he's living a wayward life, he still knows the importance of saving his children's souls. He will try to insist that his divorce won't negatively impact his children, but he can't argue against God's word, and it says that it will and that it does. Deep down, he knows he's setting up the odds of that happening. Remind him, and don't let him ignore how his decision influences their lives immediately and long-term.

If he cries that his wife could never forgive him. Let her honestly admit, that he may be correct, but she's willing to pursue counseling to help her forgive him and to work to change things so they again feel love for each other. She's willing to try. The question isn't about her. It's will he try?

SHOW GOD FORGIVES AND FORGETS WITH REPENTANCE

After reminding him of the many Scriptures where God condemns adultery, with each one wrapped in a demonstration of the speaker's love for him, and discussing the impact his behavior continues to have on his family, share Scriptures that tell of God's loving forgiveness. He needs hope and assurance that God will offer him full forgiveness with change. They should select Scriptures of forgiveness that mean the most to them.

Many adulterers fear others consider them bad, unworthy, and corrupt. Realizing others know and still care about them in spite of what they've done, may turn the adulterer back to the Lord. A great sense of freedom overcomes them when they realize that the people confronting them still love them and that God will forgive and forget his sin.

Realizing others know and still care about them after what they've done, may turn the adulterer back to the Lord

Only with God's word working through the group's confrontation will he yearn to be restored. He had chosen a path disapproved by God, but with change, God still has a positive plan for him, *"Plans to prosper you and not to harm you, plans to give you hope and a future,"* but right now he can't envision such a life without his lover (Jer. 29:11). But if he does what God requires to withstand this trial of his faith, he is promised a crown of life (Jas. 1:12). His test is just more challenging than that of many others right now.

The group who meets with him must be willing to accept that no matter the outcome of the confrontation, the ultimate decision of what he decides remains solely his. If he refuses to change, they bear no personal guilt for his choice. They can only continue praying for his heart to soften. The rest is up to the Lord.

WHAT YOU DO IF HE WANTS TO CHANGE

If he says he wants to change and return to the Lord, insist he phone the adulteress in the presence of everyone. The more who hear him end the affair the more he knows will be holding him accountable for keeping his word. Hand him a note of what he's to say to the adulteress, and ask him to repeat what it says and then immediately hang up. If the woman cannot be reached, oversee his writing her a letter that's not over four lines that are formal and cold. Insist you will mail it for him so you can assure all who confronted him that he kept his word.

Make an appointment for him and his wife to see you as soon as possible. You need to help them prepare for the long months of turmoil and pain they face as she attempts to come to grips with what he has done. Explain that he will have to write her a letter detailing every aspect of his affair, and allow her to ask dozens of questions that he won't want to answer -- but must. Without confronting all that happened, she can never fully trust him again and without trust she can't love him the way that's required for having a solid marital relationship. (See Chapter 7).

WHAT IF HE REFUSES TO CHANGE?

Caution that if he doesn't try to save his family, he will later regret the decision. Any decision made under Satan's control cannot be one that is right. Because Satan currently controls him and his adulterous partner, it's unlikely their relationship will last very long. Once together full time, they will see the illicit person's serious faults and flaws. They may then experience deep remorse for having stayed together. Regret, guilt, tainted trust, and unresolvable differences are reasons the divorce rate is much higher for couples who marry following an illicit affair.

Any decision made under Satan's control cannot be one that is right

If he shows no intent of ending the affair, explain that the entire church must be told. And it's in hope that enough people praying for his change will cause him to choose to save his soul.

POSSIBLY MEETING WITH HIM AGAIN. If his heart is dead, the third and final step in Matthew must be followed, but if he shows the slightest possibility of change, the group needs to meet with him again. Jesus didn't say how many times this confrontation might take. But obviously it should not be over a couple of times. He must be forced to realize that it's now or never, that there's no more excuses. Each delay continues his sinful condition, pains the Lord, and creates more devastating memories for his wife and children. It's in or out of the marriage and now.

The scale of 1-5 below is provided to help determine if another meeting could possibly save him or if his heart shows only hardened rebellion. If his answers best resembles the words in 1, his heart is hard, but if it's a 2 or 3, there's a flicker of hope.

1	2	3
I love her	I know it's wrong,	I know it's wrong but don't think I can stop
I'm marrying her	I can't stop	I have tried to stop and couldn't
I need to be happy	I don't know how	My wife could never forgive me
Leave me alone	I hate doing it	Help me change

If his comments fall in #2 or 3, another meeting might prove worthwhile. You can't risk not trying again to convince him to return to the Lord. However, if his every response consistently fall into #1, he's confirming that his heart has frozen hard, and he has no intention of leaving the adulteress.

If he offers no glimmer of doing what's right, the group should not plead, beg, or demand that he change. Only if the decision remains entirely his own will he work on saving the marriage and remain faithful to the Lord. The group explains they will pray for his change, but until he agrees to work on his marital relationship, spending more time together proves wasteful and fruitless. If he chooses the adulteress, the next step is to expose his sin before the entire church for their assistance in eliciting his change. Jesus always offers multiple chances to change and do what's right.

Chapter 16

PREPARE FOR CHURCH ASSISTANCE

"*He insisted he isn't going to change. He plans to continue being with the other woman. At least for now, you must accept he has chosen to live in sin. You must put financial care of yourself and the children first.*" It's the counsel a woman needs if her adulterous husband failed to respond favorably to the group who confronted his sinful behavior. The wife needs to make preparations as if he's going to ask her for a legal separation or divorce. With such a hardened heart, she may discover that he has emptied their bank accounts, stopped all insurance payments, and removed his name from all utility bills and credit cards. Once he makes the decision that his marriage is finished, many men react as if they no longer care for their families, not even their children.

Counsel her to accept her current reality. Her one-on-one approach did not work, and he refused to listen to others she took with her to confront him. It's time to plan for the worst. She must turn her attention to care for herself and the children. She must make their future her first priority. If her husband later repents, she can undo things. But at this point, he is showing everyone he wants out of the marriage, not in.

EXAMPLE. Julia refused to heed advice to put financial care of herself and her children first. She told herself, that even if her husband did leave her, he would feel enough guilt to share all assets fairly. Instead, he immediately moved out and broke into the home twice while she was at work, taking valuable things that rightly were joint property.

Finally, discovering all bank accounts were empty, and her paycheck had automatically deposited the prior day, she admitted how wrong she had been not to act quickly. Until her next paycheck arrived two weeks later, she had no money to buy groceries. She borrowed money from her parents for gasoline so she could drive to work, and pleaded with the utility company to let her pay the electric bill late. After this, Julia accepted her fate, and she found an attorney.

Finally, Julia listed all their assets, and one was a rental property they owned. Her attorney asked the judge to order that all checks for making mortgage payments on this property require both her signature and her husband's. But months later, after talking with the bank, Julia learned that each month he wrote the mortgage payment checks for $100 above the required amount and kept the cash back. She then discovered that he filed joint income taxes and forged her signature. When she heard through the children that he received a huge refund, one of her elders, a CPA, offered to refile and force him to pay back a portion of the money.

By the time Julia accepted that her husband had no intention of dividing marital assets fairly or legally, she had experienced losses that could have been avoided had she been advised to find an attorney immediately to guide her. She needed to act first, not wait and react to her husband's decisions.

COUNSEL HER TO MAKE IMMEDIATE CHANGES

As you counsel a wife trapped in a similar situation, insist that her immediate focus must be on financial care for herself and the children. She should act immediately and without her husband knowing. Remember, he's no longer making decisions that show he cares about being moral or honest. If he starts the separation process first, he may have no motivation to treat her right. Likely, he's upset about being confronted by relatives and friends, and she will receive the blunt of his ire.

While she needs to act first, she should ensure she does not treat him wrongly. She should do nothing that gives the appearance of being dishonest or illegal.

She may find this extremely uncomfortable, but unless she cares for herself, she will find that she's unable to provide for the children. While your role is to encourage her to find good legal help a list of things she needs to do and do them as quickly and as quietly as possible is provided. Explain that marriage is about love; separation and divorce are more about money. The list is offered, so as you counsel her you can ensure she does what the attorney recommends. She will dislike doing most of these tasks, but she must put the children's care first and that requires that she has the money to do so. This list lets you know how most attorneys advise someone facing an unwanted divorce.

Marriage is about love; separation and divorce are more about money

Suggest that she may need to withdraw <u>half</u> the money in all bank accounts and ask for copies of account records from the past five years. She can open an account in her name, but it would be wise to use a different bank. Remind her that her attorney will not work free, and she is now responsible for continued upkeep on the home.

If unemployed, suggest that she immediately begin looking for a job. If he reacts first, she will discover that, until attorneys settle numerous conditions, it is possible that she will receive no on-going support money, not even for care of the children.

Encourage her to immediately find an attorney/ Below are a list of things the attorney will likely require her to do.

-If her state allows, she needs to file for legal separation, and ask that her husband continue providing financial support for her and the children. Ask that she be granted custody of the children, and learn what visitation rights and alimony payments, if any, are required in her state.

-Contact the credit card companies and ask that her name be removed. She needs to request a copy of the prior year's statements. If they have credit established elsewhere, she needs to request that her name be removed. She requests a copy of the past 12 month's statements. At a minimum, she should send written notice that she will not be responsible for future charges.

-Ensure her name is listed as co-owner of their home, automobile, and all other assets they own. If not, determine if her name can be included.

-Gather copies of every document pertaining to their daily life: insurance records of both personal and automobile policies, all investments such as stocks or bonds, telephone and utility bills, their retirement records, prior tax records, payroll stubs, etc.

-Monitor their credit report and take note of any outstanding debts. Obtain a copy of their credit report and pay close attention to any outstanding charges. Until the divorce is finalized, promptly deal with any unusual charges.

-Make copies of every document and either give a copy to someone she trusts for safe keeping, or open her own safety security box at a bank different from the one he uses.

-Take pictures of all antiques, furniture, tools, gold or silver coins, and other valuable items. It's not uncommon for such things to go missing if he files first.

-Separate anything owned before the marriage, including gifts from her family given solely to her. Things acquired during the marriage are usually consider marital property.

-Change all passwords and create a new email address. This allows her to talk with her attorney and family without her husband reading what's said.

-Begin packing all of his possessions if he hasn't already left. Do not remove them until the elders make an announcement to the church.

-If he has already moved out, change all locks and do not hide a key outside nor give one to the kids or he might use them to obtain a copy.

-Adjust her lifestyle, and stop all unnecessary expenses.

If he repents after the church announcement, all of the above steps can easily be reversed. But if his heart has become as hard as stone, she has acted to ensure she can for herself the children without becoming a burden on her family or the church.

PREPARE THEIR CHLDREN
Offer to help her explain the situation to the children. You may offer support, but do not tell them for her because she can

better predict the children's reactions. Before doing this, coach her to ensure nothing is said to imply that the children should dislike or hate their wayward father. God is a God of love who pours His love into our hearts. Teaching children to hate their other parent is child abuse. Such teaching is also a type of revenge that tends to backfire once the children are adults. Once grown, children alienated by one parent tend to resent the one telling them their other parent was bad, more than they do the one who committed the wrong that caused the divorce.

Teaching children to hate their other parent is child abuse

Explain that Satan has taken away their daddy, and he is not living as God wants. Reveal the truth that he has fallen prey to Satan's temptation, wants to be with another woman, and refuses to listen to anyone. Explain they tried counseling, others talked with him, and at this point, he listens to no one. Based on the ages of the children, she will know how many details to include.

Do not minimize his sin. The children must know there is another woman or their minds flood with things she might be doing wrong. She must not lie to them, or they will have trouble trusting either of them and question if anything they are told is the truth.

Explain that his sinful behavior is going to be shared with the entire church, and if he doesn't change, then he has to leave their home. Give the children the option of attending worship elsewhere for the next few weeks to avoid as much public exposure to the fallout as possible.

Explain if the church announcement has him changing, she will insist he goes for counseling. She promises if this happens, she will do her best make the marriage work and keep the family intact.

Chapter 17

TELLING THE CHURCH

If the adulterer refused to repent after the confrontation by those helping his wife, it shows he has no desire to reconcile with her and plans to continue seeing the adulteress. It is time for the elders to practice Matthew 18:17. *"If he refuses to listen to them (the confronters) tell it to the church, and if he refuses to listen even to the church, treat him as you would a pagan or a tax collector."*

Leaders in Jesus' church don't always have the luxury of serving only in a loving, supportive role. They also are charged with protection of the flock from attacks by Satan. They must address issues that require a challenging, disciplining position. The leadership must serve as needed and as clearly mandated in Scripture.

The estranged wife should ask the elders to practice Matthew 18: 15-17. She needs assurance that they want to help save her marriage, and she requires support to remain faithful herself.

After a separation, the majority of women struggle going alone to public places. In fact, I have never found a woman who didn't. They fear people will blame her for the marriage's troubles, and they carry a strong sense of shame. Multiple women have shared that the hardest part after a separation was attending worship. They felt so abandoned by other members that it was easier not to attend. The elders must ensure that her spiritual condition doesn't crumble.

ENCOURAGE THE LEADERSHIP. Offer to go with the wife to meet with the elders while she asks for their support. Let her do the talking as she explains the prior attempts that failed to have him change.

The elders are a big determiner of the amount of support she and the children receive. For the next few weeks, an elder and his wife can sit with her and the children during each worship period. Their presence shows public support that the wounded spouse and children desperately need at this time.

No matter what another might tell her about her husband's misdeeds, she must realize that Satan uses gossiping people to inflict more hurt in hope she won't want her family reunited. The husband returning home to the Lord and to her is the last thing Satan wants. Remember his goal is to hurt the Lord by using people whom God loves.

INSIST THEY ACT QUICKLY. As her counselor-minister, press the church leadership to address the problem immediately. Some may offer reasons for waiting a while, but speed matters. Her husband is still uncomfortable from the confrontation by the group, and the more he's soaked in negative attention for his sin, the more opportunity there is for jarring him into the reality of his condition and repentance. Every minute they delay, the adulterer risks dying in his sin. Equally important is the faster things move, the less heartache that develops for the wife and children. Encourage them to act and act now

EXAMPLE: SIN IGNORED BY THE ELDERS: When Doris' husband left her and their three small children, he continued attending all church services. Only now he brought along his new lover, and no matter where Doris sat, he and his mistress sat behind her and the children. Doris pleaded with the leadership for help to stop such treatment. The situation was destroying her young, impressionable children who begged not to attend. But the leadership was too weak to do what's right.

Because the elders failed to address his sin, the young minister and his wife helped Doris relocate to another town. Then the minister resigned. These elders betrayed Doris, her husband, and the minister, by acting counter to the Lord's command.

Scripture says, *"When the sentence for a crime is not quickly carried out, the hearts of the people are filled with schemes to do wrong"* (Ecc. 8:11). When sin is ignored, some members think the church tolerates such behavior, and they view the leadership as weak and ineffective. The possibility of spreading sinful influence is why Ananias and his wife had to die when they lied about giving money to the apostles. Peter told him, *"You have not lied to men but to God,"* (Ac. 5:4). Their young, weak church couldn't risk sins such as lying contaminating others by thinking it was acceptable or ignored by God. The couple's immediate death served as a deterrent for others choosing to sin. *"Great fear seized the whole church and all who heard about these events"* (v. 11).

Jesus demands holiness in His church. All believers sin, but continued willful sin, is condemned. Scripture warns to avoid evil companions because of their possible influence and how those doing wrong often exert the stronger pull. After telling the Corinthians to expel a man who was sexually involved with his father's wife, Paul warned: *"Don't you know that a little yeast works through the whole batch of dough? Get rid of the old yeast that you may be a new batch without yeast"* (1 Co. 5:6-7). Otherwise attitudes of there being 'horrible sins' vs 'not so bad sins' develop. Soon, so many may become involved in sinful activities that God turns away from that church, as He threatened the churches in Revelation.

Scripture warns to avoid evil companions, because of their possible influence and how those doing wrong often exert the stronger pull

REASSURE HER IT'S THE BIBLICAL WAY

Jesus' command in Matthew is not a stand-alone directive. Multiple Scriptures support Matthew on withdrawing fellowship from someone trapped in sin and refusing to change. Paul tells the Corinthian church to expel a member who had taken his father's wife, and shames them for tolerating such sin. He directs, *"Hand this man over to Satan, so that the sinful nature may be destroyed and his spirit saved on the day of the Lord"* (I Co. 5:1-13). Paul was upset because the church failed to take action without his needing to tell them. He told Titus (3:10) to warn a divisive person in the church two times and if he refuses to change, then have nothing to do with him. The Thessalonians were instructed to keep away from every brother who is idle (2 Thess. 3:6), and anyone who refuses to earn the bread he eats, *"Do not associate with him, in order that he may feel ashamed. Yet do not regard him as an enemy, but warn him as a brother"* (v.14-15).

Scriptures explain that believers are to judge disputes between brothers (or sisters), but they are told not to judge those outside the church, for only the Lord judges outsiders. *"I say this to shame you. Is it possible that there is nobody among you wise enough to **judge a dispute between believers**"* (1 Co. 6:5, my emphasis)? *"The very fact that you have lawsuits among you means you have been completely defeated already (v.7).* Scriptures oppose believers going to court, but asks, instead, that differences be judged by other believers (v. 1-8). Paul instructed believers with unresolved differences to seek counsel from trusted, neutral Christian advisers. Then he immediately emphasized that the sexually immoral will not inherit the kingdom of God (v. 9-10). This command is surely relevant for marital conflicts today with the divorce courts being among the busiest of all courts.

GOAL OF A CHURCH ANNOUNCEMENT

Judging the adulterer as sinful is to have him change and save his soul. He needs to be shaken from his complacency and have no choice but to face the magnitude of his sin so he can be forgiven. The goal always remains restoration to the Lord.

The church leadership's goal must be that on judgment day he is at peace with God, and hopefully, today with his wife. Making such an announcement to the entire church body isn't a pleasant situation for the leaders. In fact, expect them to dread it. But it's a requirement that God's word says must be taken.

The church leadership must lay down their lives and seize every opportunity for saving the souls of wayward members.

The church leadership must lay down their lives and seize every opportunity for saving the souls of wayward members

The leadership's announcement to the church body about the adulterer's hardened heart should cause each member to view his sinful condition and possible excommunication as a personal loss for them. The message should create a deep sense of responsibility in all members to help save the man's soul. Each person hearing the announcement should be left aching so intensely they can't help but remember to continually pray for his change. Every member who sees him during the week should express how they love him and plead for him to come home.

Hearing the announcement from the pulpit is like driving a nail into the wife's heart. If she cannot stand to hear this, it may be best for her to stay home and spend the time alone with the Lord or attend worship elsewhere.

IF HE RESPONDS, WANTING TO CHANGE

If the announcement has him repenting of his affair, the members should welcome him back as God says prodigal sons are to be treated. Heaven celebrates his return with a party, and the church should treat him as though they are joyous about his decision and all is forgiven. As Paul wrote the Corinthians (2 Cor. 2:6-7) who had expelled a brother and it caused the brother to repent: *"The punishment inflicted on him by the majority is sufficient. . . Forgive and comfort him, so that he will not be overwhelmed by excessive sorrow."*

However, counseling with him needs to occur before things are right with his wife and children. They have not only been betrayed, but everyone in town knows and that causes them additional humiliation. They need to know with certainty he has changed and commits to being faithful to them. It is time to turn back to Chapter 7 and follow its guidance.

This man could benefit greatly from joining a Christian accountability group. He withstood confrontation, and likely, he needs strong encouragement to remain faithful and keep his promise. Such a group would ensure someone was regularly monitoring his faithfulness.

The wife needs additional prayers to hold her head high as she tries to regain a semblance of a normal marriage. Hopefully, other women in her church will reach out to befriend her and let her know they love and appreciate her.

Once their marriage is fully restored, you may be able to convince her to help others in a similar situation. She knows the struggles such women face and how to hold to the Lord during trying times. Perhaps, the time will come when they can work as a couple to help other believing couples overcome their struggle with adultery.

IF HE DOESN'T CHANGE, HE'S SHUNNED BY ALL

After the elders' set timeline, if the adulterer still refuses to repent, he's no longer considered a believer or member of the church. According to Jesus, all believers *"treat him as you would a pagan or a tax collector"* (Mt. 18:17). That means that all believers shun him. They do not include him in social events, nor treat him like a long-lost friend if they accidently meet. During Jesus day, if a pagan or tax collector was headed their way, they crossed the street just to avoid being near them. And this man is now avoided in similar ways by believers.

THEY PRAY. At this stage, all have fulfilled what Scripture requires for saving his soul, except to continually pray for his change of heart. Throughout this process, the goal remains restoration, never punishment. Although, he's no longer befriended, he still has a church full of believers praying that he will miss the Lord and Christian friendship so much that he wants to repent and return.

If your church fulfills its duty of service, the wife will receive notes of encouragement and love. Ensure the elders end their announcement with words that encourage this.

COUNSEL HER THAT IT'S TIME HE MOVED OUT

Kirk: Counseling an Adulterer Saving a Marriage

By the time the entire church is informed of the adultery, many men will have moved from their homes. If he hasn't left, tell her it's time for her to remove his things from the house. I've seen this handled in various ways.

One woman deposited his personal items in his mother's front yard because the mother supported his relationship with the other woman. Another filled garbage bags with his things, drove to his place of work, and dumped them into the back of his truck. Afterwards, they phoned to explain where their things were.

Regardless, of how she removes his things, she must do what's right. She does not destroy any of his possessions, and she includes everything he's likely to get in a divorce such as his tools, tennis racket, pictures, toothbrush, bar of soap he used, clothes, and gifts he received from his family. If it's rightly his, or if he's the only one who uses it, she puts it in his box. If some items are expensive and were purchased with joint money, she can take pictures of them, and let the attorneys settle financial differences later.

Afterwards, she should treat him as if they are already divorced and not allow him inside the house for any reason. If he breaks in, insist that she should obtain a restraining order for protection.

Encourage her to follow the required child visitation order precisely. She should have the children ready for his pickup on visitation day.

She should spurn him. The hope is that her estrangement is to make him miss being a family. The goal of isolation remains restoration of the relationship, not revenge. He has to think he isn't missed and to miss that he's not being missed.

The goal of isolation remains restoration of the relationship, not revenge

He should not help with any house maintenance problems but provide only financial support. If he phones, she should hang up immediately without talking, and speak only to him if one of the children is taken to the hospital for something serious. She keeps a lengthy emotional distance from him and acts as if their relationship is completely severed with no hope of restoration. If it's on again, off again, he may find enough comfort to feel it isn't necessary to return and stay permanently. His missing living as a family is the only remaining hope that's left to have him change.

Chapter 18

DIVORCE OR NOT?

"*How can you prepare for divorce when it's the last thing you want?*" the abandoned wife may ask. As her counselor minister, tell her that the choice is now hers. If she still hopes to salvage the marriage then she cannot focus on divorce just yet, that it's not time to call it quits. There's always opportunity for the Lord to work. The decision to divorce or delay in hopes of his change must remain hers exclusively.

As her counselor, as long as she hopes to save the marriage tell her not to mention divorce with anyone. The wounded wife needs to pray multiple times each day about their marital relationship. Encourage her to watch the movie War Room as it shows how to depend on the Lord during such a crisis.

Explain that her best hope is to deprive the adulterer of emotional contact with the family so he wants to come home enough that he will change. Her goal at this stage is to show him all he loses by not living as a united family. Often loneliness and isolation work wonders, especially if his adulteress is not available for permanent, full-time comfort. However, she may feel so distraught and tired of the endless hurt that she wants it over. Or he may decide that he wants a divorce and there is little she can do to stop him.

WHEN DIVORCE PROVES APPROPRIATE

She may insist she wants a divorce. She has done what scriptures require, and just wants the pain to end. Remind her that loving another always involves risk. The only way never to be hurt by another is to live her life in total isolation, but that also means living without all the love another human provides.

While a few adulterers divorce their wives and marry their adulterous partner, most do not. And of the ones who do, the majority of such marriages eventually end with divorce. The divorce rate for second marriages runs around 65%, well over half. Some men leave this lover for another, thus going from woman to woman. Or he realizes his sinful error and wants to return home to his abandoned family.

While most sources quote the divorce rate as leveling at around the 50% mark that percentage is deceiving. For born-again Christians it is 33% and even lower for couples who attend church nearly every week and read their Bible regularly. With Jews it's only 3%. The rate is inflated by non-Christian faiths (74%) and atheists and agnostics (65%).

If he serves her with divorce papers, and she has not completed all steps provided by Jesus in Matthew (18:15-17) and she possibly can, for her peace of mind, she should try. This lets her know she has done all by Jesus' standard. But it is not always possible, and God doesn't expect us to do the impossible.

HELP HER SURRENDER COMPLETELY TO THE LORD. For several weeks, expect this period to prove difficult. She will likely suffer depression as she realizes there are many things associated with daily living that she depended on her husband to handle. But more importantly, she needs help to learn how to completely surrender her relationship to the Lord. Help her realize that she no longer needs a man, especially not an unrepentant, straying one. She wants him and prefers being with him, but she can learn to depend fully and totally on the Lord. She can function successfully without her husband. Right now, she finds that a frightening idea. But once she accepts that God will care for her and realizes she can survive alone, she will experience an emotional freedom.

Remind that her husband was meant to compliment her, not complete her. Many women hold a false belief that they need a man to complete them, but completion is God's job. She can find great satisfaction through her own development in the Lord, her work, her children, and pleasurable adult activities whether she has another man in her life or not. Even if she remarries, the more fulfilled she is by what she can do separately, the more intimate and happier she can be while sharing life with a man. Most husbands are relieved when they are not required to be solely responsible for their wife's happiness. With God's help, she can care for her own needs and desires.

God did not create a husband to meet his wife's deepest needs, because God knew there would be times he would fail. If her husband could meet her every need, she wouldn't need God.

If her husband could meet her every need, she wouldn't need God

"The Lord will guide you always; he will satisfy your needs in a sun-scorched land and will strengthen your frame. You will be like a well-watered garden, like a spring whose waters never fail" (Isa. 58:11). *"For **your Maker is your husband**- the Lord Almighty is His name. . ."* (54:5, my emphasis). When she responds to the Lord as He wants, she will live blessed.

By depending fully on the Lord, she will develop a new strength. If she and the straying husband divorce, her new found strength won't let him take all their money and other possessions, and it safeguards against his taking the children completely away from her. She will know how to stand up for herself if he dares to try. If he should change his mind and want to come home, or if he doesn't, her learning to depend on her trust in the Lord will prove one of her most valuable assets. She can face whatever lies ahead, whether it is an unwanted divorce or working to build a new and different relationship, she will know the Lord is with her.

COUNSEL IF HE WANTS TO RETURN HOME

Most often adulterous relationships simply end. They finally see the other's faults and flaws and don't like them. Her annoyances tend to cause worse hurt than the issues he faced at home with his wife and kids. Or the adulteress won't leave her husband, and they tire of having to sneak to be together. Or her husband threatens him, and he bails. Often, his children reject him, and it's more than he can handle. Some miss their relationship with the Lord, worry about going to hell, and they want to return. Regardless of what causes the affair to end, when it does, many want to move back home.

If he regrets his sinful lifestyle, the betrayed wife should expect him to call or send her a note asking if they can work out things. Under no condition should he be allowed back into the home as if nothing happened. He still has many changes to make before proving trustworthy. She cannot risk putting herself through another long, painful battle, nor of the children having a parent whose life-style displays a revolving door.

He still has many changes to make before proving trustworthy

When a man returns home because he's lonely and feels abandoned by his lover, the marriage rarely proves successful. The same issues he hated during their marriage are still present. Nothing has happened to change how they relate, except she has grown wiser and stronger, and he is unlikely to appreciate the new her.

Yet, she's also lonely and tired of acting as both mother and father. She must not allow her emptiness or overload of responsibility cause her to let him return without proven change. Otherwise, he's likely to leave again once he becomes annoyed with things at home and another cute woman says something that boosts his ego.

The wife needs to ensure he has changed and will never betray her again. Remember he didn't care enough to break it off by phoning the first woman, so she has no reason to trust he would react differently if another willing woman surfaced.

COUNSELING FOR HIM. Before she considers them being together, he must go for counseling alone. After he's been in extensive counseling to address the reasons that contributed to his leaving, she can consider joining him for marital counseling. Their joint counseling should be sufficient to ensure they are ready to live together.

She has to remember how many months he stayed with his lover before the affair ended. It takes time for marital bonding to reoccur and for him to completely erase desire of the other woman. She must stand her ground no matter how he might hook her emotionally during a particular counseling session, because she needs any reconnection to last a lifetime and not become his occasional one-night-stand.

They need to begin dating – all without sex. It will tell her a lot about his willingness to see her without insisting they go to bed and having everything on his terms. She needs to evaluate if he honors her requests as an equal partner or if he's wanting control. Remember Satan controls his thinking until he is fully restored with the Lord.

HE MUST RECONNECT WITH THE LORD. She must know with certainly that he has changed. And that includes his going forward at church to admit his sin and asking for prayers to remain faithful. If available, he needs to join an accountability group at his church, or if they do not have one, ask someone from the group who confronted him to hold him accountable. Weekly, this partner assigns him Scriptures to read and then questions him to ensure he's studying. He should agree to have his accountability partner phone his wife and give her updates on his progress or lack thereof. Or that may be a role you fulfill.

During this time, he should be present every time the church doors are open and offer to help other members as their requests arise. He needs the influence of other believers. Until he proves his commitment to the Lord, she should not believe he will remain committed to her. Only by drawing closer to God will he yearn to be with her and know the faithfulness this requires.

He has to lay his sins at the cross of Jesus and leave them there. Just as the woman caught in adultery was brought to Jesus, the Lord waits to forgive this man. The adulterer must not continually remind himself of his sin or that has him placing himself above God's authority to forgive. Recall what Jesus told the woman at the well: *"Neither do I condemn you. . . Go now and leave your life of sin"* (Jn. 8:9-11). Jesus expected her to change, and by doing so to know: *"There is no condemnation for those who are in Christ Jesus"* (Ro. 8:1).

In his talk at the American Association of Christian Counselors, Dr. Clark offered an excellent idea for ensuring the adulterer's trustworthiness. Dr. Clark tells wives to refuse to allow the adulterer to move home until he proves he's sincere. He demonstrates his commitment by visiting her attorney and signing an affidavit that says if he leaves her again or has another affair, the house, car, and all assets, become exclusively her. He agrees to keep her insurance paid in full, provide her a sizeable alimony, and allow her sole custody of the children. That contract would serve as a powerful deterrent to keep many a man faithful.

The couple now needs to address the many issues hindering their closeness. It's likely that both have complaints about the ways the mate responds to things important to them. When these aren't addressed they create a built-up of hurts, and the spouse begins to think, "He/she has to know and doesn't care how it hurts me." This couple needs to learn to be intimate with each other, and to find ways to stop behaviors that cause the other pain.

Encourage them to attend marriage and parenting seminars and become avid readers of marriage books. Suggest they discuss what such ideas mean to them, what parts fit their situation and why, and what ideas don't.

During their months of joint counseling, they need you to lead them through the process described in Chapters 7 - 13.

- Write a letter to her that details the affair (provided she needs more details. After this amount of time, she may know all there is to know through gossip)
- Prepare for her emotional reactions (with this time delay, there will probably be much less drama)
- Work to resolve conflicting issues
- Learn to create intimacy

Recovery for all couples plagued with adultery involves a slow, painful process. Yet the vast majority of couples who work to save their marriages say it was well worth the struggle and report being thankful they stayed together because their relationship was better than they ever hoped. And you helped them get there.

Chapter 19

OTHER WAYS ADULTERY REQUIRES HELP

If you have been doing counseling for a few years, you know that you cannot predict what type problems you will face. There are multiple ways an affair can produce pleas for your assistance. Five alternatives are offered below to help you prepare.

-1. What if she comes thinking her husband may be involved with another and he denies it?
-2. What if she wants to make the marriage work for the sake of the kids?
-3. What to do if he wants to use you to tell his wife he wants a divorce?
-4. What if he insists that you keep his affair a secret?
-5. What if the wife doesn't know about the affair, and he hopes to save the marriage?

SHE FEARS HE IS HAVING AN AFFAIR BUT HE DENIES IT
"*My husband is seeing another woman. I found notes from her in his gym bag. It shows they are in love. When I asked him about it, he said the notes belonged to his friend, Joe, but I*

don't believe him. That note explains a lot. I thought all this time that he was at the gym working out or at his job working overtime. I bet the times no one said anything when I answered the phone were her calling. How could I be so blind? And now he keeps lying about it. Why won't he just be honest and admit it?" the sobbing wife explained as she stared at the floor.

If the wife comes to you thinking her husband is involved with another woman, and asks what she should do, insist that she must have valid proof. Has she seen them together, or maybe, another who saw them told her? To be certain that her fear is accurate, encourage her to identify specific data. I counseled one woman who insisted her husband was involved with another woman because of his increased time away from home and how quiet and sullen he had grown. His problem wasn't another woman. He had cancer and didn't know how to tell her. Accusing someone of adultery is a serious charge, and she should be certain before risking the damage it can cause the marriage.

An affair can usually be determined by examining five ways the adulterer has changed. She needs to record changes in his time, money, secrecy, ways he treats her, his appearance, and the frequent mentioning of another woman's name. Changes in several of these could raise enough concern to ask him. The wife should consider six possible changes listed below in how he behaves. .

Time away from family
Additional spending
Increased secrecy
Changes towards her
Changes in his appearance
Mentioning another woman too often

TIME AWAY. Is he taking more trips without her? Does he appear to have too many reasons to be away from the family? Ask her to document times, dates, and how long and how often he is away from home without someone in the family along.

ADDED SPENDING. Has she checked their bank account for unusual withdrawals? Is she seeing unexplained charges on the credit card bills? Presents and motel rooms add up quickly. Secretly spending money is a good indicator. She needs to keep a record of all that's unexplainable.

INCREASED SECRECY. Is he suddenly moving the computer to a room so he can be alone? Or turning it off the minute she walks into the room? Does he take the phone to the bathroom or outside on the porch to talk alone? Does this happen on a regular basis? Has he changed the passwords on his accounts?

CHANGES TOWARDS HER. Is he suddenly no longer interested in sex or has he shown an increased interest in new ways of lovemaking? When did this begin? Are they talking less and arguing more?

CHANGES IN HIS APPEARANCE. Is he suddenly changing how he dresses? Where he was once comfortable with informal casual jeans/shorts does he now need a neater attire? Has he changed his beard/hair/cologne? When did this start?

MENTIONING THE OTHER WOMAN. Does he frequently quote things another woman says? If you say something negative about her, does he defend her? Does he note things about her that he ignores in other women? Does he seem to always have a reason to talk with her? Does he have reason to phone her and does he know her phone number by memory?

Help her determine any patterns in his changes. If it appears she is correct, she needs to confront him, but she needs numbers to support her claim. You do not want to be party to accusing another of adultery if the wife is just angry or the irrational, jealous type. Once she can back up her fear with data, arrange a meeting for her to bring him to see you so she can express her concerns and if necessary, to present her evidence.

If he denies having an affair, and you believe him, tell him that there is only way to rebuild trust with his wife and that is to stop all actions that she has recorded. He needs to double the amount of time he spends with his wife and do nothing in these five areas that could display an appearance of distrust. They may just need marriage counseling so they learn to do more together and to stop doing the things that create hurt for the other. If so, skip to Chapters 10-12.

If he admits to an affair, insist he must stop all contact with the other woman. If he denies having an affair but her evidence proves otherwise, treat him as if he is in a full-blown affair, just as you would any other. Insist that he must end the affair immediately, and follow the same steps as others for saving the marriage. Go to Chapter 6 and being working with the wife to have him change.

If he's guilty, he has learned what every adulterer should know: Your sins will find you out. Eventually, someone always knows, and at some point, the victimized spouse learns too. Because God loves him, God ensures that his adulterous sin is exposed so he can repent. Every sin faces consequences, *"For a man's ways are in full view of the Lord, and He examines all his paths"* (Pr. 5:21). Hopefully, he will change in time to save his family.

STAYING TOGETHER FOR THE KIDS' SAKE

"I know my husband has been unfaithful. He says he no longer sees the woman and I believe him, but I am very angry and at times I want to leave him. But I know it's better for the children if we work out things. I am committed to staying with him provided he proves I can trust this won't happen again. We need your help, because right now, I don't trust him at all. I don't even trust him to care for the dog, let alone be faithful to

me." After counseling several women whose husband were caught in adultery, you will realize this is a typical reaction.

Most women do not want a divorce if they believe they can learn to trust him again. Men will divorce their wives who have committed adultery, but women try to forgive and hold the family together.

When a couple comes for counseling with the wife knowing about the affair, it's likely that, at least for now, she has decided to remain in the marriage. They need you, as their counselor, to instill a strong sense of hope that things can change, and the attraction he feels for another can be refocused onto the wife. You need to build hope that the marriage can and will be good, and things can improve so they meet each other's needs. He needs to realize that what he feels for the other woman isn't love, but an emotional dependency he has allowed to grow.

Adultery happens most often when a couple lives with unresolved issues, so they must commit to talking openly and vulnerably. Remind them that Satan uses their problems to have them believe things will never change. Satan is the father of lies, but the Lord works all things for the good of those who trust Him (Ro. 8:28). Their relationship can be as rewarding as it was when they dated if both commit to working on their differences. Keep reassuring them that God will ensure that things can and will produce the marriage they both desire. As James wrote, all they must do is ask and obey (4:2).

How the wife learned of her husband's adultery doesn't matter. She knows, and now she must demand that he inform the other woman that they will never again contact each other.

Ask if she knows enough or needs to know more details to stop fearing that someone else might tell her more. If she wants more information, have him write a letter explaining the entire affair. A description of how to write such a letter is described in Chapter 7.

He must work on bonding with the Lord and renewing his marital relationship. The adulterer needs to know that for the next several months, his wife will continually monitor his behavior. He only has this one last chance to prove he's worthy of her support.

No matter what brought them for counseling, the first action must be to ensure that the affair has ended. Even if he insists that he and the adulteress have stopped seeing each other, ask how long it's been since they talked. If you are not fully convinced that it is 100% finished, then require him to make that uncomfortable phone call to the adulteress and end the affair permanently.

SEE A PHYSICIAN. Insist they both must be tested for AIDS and STDs. Expect him to protest and insist there's no reason, but refuse to accept his argument. He has no way of knowing if his mistress has slept with others. Even if she hasn't, maybe, her husband has, and he could have passed an infection to her. Insist they go together to their physician, and he should be the one examined first so he explains to the doctor the reason for their testing. Until the test results are known, all forms of sexual intimacy should be avoided.

For a sinner to change, he must experience emotional devastation, and such brokenness requires guilt, shame, and a loss of what he once enjoyed. Hopefully, telling the doctor initiates shame for this man.

Brokenness requires guilt, shame, and a loss of what was once enjoyed

Counsel him to expect his wife to have times when she needs him to repeat telling details of his affair. She asks because she seeks reassurance the affair is over and that he loves only her. He must not become defensive, but be thankful she stayed with him to ask.

HE WANTS TO USE YOU TO ASK FOR A DIVORCE

Likewise, some men make appointments for counseling so they can bring their wives and inform them of their adultery and ask for a divorce in your presence. They want to use you in hope their wives won't react so emotionally. Often this does help a wounded wife absorb the information slowly and carefully, but it still causes her deep suffering that hurts for a very long time.

Remember that this is a man who wants a divorce and hopes seeing you will let him walk away from his family with less drama and remorse. He just doesn't have the guts to tell her alone. His using you to reduce his guilt highlights the depth of this man's spiritual deficit.

Regardless of his motive for initiating counseling, you should allow only one option and that's his ending his adulterous relationship. Refuse to discuss divorce. If he says he wants a divorce, divert the attention to the need for him to end his affair by explaining how short-lived a marriage to one's illicit lover is and how most who do marry their adulteress later regret such a decision. Explain why his desire for a divorce is sinful, and that you will only be party to his phoning and ending the adulterous relationship. Keep the conversation focused on him calling the adulteress to tell her their relationship is finished. Give him no other alternative. The difference in this example is he has put you and his wife in the position of being together to overhear the phone call to his adulterous partner.

Expect him to protest and attempt to keep saying how unhappy he is in the marriage, but refuse to listen to any critical complaints. His wife doesn't need to hear him claim that things are her fault. Tell him that at this point, all marital problems are his fault because they cannot be resolved as long as he's involved with someone else. Interrupt him, no matter how often you must do so, to keep him focused on ending the illicit relationship.

Promise that you will work with them to improve their marriage or refer them to another for counseling, and with Jesus' help differences can be resolved. Remind them that when both are obedient, God can do more than they can imagine or dream.

If he appears to accept your words and offers to call the adulteress from home, refuse to accept his plan. He involved you in this matter, so you have a right to disagree. Likely, he's trying to find a way to avoid phoning. What he's asking is, *"Let me continue in this sin for a while longer,"* something you cannot morally agree to do. Insist that he phone her from your office, or he needs to leave because you cannot agree be party to his sin. Offer to support the wife, but without change, he no longer has a reason to stay.

IF HE REFUSES TO PHONE. He may surprise you by insisting that without him his lover won't learn about God and go to heaven. Some do plead this as a reason to continue seeing the adulteress. But the truth is, if they remain together, neither of them are destined for heaven. The only helpful reply is that he must never see the adulteress again. If he knows enough to teach her God's word, he knows Jesus' teaching on adultery and knows he cannot help save her soul while living in sin. From this moment forward saving her soul is God's role. God can't reach her as long as their sinful relationship blocks His way.

He has proven he cannot live a Christian life on his own strength. His sinful nature controls him, and he has failed (Gal. 5:16, 17; 24). He cannot bring another close to the Lord if he isn't first there himself.

It's time for him to hear the truth and with the plainest of words. Refuse to allow him any retreat into Satan's bag of lies. He should phone the woman and end the adulterous relationship from your office and do it now. Do not cave.

If he refuses, then you need to stand, walk to the door, open it, and tell him to leave, and to expect serious consequences at home from his wife.

Ask the wife to stay, and coach her on how to tell him to either leave their home or she's to shun him as he lives in the house, as Chapters 5 and 6 explain. She should see a physician for STD and AIDS testing and refuse to have sex with him until he ends the affair and their physician says they both are safe.

If he refuses to leave your office without his wife, explain in his presence how she needs to isolate herself and the children from him. Open your Bible and read the appropriate Scriptures. This reinforces her actions by knowing she's following God's word, and lets him hear you read that she's doing as the Lord commands.

Offer to continue seeing her. Tell him that you cannot continue working with someone who has no desire to change and serve the Lord. However, if he shows a slight possibility of repenting, use what he said and remind him of what he stands to lose by continuing in sin and gains by stopping the illicit relationship. Keep insisting that he make the phone call to end the affair. But if his reaction reveals only a hardened insistence on divorce, remind him that the day he realizes his need for the Lord you will gladly counsel him, but until that day, there's no longer a reason for him to see you.

> **Tell him that you cannot continue working with someone who has no desire to change and serve the Lord**

HE WANTS YOU TO KEEP HIS AFFAIR A SECRET

If the adulterer sees you without his wife, no matter his argument, insist he can learn to love his wife again and have his needs met at home, including the ones his mistress currently provides. However, if his mind is locked on divorce, don't expect him to listen. With some men, you can crack their defenses by asking them to repeat word-for-word what you say about his eternal condition and what he stands to lose. Others may refuse and respond angrily.

Stress that he must tell his wife about his affair. With any form of sexual betrayal, an adulterer wounds his wife. Even if she doesn't know there's another woman, she realizes that as a couple they no longer interact as closely as they once did. She definitely recognizes that her husband is behaving differently. Remember it is a thousand times better for her to learn of his adultery from him than from another, and eventually she will hear. It's only a matter of when, where, how, and from whom.

Affairs cannot be kept secret for long. Insist that you cannot be party to covering up sin. Explain that God says to expose sin, and you live striving to follow God's word. Ask him to phone the adulteress from your office and tell her they are finished. If he refuses, insist that he go home and immediately confess his sin to his wife, and then with the wife listening, phone the adulteress and end the affair. Give him a copy of what he's to say to the adulteress.

Make an appointment for him to return with his wife. Ensure him that you will support him as he explains his affair. If he cancels the appointment or is a no-show, phone his wife and ask her to come with her husband to see you. Explain there is something that you need to discuss with her and her husband together. Do not tell her what he needs to explain, that is his responsibility. Sometimes being forced to face his wife with such painful facts causes him to retreat from an idea of divorce.

If the wife comes alone or phones and says her husband refuses to come, insist you can't see her alone, that both must be present. Clarify that it's imperative that you see them together – and immediately. Do not tell her why and betray his confidentiality. You can be sure that she will badger him until he admits why you are insisting. And if he continues refusing, she will probably guess why. This way she knows without you telling her.

Only the truth can set their relationship free of Satan's lies, mistrust, and sinful wrongdoing. For his restoration with the Lord and to possibly save his marriage, he must genuinely confess everything to his wife and to the Lord, repent, and then allow the Lord to heal them.

Refuse to hide an on-going adulterous affair. When a wife learns of his adultery through the grapevine and realizes you know, she will feel betrayed by you as well. She will likely feel angry for you not telling her sooner so she could have avoided some unnecessary gossiping humiliation.

If she learns of the affair and he still refuses to come for counseling, coach her on how to isolate him from the family, with hope that he will change. If he does return with her to see you, have him write the letter to his wife that explains every detail about the affair. What the letter should include is explained in Chapter 7. Only by fully knowing what all the affair involved, can she finally rest assured there's no trailing gossip and that it is finished.

HE WANTS TO SAVE THE MARRIAGE

Some men who hope to salvage their marriages arrange counseling to have another present as they tell their wives about their affair. Likely, this man's affair has terminated. Often, it's the adulteress who ended it. Regardless of whom was responsible, it's over, and he wants to remain married. Question him about when it ended, and how, until you are convinced it truly is finished. If there's any doubt, then he must phone the adulteress and ensure she knows they will never again meet or speak.

If he calls the adulteress, coach him on what he should say, the firmness with which he must speak, and that he must hang up immediately before she can respond. He should sound cold and definite so she believes the ending is permanent. Any hesitation shows he isn't ready to stop seeing her.

Some men argue they need to say more or say it's over in a kinder way. They may want to apologize to her or ask her to forgive him. This is especially true if he was a minister or an elder in the church. But stand your ground. You must give him no opportunity to do this. Hand him a note and insist he says exactly what is on it. Tell him he's to hang up after the last word on the note. Any added conversation can trigger their emotional connection, and their emotional bond must be severed for the marriage to survive.

Explain that he needs to prepare for the adulteress to contact him one more time. She will seek assurance that he ended their relationship without duress, and it's over because it's what he wants. He must agree that if she phones, he will immediately hang up without speaking.

Tell him that he must commit to doing whatever is necessary so they never see each other again. That may require finding another job, a new church, even moving to another state. He must be prepared to allow his wife to know where every penny he spends goes and to know where he is every minute for the next six to twelve months. Listing these boundaries in the wife's presence provides her additional reassurance that the affair has ended.

Explain that he must prepare to share every detail of the illicit relationship with his wife, many he would rather not remember. Require him to prepare a letter listing everything about the affair as detailed in Chapter 7. He cannot risk his wife hearing new, unknown, sordid tales from others. .

Insist that it is especially important that he retraces in his mind how one thing led to another, a timeline of how things progressed. This lets him explain his weaknesses to his wife and shows he now knows how to protect himself from similar, sinful situations in the future. He forgives himself faster knowing he will never again be so vulnerable or act so stupid.

Kirk: Counseling an Adulterer Saving a Marriage

Explain that the details of his affair will cause unbearable pain for his wife, and many women respond with attacks and criticism. He must be prepared not to react defensively but keep repeating, *"I am sorry. I will never betray you again. I want to save our marriage. I will do whatever it takes to win you because I love you."* Prepare him that the next few weeks, more likely months, will be filled with days of closeness and days of her reacting with anger and pain.

BRING HIS WIFE. Schedule a time for him to return with his wife, preferably within the week. Meanwhile he is to write the letter detailing the affair and bring it to the next session. The longer he waits the more likely she will learn things through another. Book them a double session as this will be an emotional experience for all.

Wounded wives need additional counseling as they decide if they remain married. Refuse to let them make such a serious judgment during the session when they learn of his unfaithfulness. The shock produced by such news limits their ability to rationally make decisions that carry such long-lasting consequences. If they appear overly distraught, they may need to see their doctor for medication to ease their anxiety. They need full mental control to decide what to do next. Let them leave counseling knowing when they can see you again, preferably within the next few days.

Kirk: Counseling an Adulterer Saving a Marriage

Explain that their next few weeks will prove a very emotional time as the wife adjusts to a man whom she no longer trusts. She will rage with anger, sob with indescribable hurt, and vacillate between wanting more closeness and wishing she could kill him.

Chapter 20

AGES AFFAIRS ARE MORE LIKELY

According to Daniel Levinson, author of *Seasons of a Man's Life* and a mentor during my research of women's adult life cycles, married couples face critical periods when they experience a yearning for something different. It's when one partner craves a new and different challenge. The person may seek something more stimulating, or they want to reduce their level of responsibility.

Research for my dissertation proved this occurs at definite ages for women, just as it did for the men Levinson studied. Fortunately, the timing tends to differ for men and women, or they might destroy each other because such transitions can create unbearable marital turmoil

These turbulent transitional periods lasted four or five years as the ones seeking change wrestled with decisions that would satisfy their cravings. During these stormy times some couples grew together and others apart. Afterwards those still together settled into stable and fairly comfortable routines.

THE 20s

Most couples still marry while one or both are in their 20s, and they face the most marital challenges. Successful marriages require serious consideration of the partner's feelings rather than just pursuing their own desires. The couples who tend to experience more problems are those who marry at younger ages and/or those who are considerably much older and have not been previously married. Having primarily focused exclusively on one's self, and now becoming a couple, they find it more difficult to blend in another's wants and wishes.

New husbands often put other people or their activities ahead of his new wife, but in Deuteronomy 24:5, God says for the first year a new wife should be the exclusive center of her husband's attention. Too many men marry thinking their social and pleasurable activities will continue as before, and the only change is they can now have sex any time they want. Parents fail to explain that unless he tones down his routine, he sets up unnecessary arguments. God says a husband's new wife should be his main attention during the first year because God knows how vulnerable a new wife feels when she is displaced by other people or his activities exclude her. He needs to prove that she ranks first in his life to establish a trusting, bonded relationship.

If she's always fighting to have first place, her continual failure leaves her tired of trying, and she questions if she married the wrong man.

Her blunder is not responding warmly to his sexual advances, especially when she feels upset with him, because, after disagreements, sharing sexually is how many men reconnect. If she withholds sex to punish him, she disobeys the Lord. God says a wife's body no longer belongs to her because of how vulnerable a man is to other attractive women when he hears a string of, "*I can't while so upset*," or "*No, not tonight*" (1 Corinthians 7:3-5). He thinks I married to have sex when I wanted, and I am tired of being rejected. His ego deflates.

After multiple disappointments, the traits newlyweds initially found appealing in their mates begin to create annoyances. What she called generous while dating becomes viewed as wastefulness. What he considered supportive, he now labels manipulative. They argue about these aggravations instead of what's really bothering them and many find it easier to leave than to continually try to have their mate meet their needs. Or they pursue an illicit affair partner to satisfy their emotional emptiness.

AGES 30-35.

My research found that women aged 30-35 typically experience a craving for a new, stimulating challenge. If she is a homemaker, she no longer finds PTA, charity work, and teaching children's Bible satisfying. She tells herself, *"If I am going to work full time for these, why not do something to bring home a paycheck?"* Her entering the work force, perhaps for a first time, puts her with men who dress nicely and pay her compliments that she missed receiving at home. For too long, she centered on small children who express demands, not appreciation. In addition, her change creates added stress on her husband. Now she expects him to contribute more to childcare and housework, and this causes more arguments. Then both feel cheated in their relationship and blame the other.

If she had previously been employed, she realizes her reproductive clock is ticking and desperately wants a baby. I interviewed one woman who traveled to South America to adopt a child because her locale did not permit single women to adopt. While she had a special man in her life, he wasn't sure he wanted children, and for them to marry now required him to accept this added responsibility. If he left her, she had to decide if she would attempt to rear a child alone or actively pursue finding a man who wants a ready-made family. Neither seemed good choices.

According to Levinson, men in their 30s want the freedom to focus on reaching the peak of their careers, not daily face a woman expressing a desire for a life change. He seeks that envious promotion, or hopes to write a best-selling novel, or have the highest order of sales in his organization. Consistent with God's punishment for Adam, work remains his dominant focus, with an added hope of becoming noted.

Having his wife make an unexpected change of going to work or quitting her job to have a child distracts from what's most important to him. He feels cheated that she withdraws his needed support. He wants the freedom to focus on peaking in his career, and she feels used if he disapproves of her change.

The thirties can prove a very turbulent period for both mates. If an outsider comes along who supports either of their desires, they can easily turn all attention to this person for support and ignore the spouse. Thus, an affair blossoms.

MEN AGES 40-45.

About the time their wives again appear stable and contented with their prior change, men reach mid-life and many encounter a mid-life crisis. Feeling he's peaked in his career, he questions what's left for him to accomplish. He hunts new outlets, but his wife rarely receives his idea of selling their home and moving to an island any better than he welcomed her earlier change.

She considers them too old to drive a convertible, with the wind blowing his new shoulder-length hair and gold chains lining the neck of his unbuttoned shirt. She tends to have no appreciation for his losses and feels contented in the middle of her stable period, and this leaves him feeling lonely.

He's trying to recapture some of his remaining youthful spirit, and feels cheated as if every penny and all time always goes to doing things for others. He yearns for all the personal desires and dreams that caring for others caused him to miss. He often feels this is his last chance to satisfy earlier goals. Levinson found the men who navigated this transitional period successfully, took younger men under their wing and taught them the ropes of their career or a sport. They learned to find success in other's accomplishments. Other plunged into a new career or part-time work with their church.

Wives navigate this crisis best by purchasing scarfs to protect their hair so Satan doesn't bring another woman to ride in that new convertible with him, because many men resolve this transition with affairs and /or a divorce. And he often finds that he's attracted to a younger woman, some as young as his own daughters. Her age helps him feel more youthful and distract from how he is aging.

THE 50s AND 60s.

Transitions during 50s and 60s appear to struggle with very similar issues. Both men and women report going through periods of feeling an urgency for change. However, most of these periods were much briefer than at previous ages. They become consciously aware that death lurks around the corner, and there are numerous desires they still haven't fulfilled, things they haven't tried but always said they would.

For a woman, it's her time to brag of success. She feels wiser and smarter and wants to set the world afire, be it a career goal or working more for the Lord. The kids are gone and their absence means she is finally free to tackle more and do more. She no longer has to live with goals that are postponed until the kids were gone. She feels free at last. If her husband fails to support her in her new challenges, she may find some man who will, especially because he's now ready for a slower pace, enjoying fun times, and creating lasting memories together, not taking on new challenges. He's tired of big challenges. He's been there, done that, and doesn't want a repeat.

For him, the kids' absence provides an opportunity for them to grow closer as a couple. He sees advertisements about men losing their sexual prowess and thinks, "It's now or never for us to enjoy our last days together." More couples are divorcing later in life and most of these divorces are initiated by the women who are not ready for a retirement home, but neither is she ready for every weekend filled with sex. He feels neglected, and too often, he seeks outside companionship during the weekends she is working.

THE 70s.

This stage of life brings health concerns and the need to find activities to replace strenuous sports. The mind thinks they still can participate in skiing or tennis, but the body proves them wrong. Acceptance of limitations and finding pleasurable outlets prove a dispiriting challenge. Facing one's own death becomes unavoidable, as they attend funerals of friends their age. One's own death can no longer be ignored.

Without open communication about different desires and a commitment to live as God commands, many older couples face affairs or divorces. Some appear almost as vulnerable as newlyweds. But divorce and remarriage never pushes death to the background. It may temporarily distract, but the reality of what lies ahead cannot be permanently removed.

Transitions at any stage can create chaos because of how we address changes we don't like. God explains how to have good marriages, but we want to do things our way, not God's way. Without compromise, both spouses sin and kill their love for each other. It begins when one mate begins continually emphasizing the small annoying things the spouse does while ignoring those their own irritating habits. The more they focus on frustrations, the more they tend to become hyper-critical and create never ending arguments. Yet, Scriptures say to do **everything** without complaining, arguing, or grumbling (Phil. 2:14; Js. 5:9). They forget that they cannot focus on the negative they dislike and the mates' good qualities at the same time, and that their focus is controlled by them, not the spouse.

It is interesting how the ratio of cheating and divorce varies by gender and by ages. Such numbers tend to come from therapists and attorneys, but these cannot include those who are able to keep their sinful transgressions a secret. However, the discovery of the Ashley Madison website, where married people anonymously pursued sexual relations, revealed some interesting facts. The number of men and women in their 30s who used this website was evenly divided. In the age 40s stage, men out-ranked women 3 to 1. The ratio of users in their 50s was 4 men to 1 woman, and in the 60s it ran 14 men to 1 woman.

A woman's straying is greatest in her younger years. This underscores the importance of a newlywed husband giving his wife his full attention during the first year so she feels bonded, loved, and knows she is holds the top priority in her husband's heart. Without feeling first, she wants to find another who will make her his primary priority.

As women age, they show less and less interest in other men, while the percent of men having affairs remains fairly constant, regardless of their ages. Men at all ages are more likely to seek a divorce attorney than a therapist when they learn of their mate's affair. Women, especially if they have children, prefer working out things. Few men forgive. Most women work to try.

However, it's not the frustrating irritants that lead to divorce. According to research by John Gottman, author of *What Predicts Divorce,* the problem isn't what we argue about or even how often we disagree. Rather it is how we behave as we disagree. If we use attacking tones, hurtful labels, and continual putdowns we are headed for divorce. In fact, querying hundreds of married couples conducted over a 20-year period, Gottman discovered that the happiest and best satisfied of long-term married couples had three issues they never resolved. They learned to focus on the good aspects of their relationship and refused to allow the disagreeable matters to become the center of their focus. They learned to live happily without the three issues being resolved. They found ways to work around them so they no longer impacted or interfered with their one-on-one closeness.

What contributes to a couples many trials is a lack of understanding of Biblical priorities. Instead of keeping God first, spouses second, minor children third, jobs fourth, parents fifth, and adult children next, and then others, many let other demands control their daily schedules, time, and money. Certainly, having a sick child or dying parent bumps to a higher priority, but only temporarily. However, if we put career advancement or helping others before our relationship with God and our spouses, even if it's heavy involvement in *church work*, we need to do a deep, self- evaluation because that has us acting like Martha, not Mary.

I envision Martha thinking, "But Lord, I was serving you and your friends. You were hungry, and I fed you." Picture her shock as Jesus explained that her priorities were skewed. She placed caring for others as more important personal time with the Lord (Lk 10:41-42). If we lose our spouse because we want to become noted or even while trying to save others' souls, I fear the Lord's warning about being blind and guilty of sin must surely apply (Jn. 9:41).

Adultery always leaves a painful string of permanent consequences. *"A man who commits adultery lacks judgment; whoever does so destroys himself. Blows and disgrace are his lot, and his shame will never be wiped away"* (Pr. 6:32-33). And so it is with sexual, emotional, or spiritual adultery.

Putting God first by talking often with Him, studying His Word, and surrendering to His control of our lives, while keeping our spouses second with time, energy, money, emotional, sexual, and spiritual support ensure that God blesses our marriages. And we avoid continued arguments about the many changes each feels driven to make as we advance through our adult life-cycles.

We can find ways to support our spouse's changes, not because we like what's happening, but because we love our marital relationship and love the Lord. Wearing the name of Jesus Christ(ian) is a commitment to keep first priorities first and keep our consciences clean (1 Pe. 3:21). If we claim to belong to Christ(ian), He expects us to act like it.

Chapter 21

LEGALLY PROTECT YOURSELF & THE CHURCH

The courtroom rang with a deafening silence as the judge announced his ruling in favor of the plaintiff. As he slammed his gavel on the desk, the elders and minister sat stunned, unable to move or speak for several minutes. Afterwards, the minister and elders mailed letters to other churches seeking donations to help pay the enormous expenses incurred from the lawsuit.

The suit resulted when the minister shared with the elders that a female member of their congregation confessed to having an affair. An elder repeated this information to his wife, and you can guess the rest of the story.

When the woman discovered others knew, she immediately found an attorney who sued them all. She thought she had confidentiality protection between herself and the minister. She would never have revealed her affair had she known the minister would repeat it to others or that an elder would tell such a private matter to his wife. Confidentiality was broken once the minister repeated information shared privately with the intent that it not be further disclosed with anyone.

As this case proved, unauthorized disclosure of confidential information can create a serious legal liability. No longer is confidentiality just a moral and ethical issue; today it's also a legal one that ministers and elders need to understand. U. S. Supreme Court Chief Justice Warren Burger is noted for saying the courts overflow today because churches and families have failed to teach how to respond to conflict in a godly manner, and he ruled that a minister or pastor who repeats information obtained during a counseling session could be sued for invasion of privacy or defamation.

People who seek counseling with ministers expect that what they share will be held in the strictest of privacy. They want to disclose personal concerns without fear of the information leaving the room. Conflict occurs when a church member's expectations and the clergy's practice of confidentiality differ.

CONFIDENTIALITY: EXCEPTIONS--LIMITATIONS

While confidentiality is clearly defined in some churches, in others it is not. Many members do not understand there are legal exceptions and limitations to confidentiality. They enter a minister's office unaware that in some instances preachers are bound by law to reveal what they hear, so they assume that anything they share will be treated in the strictest of confidence regardless of what's disclosed.

Irrespective of how strongly a minister may desire to uphold the firmest of confidence, legally, he may be unable. Depending on the issue, the laws surrounding private communication may supersede the person's right to keep secret what is said.

Irrespective of how strongly a minister may desire to uphold the firmest of confidence, legally, he may be unable

Discussions between lay members and a minister are legally considered *clergy-penitent privileged* conversation, which means that the conversations between ministers and counselees are non-admissible in a court of law. In all states, the privilege is for the protection of the person who discloses private information. Half the states allow ministers to also assert privilege and not share in court what was privately disclosed. This means that clergy must maintain client confidentiality, privacy, and privileged communication to the fullest extent allowed by law and the church's rules and policies. However, there are certain provisions that make the protection of privileged confidentially conditional. For example, all states define communication between clergy and parishioners as privileged only if the confidential communication is shared with a minister who is acting exclusively as a spiritual advisor. This includes written correspondence and phone calls.

PRIVACY. In some states, even conversations that are limited to spiritual matters may not be considered privileged if a third party is present or if others could hear the discussion, such as when the office door remains open. It matters not that parishioners may think such talks are privileged, because privileged communication needs to take place in the traditional church setting where privacy is maintained. In these states, it could put the counseling of couples on shaky ground. While the conversations of couples is confidential, what they say may not always be recognized as clergy-penitent privilege.

PUBLIC DISCLOSURE. Likewise, talks in a social setting may be confidential, but the courts do not consider them privileged. To avoid such confusion, if during a public or social meeting, a minister is told about a personal or sensitive issue that could ultimately create a legal matter, he should ask if the person is bringing up the matter as his friend or in a spiritual capacity. If the person thinks the minister-counselor is listening as a spiritual advisor, it would be best to explain that what's said in such a setting is not privileged, and he could be forced to share such details in court. He can avoid this risk by scheduling a private, confidential meeting to discuss the topic and immediately change the subject.

ABUSE REPORTING. All states make it mandatory for ministers to report any reasonable suspicion of child maltreatment. The minister is legally bound like others in helping professions (doctors, dentist, therapist, teachers, etc.), to report if a child under age 18 is currently being neglected or abused physically or sexually. Clergy are considered required reporters no matter where or how they learn of the mistreatment. In some states, even neighbors, friends, and relatives are required to report child abuse, and some states consider it abuse if a child is under the care of anyone who uses drugs.

All states make it mandatory for ministers to report any reasonable suspicion of child maltreatment

All states grant mandatory reporters *limited liability immunity* for those who act in good faith. They cannot be sued, even if the allegations prove false. States protect the identity of the one reporting unless there's documented malicious intent.

While the requirements for reporting may differ, all 50 states have enacted child abuse laws, and each state has a hotline number for reporting abuse. The national hotline number is 800-422-4453 and can be used no matter where the reporter lives. All calls are anonymous, and contact for other support services are provided.

Each state's requirements are listed in the website: www.childwelfare.gov. It is imperative for a minister to know his own state's legal requirements and abide by them. If the minister's state considers him a mandatory reporter, his failure to report makes him subject to criminal penalty and in some states civil liability. Attempting to handle child abuse with church discipline is not considered sufficient legally.

Ministers who live and/or work in one state but counsel people living in another state should abide by the regulatory statutes of all such states. If these differ, he should use the one with the most restrictive regulations and explain all requirements to those he counsels.

HOW COURTS HANDLE LACK OF REPORTING

Mandatory reporting often includes reporting abuse of the elderly. In the majority of states, clergy are also required to report if those they counsel reveal they are suicidal or detail a plan to cause real harm to another. In these situations, the minister is required to notify the police, and if the person threatens to kill or harm another, the one in danger must be warned.

A psychologist lost his license and received a jail sentence for failing to warn an intended victim after a man he counseled revealed plans to kill the victim. The psychologist notified the police and attempted to warn the intended victim, but when he didn't answer his phone, the therapist notified his parents. Because the person was murdered, the judge ruled that the therapist had not given sufficient notice and should have done more to warn the deceased man.

Previously, some courts have held ministers to the same standard as licensed professionals when threats of another's life are revealed during counseling. Ministers need to disclose to everyone they counsel what they are required to reveal before counseling conversations begin.

Ministers need to disclose to everyone they counsel what they are required to reveal before counseling conversations begin

AGREEMENT FORMS

Ministers or elders who engage in counseling should have everyone they counsel sign a counseling intake-agreement form before any discussion begins. Examples of several such forms are provided in Appendix A. These forms can be copied and modified to fit each counseling-minister's specific needs. Ensure the form includes a place for counselees to check the type of issue for which they seek help (e.g. individual spiritual help, depression, anger issues, family, parenting, marriage, etc.) and sign it.

Any form used should include the issues not covered with *clergy-penitent privilege*, and list the specific issues that a minister is required by law to report. It should also address church policies that require special attention. All such waivers of the privilege communication (e.g. child abuse) must be clearly and specifically detailed so the lay person understands that not everything shared in private is guaranteed legal confidentiality.

The minister needs to explain exactly what is considered confidential, what is not, and who else, if anyone, needs to know, and under what circumstances. The minister can explain that he will do his best to keep what he's told in strict confidence, but there are certain conditions in which the law and/or church policy says he cannot. Knowing this in advance places the burden of what's shared and how much on the counselee, instead of the minister.

ADDITIONAL FORM(S). Anyone who has done counseling knows that a counselee can begin talking about one issue (questions of faith, drug dependency, own sexuality, etc.) and without notice, immediately switch to sharing concerns about an entirely different issue (teen discipline, marriage issues, problems with a boss, etc.). When this happens the person(s) should be asked to sign a second form or modify the original form by including the new, additional reason for counseling. The counselee who discloses new information needs to understand if they are opening an area that requires legal reporting or that isn't covered with privilege.

Because state laws differ regarding the counseling of married couples, having such a form signed by each person is necessary because not all marriages can be saved. Some couples will face a divorce judge. A signed document does not change the confidential nature of the verbal communication or written records of the counseling sessions, but it does prevent one member claiming their conversations were privileged, while the other asks the court to force the minister to testify on his behalf. If both parties waive their right to privileged confidentiality, then all information shared is subject to possible disclosure. If requested by the courts, the minister has no legal ground for withholding disclosure. However, the minister remains bound to hold all communications and records confidential and not disclose what's said to anyone else.

If both parties sign that their sessions are to be considered privileged, the courts are more likely to honor this, no matter that one party later changes his mind. Both signing for privileged communication reduces the worry about being compelled to testify in court so long as copies of their intent and signatures are kept in a secure place.

Preachers and counseling elders must abide by what their written agreement says and tell no one who isn't listed, and that includes their spouses, other elders, or friends. One minor slip of the tongue could land them in serious trouble.

WHEN AFFAIRS ARE INVOLVED

When people come to a minister seeking counseling because one spouse is involved in an affair, it places the counseling minister in a precarious position. Certainly, the adulterer has a spiritual problem and needs spiritual advice and guidance, and such individual counsel is covered under privilege. But counseling about an affair rarely involves a single person's adherence to God's Word. Many discussions must focus on the spouse and problems in the marriage that contributed to the affair. Therefore, they need to protect themselves, by ensuring those they counsel know before they share private information what could be revealed to others, and if shared, with whom, and for what reasons.

When doing such counseling, I make it very clear up-front that if the person is having an affair, I will not keep it a secret from their spouse. I will do nothing to protect nor hide the sin (Eph. 5:11). I insist that the person cannot return to the Lord and be spiritually forgiven nor the marriage saved unless the affair is stopped and then openly addressed. I explain that saving the person's soul is my goal, but marriage problems require discussions with both spouses, and some states do not honor privilege communication with both partners present. I also stress that the marriage may or may not be salvaged, and full responsibility for the marriage succeeding belongs to the couple, not me. My limited role is to explore, invite, encourage, teach, and many times, insist. I do not have fairy dust or a magic wand, but I do rely on God's Word.

In addition, although I have no way to enforce such a request, I always begin counseling with married couples by asking them to agree to attend a minimum of 12 counseling sessions. From my experience, I find one party will come to one counseling session, two maybe, and then say, "We tried counseling, and it didn't work either." Such behavior shows they didn't want the marriage saved. I make it clear that I don't want to be used like that. In these type cases, one party is usually trying to ease the conscience and/or to have others think they have done all they could to make the marriage work. I have found that it takes at least three or four sessions for a couple to stop finger pointing and talking about each other's flaws. Only then do they begin talking to each other in ways the other can listen.

MINISTER'S NOTES

A minister counselor needs to attach each counselee's counseling agreement form to his own personal counseling notes. At the very least, his notes should include dates, times, topics discussed, agreements, and recommendations. Some professional organizations recommend using only a person's first name in written notes. All notes and release forms should be stored in a way that safeguards them so no one else sees them, and are later disposed of in ways that maintain confidentiality such as secure shredding.

After researching multiple professional organizations' ethics, I found no consistency for how long counseling notes should be kept under lock and key, except for psychologists. They recommend keeping counseling notes for seven years in case a court or person later needs them, but even they offer possible reasons for both longer and shorter times.

PASTORAL LICENSING

The American Association of Christian Counselors (AACC) states that ministers who offer pastoral, marriage and family therapy, or other counseling services are exempt from licensure requirements so long as their services are authorized by the local congregation/church. Groups such as AACC, the American Association of Marriage and Family Therapy, and Licensed Professional Counselors insist that if a minister accepts payment or barter of any type, he must be licensed by his state. This is required even if he only counsels part-time. If there is a charge for any materials used, whether assigned fees or voluntary donations, they must be payable to and deposited in the church's account, not the minister's. Otherwise, he must be licensed.

Some ministers choose not to join professional counseling groups because these organizations have written codes of ethics that all members must agree to abide by, which may differ with beliefs of the minister and his church. If a conflict arises, the minister could be hurt by negative public press if the organization publicly chooses to challenge such differences.

For example, The American Association of Pastoral Counselors states a minister cannot discriminate against or refuse employment, educational opportunity or professional assistance to anyone on the bases of race, ethnicity, gender identity, sexual orientation, religion, health status, age, disabilities or national origin; provided that nothing herein shall limit a member or center from utilizing religious requirement or exercising a religious preference in employment decisions. Based on these requirements, a minister could be challenged if he refused counseling to someone who occasionally attended his church and called themselves a member, but was not considered a member by the church leadership or minister, and the church only allowed counseling of members. The minister would likely win the challenge if his church had a written policy stating he could only counsel members, and it defined what was required to be a member. But without such a policy in place, should the matter be publicly challenged, his and the church's reputation could be negatively impacted.

In an effort to help alleviate such concerns, the American Association of Christian Counselors (AACC) has established separate standards for ministers who have counseling as a part of their responsibilities. AACC list ministers' conduct as separate and distinct from licensed professionals in the field. Their code of ethics for clergy states:

> "Pastors and unlicensed minister- counselors - - by law and/or regulation – are not typically required or held to the same standard of professional conduct as licensed practitioners. Nevertheless, they recognize possible moral and/or ethical imperatives that may still exist as part of the Judeo-Christian ethic."

AACC further states that pastors and ministerial counselors are responsible to ensure they do not aid or abet the use of unlicensed, untrained, unqualified, or unethical counseling or lay help. Lay help includes those with no official counselling training. When a minister requires additional assistance, they recommend pursuing consultation and /or referrals to professionals.

All ministers would be well served to familiarize themselves with the American Association of Christian Counselors Code of Ethics since courts have previously made legal determinations by using standards set by national associations. AACC provides minister's a special definition so their responsibilities can be considered different from licensed and paid professionals working in the field.

In addition, organizations such as AACC can aid ministers in developing their own set of written ethical standards. Copies of AACC Code of Ethics are available on line at http://aacc.net/files/AACC%20Code%20of%20Ethics%20-%20Master%20Document.pdf

Once logged into this site, scroll to pages 48-50 where it discusses ministerial counseling ethics.

LEADERSHIP RESPONSIBLITY

Church leadership must recognize their need for the strictest of confidentiality. The elders must consider how they will handle a person confessing a sensitive, sinful behavior in a classroom Bible study setting and know how to address the ethical and/or moral responsibility of privilege in a way that best honors the person's request that what's told is to be kept confidential. If the employed minister refuses to counsel, marry, or deliver a funeral sermon for someone, what limits do the elders have in writing that support such a decision? If the minister asks for assistance in referring a person/couple for additional counseling, what resource will they recommend? If a couple cannot afford counseling will church funds be used to help? Will each person who needs financial assistance be given the same or will it be based on individual need? Who would assess such need? If the minister counsels someone who refuses to give up a sinful lifestyle, will the elders be told, and if so, how will they respond if. . .

*The elders should decide how they will respond if t*he following situations occur and create in advance written policies and procedures. For example, what policy seems appropriate for the following?

-Someone reports unethical behavior of the minister?

-If asked to provide a reference for a minister that's guilty of an immoral, unethical act?

-A wife seeks assistance in dealing with her husband bringing his adulterous partner to worship while they are still married?

-If full membership and involvement is demanded by someone whose lifestyle shows they practice what the church believes is sinful?

-If fellowship is withdrawn from someone, what will the congregation be told so all members share a stake in helping the person change and live right with God?

-What written guidance/expectation is provided the minister and each person who holds a church position? Will it include written expectations of the minister's wife, as many now include?

-If the minister is expected to do counseling, will he be granted time and money to pursue training with a counseling focus?

-If there's report of a serious problem in the church and a news agency phones for an interview, who will respond to the call?

-How will fraud/theft be handled?

-What preparations are in place if a shooting or an abduction occurs (for example, do children's rooms have doors that lock from the inside and a way to alert additional help)?

-Concealed guns are allowed, how do you ensure carriers are certified?

-What involvements will a registered sex offender be allowed and which denied?

-What policies cover extended facilities (camps, educational centers, external facilities rented for church use, cell phone use while operating church vehicles, etc.)?

-Who can take pictures of children/adults involved in church activities and how can they be used?

-Will video cameras be used for security and liability protection?

The above list is offered as a starting point for elders to think about issues that need serious consideration. While writing such policies can seem overwhelming, there are groups who, for a fee, help churches develop procedures to fit their needs. See such examples in Appendix B developed by AG Financial group. This company is primarily an insurance company that offers this type support throughout the U.S. There are many other companies and attorney groups who do the same.

EXAMPLE. A lawsuit that shows the need to have firm policies in place is Fort Des Moines Church of Christ v. Jackson. At stake is the freedom of churches to teach their religious beliefs and to use their houses of worship consistently with those beliefs without government intrusion and threat of punishment. Fort Des Moines Church of Christ's motto is to love God, love people, and serve everyone. This Iowa church is active in its community and welcomes everyone to learn more about the good news of God's love and salvation. But because the church welcomes nonmembers to attend its worship services and other activities, the Iowa Civil Rights Commission takes the position that state law requires Fort Des Moines to censor its speech about human sexuality and make showers and restrooms accessible to the opposite biological sex.

The law at issue prohibits "public accommodations" from "indicating" that a person is "unwelcome" based on his or her "gender identity." Fort Des Moines welcomes everyone; but the speech ban is so broadly written as to prohibit a preacher's sermon about God's design for marriage being a male and a female. The law also compels public accommodations to open their restrooms, locker rooms, and showers to persons based on gender identity, rather than biological sex. The implication is that the law could be applied to any activity at a church that does not have a 'bona fide religious purpose' such as when the building serves as a polling place or a daily childcare facility. During such time, a church cannot do anything that might make any gender feel unwelcome.

For the first time in our nation's history, many state officials are attempting to control a church's religious teaching and its house of worship. Alliance Defending Freedom has filed a lawsuit on behalf of Fort Des Moines Church of Christ against this unprecedented overreach by the Iowa Civil Rights Commission. Their stand is that all churches in Iowa should be free to communicate their beliefs about human sexuality without government censorship and operate their facilities consistently with their faith.

For the first time in our nation's history, many state officials are attempting to control a church's religious teaching and its house of worship

At a minimum, a church needs policies in writing that address confidentiality, use of church property by members and by nonmembers, counseling guidelines, abuse, employment policies, membership requirements, expectations of everyone that received church money, and insurance, including how insurance records are handled so they meet the strict standards of HIPPA. Policies should cover prevention, protection, reduction of risks, appropriate responses, and recovery.

All answers to this limited list of questions above (and the many not included) must honor God and explain how they support a church's beliefs. Before sharing policies with the members, all written documents should be evaluated by an attorney specializing in laws pertaining to places of worship, rather than one who practices general law. While preparation of policies and procedures requires hours of work, it proves far less than what is required when facing a legal battle.

RESPONSE TO SUBPOENAES

If a minister (or elder) receives notice from the court that he must either testify or relinquish his notes to the court, he should immediately contact the involved counselee. This allows the counselees opportunity to contact their attorneys to file clergy-privilege exception and to direct all such disclosures. If the counselee fails to do this, the minister should seek his own attorney. While this does not prevent him from being required to comply, it does stop the counselee from claiming a minister's deliberate misuse of privilege.

MALPRACTICE

Today, anyone can file a lawsuit for practically any reason. Thus far, the courts have determined clergy malpractice based on what the preacher did or did not do as compared with what a reasonable minister would do in a similar situation. While few courts have permitted a claim of pastoral-ministerial malpractice, they have allowed claims of defamation, fraud, assault, slander, etc.

Specific ways a minister can protect himself include refusing payment of any type, learning the state's reporting laws, and discussing these thoroughly with each counselee before counseling begins, especially if the person reveals on the intake-agreement form something that might require mandatory reporting. This leaves counseling ministers exclusively under the beliefs and practices of their sponsoring church and the state laws.

It should be mandatory for a church to have procedures and policies in place to restrict or remove the potential for minister and leadership malpractice, and to have insurance that covers potential claims. While malpractice insurance is expensive, it proves cheaper than churches losing their good reputations and ministers and elders being left deeply in debt from a lawsuit.

Dr. Wyveta Kirk is a retried Christian psychologist. She continues to write books and magazine articles and is available to conduct retreats, seminars, and programs that are Biblically based.

Her popular, best-selling book is about marriage: Women Talk Men Walk: Have the marriage you crave, God tells how, Hormones explain why.
Her other books include:
God Wants to Say YES
Does God Really Love Me
Keeping a Promise (children's book)
Ashamed (fiction novella)
A Legacy of Love
2 Things Men Need More Than Sex

Dr. Kirk lives in Benton Arkansas with her husband, James Rodney 'Rod' Kirk, without whose help this book would not exist. He agonized over all that's required of a man for rebuilding trust after such betrayal and still continued to proof read. They worship with saints at Northside Church of Christ.

REFERENCES:

1. AG Financial Insurance Solutions. "Church Liability: Clergy Privilege, Confidentiality, and Reporting." http://blog.ag financial.org/bid/103391/Church-Liability-Clergy-Privilege-Confidentiality-and-Reporting.

2. AG Financial Insurance Solutions. "What You Need to Know about Church Risk and Child Abuse Reporting." http://blog.agfinancial.org/What-You-Need-to-Know-about-Church-Risk-and-Child-Abuse-Reporting, and http://blog.agfinancail.org/

3. AG Financial Insurance Solutions: What You Need to Know When You Let Others Use Your Facilities: http://www.agfinancial.org/blog/bid106242risk-management-resource-facilities-use-agreement/ and the free form to use: http://www.agfinancial.org/wp-content/uploads/2013/09/0e1887305_insurance-facilitiesuseagreement091510.pdf

4. American Association of Christian Counselors. "AACC Code of Ethics." www.aacc.net/about-us/code-of-ethics/

5. Andreas. Steve. 1991. *Virginia Satir: The Pattern of Her Magic.* Palo Alto, California: Science and Behavior Books, Inc.

6. https.//www.quora.com/What-are-the-demographics-of-Ashley-Madison-users.

7. Barna Research. 2008. *New Marriage and Divorce Statistics Released.* http://www.barna.com/research/new-marriage-and divorce-statistics.

8. Barna Research. 2016. *The Porn Phenomenon.* http://www. barna.com/the-porn-phenomenon/

9. Bendixen, Mons, Edward, Leif, Ottesen, Edward, Buss, David M. Jealousy: Evidence of strong sex differences using both forced choice and continuous measure paradigms. **Personality and Individual Differences**, 2015; 86: 212 DOI: 10.1016/j.paid.2015.05.035

10. Berger, Warren Justice. 1982. Annual Report on the State of the Judiciary, *American Bar Association Journal.*

11. Brecheen, Carl, and Faulkner, Paul. 1977. Marriage Enrichment Seminar. Abilene Christian University, Abilene TX

12. Clark, David. 2015. *"I Don't Love You Anymore: An Aggressive Approach for Serious Marital Sins."* Speech presented at the American Association of Christian Counselors; Nashville TN.

13. Cooper, Al, Delmonicao David L., Burg, Ron. Cybersex Users, Abusers, and Compulsivity: New Findings and Implications. Vol. 7. Is. 1-2, 2000. *Journal of Sexual Addiction and Compulsivity*

14. Enrichment Journal. Pastoral Confidentiality: An Ethical and Legal Responsibility. 11445 Boonville Av. Springfield MO (Phone 417-862-2781, ext. 4095).

15. Frederick, David A., Fales, Melissa R. 2016. Upset Over Sexual verus Emotional Infidelity Among Gay, Lesbian, Bisexual, and Homosexual Adults.

Archieves of Sexual Behavior. 40. 175-179. Doi: 10.1007/s10508-014-0409-9

16. Gibbons, Luke. 2017. How Pornography is Paralyzing the Church.. Vol. 41. No. 8. September 2017. *AFA Journal.*

17. Gilkerson, Luke. Porn Use as Grounds for Divorce: How my Opinion Changed. October 8, 2014. http://www.covenanteyes.com/2015/10/08/porn-use-as-grounds-for-divorce

18. Gottman, John. 1994. *What Predicts Divorce? The Relationship Between Marital Processes and Marital Outcomes.* Hillsdale New Jersey: Lawrence Erlbaum Assoc. Publishers

19. Heitler, Susan. Recovery from an Affair, November 1, 2011. *Psychology Today.*

20. Kirk, Wyveta J. 2014. *Women Talk Men Walk: Have the marriage you crave, God tells how,*

21. Krejeir, Richard. 2006. Research on the Happenings in Pastor's Personal and Church Lives. www.intothyword.org/apps/articles/?articleid=36562

22. Krejeir, Richard. 2016 Update. Research on the Happenings in Pastor's Personal and Church Lives. www.intothyword.org/apps/articles/?articleid=36562

23. Laaser, Mark R. 1992, 1996, 2004. *Healing the Wounds of Sexual Addiction.* Grand Rapids MI: Zondervan Books.

24. Marshall, Catherine. 1951, *A Man Called Peter.* Nineteenth Printing. New York, NY: McGraw-Hill Book Company.

25. Public Disclosure. 2016. *What is the Actual US Divorce Rate and Risk?* http://www.thepublicdiscourse.com/2015/12/15983

26. Stetzer. Ed. 2012. Pastors: That Divorce Rate Stat You Quoted Was Probably Wrong. http://www.christianitytoday.com/edstzer/2012/September/pastors-that-divorce-rate-you-quoted-was-probably-wrong

27. Vaughn, Peggy. 1990. *The Monogamy Myth.* New York, New York: Newmarket Publishing.

APPENDIX A

<u>This form is provided only as an idea for developing your own counseling agreement that fits your particular situation, your church's policies, and your state laws.</u>

Several options are provided for your selection.

COUNSELING AGREEMENT &

IN-TAKE FORM

Please read this agreement, sign and date it at the bottom. It must be completed before counseling.

DESCRIPTION OF COUNSELING: *Counseling by _____ minister is exclusively for active members in good standing of _____ church (or of _____ community)*

Your counseling process will explore three avenues of life: you the person, your situations, and the Lord's commandments. Counseling is Biblically based for both individuals, couples, and families. If your problem is outside my level of ability or skill, I will gladly refer you to another minister or professional therapist. I am unable to give financial, legal, or physical advice. My role is spiritual and how your life is centered on God's commands because I believe all people are designed to have an intimate relationship with God through Jesus Christ and then with others. Facilitating the restoration of these relationships is an important part of the counseling process. I focus on *discovering and changing unhealthy ways of relating that causes pain and distorted thinking.*

During my time with you, I will pray and read from God's Word as appropriate. Other reading materials may be suggested, and these will be at your expenses and belong exclusively to you. You may be assigned homework to facilitate personal time with God and that have ideas that often form the basis of counseling discussions. You are required to complete all homework before each meeting and failure to complete two consecutive assignments constitutes terminate of counseling. Counseling is a cooperative process with mutual responsibilities resting on both you and the minister. You should approach counseling as an opportunity for personal change and spiritual growth.

You agree that you understand the minister is not licensed, nor is he required by state law or any professional organization. You understand that the minister is not a psychologist, psychiatrist, medical physician, certified therapist, or any type of professional mental health care provider. He provides only Biblical guidance based on the teachings and authority of God's Word.

If you come wanting to discuss one issue but later include another, you may be required to sign an additional consent/agreement form before continuing that is congruent with any new counseling role, and discuss the benefits and requirements inherent in the transition. Because you may not want to share every detail of your problem, no warranty of success is guaranteed. Your decisions about how you choose to live your life remain solely your own decision.

Both you and the minister/counselor have the option of terminating counseling at any time and for any reason.

<u>*This form is provided only as an idea for developing your own counseling agreement that fits your particular situation, your church's policies, and your state's laws.*</u>

CONFIDENTIALITY: *All matters that you share will be held in the strictest of confidentiality. Confidentially is crucial to an effective and trusting counseling relationship and what you share in counseling, by phone, or written correspondence will be guarded to the fullest extent possible. All counseling notes will be held in a secure, private manner and no one else will be allowed their access.*

There are times when, as your minister/counselor, I am required to share with others the information learned during counselling. These are:

1. When, in my professional judgment, a child is being abused (physically and/or sexually) or neglected, I am required by law to report this to the proper authorities.

2. When, in my professional judgment, an adult (esp. the elderly) is being abused, neglected, exploited or abandoned, I am required to report this to local protective agencies.

3. If you express a serious threat, with intent to harm, kill, or seriously injure yourself, another, or a group, and it appears you plan to carry out such a threat, I am required to take measures to prevent the threat. This will include warning your family, your intended victim, and law enforcement.

4, If church policy/rules require me to inform the leadership or if church discipline deems necessary, this will be revealed.

5. As your minister/counselor I am not required to notify you in advance of such contact that may be required with appropriate entities

6. Whatever is appropriate for saving your soul, is what I will do.

Kirk: Counseling an Adulterer Saving a Marriage

This form is provided only as an idea for developing your own counseling agreement that fits your particular situation, your church's policies, and your state's laws.

Today's date _____   Phone home:
Phone cell:

Name   Address

Email   Birthdate

Occupation   Employer

Spouse name if married

This is your ___ marriage This is your spouse's ___ marriage

Number of children: Their names and ages:

Concern for counseling checklist: (Circle all appropriate)

Alcohol/drug use/abuse   Adultery (self/spouse/child)
Anger/frustration   Anxiety

Conflict with others   Confusion

Depression   Difficulty making decisions

Distance from God   Extended family issues

Fearfulness   Financial problems

Forgiving others/self   Guilt

Hopelessness   Jealousy

Loneliness   Marital issues

Kirk: Counseling an Adulterer Saving a Marriage

Parenting concerns   *Past abuse/neglect*

Pornography use   *Unsure of salvation*

OTHER
_____
_____

How often do you attend worship?

_____ *Read your Bible* _____

Describe your current spiritual life
_____
_____
_____
_____

_____ *name*
_____ *date*

Kirk: Counseling an Adulterer Saving a Marriage

<u>This form is provided only as an idea for developing your own counseling agreement that fits your particular situation, your church's policies, and your state's laws.</u>

I understand and agree with the following:

1. My minister_____, spiritual counselor, for the _____ church, is not a psychologist, psychiatrist, medical, or legal professional. There is no charge for counseling. His ministry is strictly a voluntary ministry.

2. Biblical ethics, church policies, state and federal laws will be honored and practiced.

3. Your initial meeting will be to determine if counseling is continued or if a referral would better serve your needs.

4. All counseling is based on a Biblical perspectives, including prayer and Scripture readings.

5. By signing this form, I authorize my minister to release information deemed appropriate to _____ (Circle one: spouse, employer, child, child's teacher, friend) I understand that my minister will not release any information to any one not mentioned, except where required by law or church policy, and by providing a written statement, I can change the release at any time.

6. Releasing information to the elders/shepherds or my church will be done with a Biblical perspective <u>only</u> if discipline deems appropriate. It is my responsibility to be informed as to the stance my church takes on this matter and to place myself in subjection to

that policy if my lifestyle moves in the needed direction for saving my soul and to return me to Christ.

7. When doing pre-marital, marital, and family counseling there is limited confidentiality, meaning the confidentiality belongs to the relationship not the individual.

8. I understand that certain statements may not be privileged communications under law and/or church policy.

9. I am consenting to resolving my problems by obedience to God's Word.

10. I know I can leave counseling at any time without giving a reason, and likewise, it can be terminated by the minister/counselor at any time and without reason. Should the problem be beyond the minister's expertise, he will refer me to another and such referral will automatically terminate my counseling contact with him.

11. Marital and family counseling may require 12 -20 sessions while other issues might be resolved in one or two sessions.

Waiver of Liability: In consideration for receiving counseling from the minister of _____ church, I have read the conditions set forth in the consent/acceptance form and agree to release and waive any and all claims of any kind against the minister, elders, or the church from any legal

Kirk: Counseling an Adulterer Saving a Marriage

liability, claim, or litigation arising from my participation in this voluntary counseling ministry.

I understand that I have no obligation to disclose this requested information and may revoke this consent at any time by informing the minister/counselor in writing.

My signature indicates that I understand and agree to the purpose of this request

_____*Name*
_____*Print*   *name*
_____*date*

APPENDIX B

HELPFUL RESOURCE FROM AG FINANCAIL INSURANCE SOLUTIONS FOR DEVELOPING CHURCH POLICIES

EXAMPLE: FACILITIES USE AGREEMENT

This Agreement is entered into this _____ day of _____, _____ by and between

_____

___
And

_____
Of Name of Church Licensee

_____
City & State of Licensee

In consideration of the mutual promises and conditions contained herein, Church and Licensee agree as follows:

1. Grant of License

Church grants Licensee a license to use the premises as follow:

A. Description of Premises

_____

B. Personal Property/Resources (if any)

_____
_____
_____

Purpose(s)

_____

D. Date(s) and Time(s) Term

_____

2. Term of License

This License shall be effective as of and continue through the dates and times described above. Licensee shall promptly vacate the premises at the end of the license term.

3. Payment Terms

Licensee agrees to the following payment terms:

A. Deposit.

Upon execution of this Agreement, Licensee shall pay the Church a deposit representing one-half of the fee for the use of the Licensed Premises. Payment of the deposit shall reserve the premises and facilities for Licensee's use. Until such deposit actually received, the Church may offer and license the premises and facilities to other potential licensees.

B. Final Bill.

In the absence of an express billing arrangement to the contrary, Licensee shall be presented with and pay a final bill prior to Licensee's use of the premises.

C. Sales Tax/Other Applicable Taxes.

The final bill shall include all state applicable taxes. Any request for an exemption from the payment of sales tax must be accompanied, in advance, by proof of exemption.

4. Terms of Use

Licensee agrees that its use of the premises and facilities is subject to the following terms and conditions:

A. Licensee shall use only the premises and personal property/resources describe in paragraph one above, only for the purposes stated in this Agreement.

Licensee shall not use any other Church property and resource and shall be responsible for any damages caused by the unauthorized use of such property or resource.

B. Licensee shall comply with all Church policies, rules and regulations.

C. Licensee shall comply with all applicable municipal, county, state and federal laws and regulations.

D. Licensee shall place no signs or temporary structure on the premises without obtaining advance written approval from Church. Any signs or temporary structures placed on the premises by Licensee shall be promptly removed at the end of the license term.

E. Licensee shall not create any nuisance or disturb the quiet enjoyment of anyone utilizing adjacent or common premises and facilities.

F. Licensee expressly acknowledge s that the sale, possession, consumption and use of alcoholic beverages, tobacco, and illegal drugs are forbidden on all Church premises.

G. Licensee expressly acknowledges that the use and possession of weapons and firearms are forbidden on all Church Premises.

H. In the event Licensee's use of the premises and facilities involves participants who are minors (including the minor children of participants), then Licensee shall be responsible for the safety of all such minors and shall place such minors under the constant supervision and control of a responsible adult. Licensee shall be responsible for conducting suitable and thorough background checks on all persons supervising minor children. Licensee shall further be responsible for obtaining a properly completed and signed Authorization from the custodial parent(s) of any minor child who will participate in

Licensee's use of the premises and facilities without the presence of his or her custodial parent(s).

Licensee understands and agrees (i) that it is responsible for all actions of its participants and guests, (ii) that any person(s) in violation of the foregoing terms of use will be expected to immediately vacate the premises of Church, and (iii) that Church reserves the right to immediately terminate this

Agreement and Licensee's use of the premises and facilities in the event of any violation of the foregoing terms of use without liability to Church.

5. Surrender of Premises

Licensee shall surrender the premises and personal property described in paragraph one above, including all furniture and fixtures, upon termination of the license in the same condition as they were delivered upon commencement of the license, normal wear and tear expected. Licensee shall be responsible for the repair and/or replacement of any Church property/resource that is damaged or removed during the license term.

A Indemnity

Church and its officers, directors, agents, members, and employees shall be free from all liability and claims for damages by reason of any injury allegedly sustained by any person or to any property that is in any way connected to Licensee's use of the premises during the license term or any extension thereof. Licensee expressly agrees to defend, indemnify and hold harmless Church, its officers, members, agents, and employees, from and against any and all actions, suits, demands, losses claims, and liabilities arising out of any such injuries or property loss however occurring, including reasonable actual attorneys' fees and all other costs of defending any claim.

7. Insurance

Licensee warrants that it carries general liability, medical, and property insurance in amounts sufficient to cover the risks and exposures resulting from its use of the premises pursuant to the terms of this Agreement. Specifically, Licensee warrants that it carries general liability insurance in the amount of not less than one million dollars ($1,000,000) per occurrence, three million dollars ($3,000,000) aggregate. Licensee further agrees to have Church named as an additional insured on Licensee's insurance policies and will, prior to the license term commencement date, provide a certificate of insurance to Church naming Church as an additional insured. In addition to any other remedies that may be available, Church may terminate this Agreement and retain any deposit paid by Licensee in the event such certificates are not provided by Licensee prior to the license commencement date.

8. Unforeseen Events

Church shall have no obligation to make its premises and facilities available to Licensee by reason of an act of God, inclement weather (as determined by Church), strike, illness, any act or order of public authority, or other unforeseen event beyond the control of Church. In such an event, Church shall have no liability to Licensee.

9. General Provisions

A. No Warranty. Church does not warrant or represent that the premises and facilities are safe and suitable for Licensee's purposes. Licensee expressly acknowledges for itself and for all persons who will be utilizing the premises and facilities in connection with Licensee's purposes that Church is providing the premises and facilities on an "as is" basis.

B. No Waiver. No waiver by either party or any breach of this Agreement shall be deemed a waiver of any preceding or succeeding breach.

C. Assignment. This Agreement may not be assigned by either party.

D. No Landlord-Tenant Relationship. Church and Licensee expressly agree that this Agreement shall not operate or be construed to create a Landlord-Tenant relationship between Church and Licensee under any circumstances.

E. Entire Agreement/Amendment. This Agreement and attachment constitute the entire Agreement between Church and Licensee and there are no oral representations, warranties, and promises pertaining to this Agreement that are not contained in writing in this Agreement. This Agreement may be modified or amended only by subsequent written agreement signed by duly authorized representatives of Church and Licensee.

IN WITNESS WHEREOF, Church and Licensee have executed this

Agreement as of the date first above written.

CHURCH LICENSEE

Signature of Church Representative
Signature
name of Church Representative   DATE

Example: Church Liability and Registered Sex Offenders (AG FINANCIAL INSURANCE RESOURCE)

One of the top questions asked about church liability has to do with dealing with known registered sex offenders who attend church. What steps should a church take to protect its members from potential harm and itself from a potential lawsuit?

First, let it be understood that a church has not been held liable for *unknowingly* allowing a registered sex offender to attend services. This information relates to *known registered sex offenders only*. Furthermore, there is no need to perform background checks on everyone in the church. The church's legal duty to proactively check backgrounds arises when someone is set apart in an official capacity as with employee's or board members, or those who work with minors in some way, as a volunteer, teacher, transportation provider, etc., or those who have keys to the church.

When it becomes known to the ministerial-pastoral staff that a registered sex offender is attending, the church can choose one of the following three responses:

> **Do nothing**. Unfortunately, this is often the approach taken by many churches. This response is not recommended due to its associated legal risks, which include the following: risk that the offender may molest a minor, liability to the church if the person will be working with minors, punitive damages for reckless or

gross negligence, liability for board members who failed to implement appropriate safeguards, negative media publicity, and the risk of a potentially uninsured claim (intentional or criminal misconduct is not an insurable risk). Bottom line: in choosing to do nothing, you carry a high risk of harm to minors and of being sued for negligence.

1. **Total exclusion of all registered sex offenders from the church.** Although it may appear harsh and unforgiving, this is a valid option that depends on the severity of the person's crimes. There are different segregations of the crimes for which a person can be placed on a state's sexual offender registry:
– Tier 1. These are the least severe sex crimes. The person is on the registry for 15 years.
– Tier 2. These are more severe sex-related crimes and the person is on the registry for 25 years.
– Tier 3. These are the most heinous sex crimes and the person remains on the registry for life.
If you have someone who's a Tier 3 offender, the best response is to exclude them from attending. Even if the crime(s) occurred decades ago, consider the age of the victim(s); if the incident(s) involved pre-pubescent or early-pubescent children, it should not matter how long ago it occurred, since such a person may be a pedophile (someone with a sexual preference for prepubescent or early pubescent minors). According to an FBI profile, pedophiles are incurable, promiscuous, predatory, and have a high recidivism rate. From a liability standpoint, the risk to minors and to your church in allowing a pedophile to attend may be too high. In addition, exclusion may be the proper response in cases where the victim(s) of the sex offender's crimes attend the same church.

2. **Conditional attendance, according to a signed legal agreement.** This means that the person is allowed to attend provided he or she complies with the conditions of the agreement. This is sometimes viewed as a more merciful response. Worded properly, this can put the church in a position to be viewed as having acted reasonably under the circumstances, which means that it may not be considered negligent. However, a couple things must be kept in mind if this course is chosen. First, this document must be drafted by an attorney and comply with any requirements under state law. Second, careful thought must be given as to the conditions stated in the policy. The following conditions often are inserted in such documents:

• The offender may not work with minors in any official capacity.
• The offender may not transport minors.
• The offender may not attend children's or teens' functions at church.
• A chaperone must be designated to observe the person at all times while on church premises, never letting the person out of sight. Restrooms, in particular, pose a risk. Many documented cases of child molestation have taken place in a restroom. Always have the chaperone follow the offender into the restroom. In general, the spouse of a sex offender would not be a good choice for a chaperone. Ushers or board members are good candidates. In the case of a minor who has sexually molested another minor, the parents or legal guardians could act as chaperones. In their absence, another designated chaperone may be appointed.

It is also recommended that churches adopt a *Zero Tolerance Policy* for violation of a conditional attendance agreement. Even a single violation should result in the individual no longer being permitted to attend. In addition, it is best to contact your insurance agent or company to review the agreement after it is drafted and reviewed by an attorney. This is for your own protection as many applications for insurance ask if any member, employee, or volunteer (past or present) associated with your organization has been accused or convicted of sexual misconduct. The last thing a church wants is to have coverage denied in the event of a material misrepresentation.

One more step should be taken before adopting an attendance agreement. Check with the individual's probation officer if they have one. Many registered sex offenders have been released from incarceration as a result of a probation or parole agreement. Some probationary agreements prohibit offenders from attending church, and if this is the case, it is essential for church leaders to know it.

When faced with the need to deal with a registered sex offender in your church, the point of these recommendations is not to eliminate risk but to reduce it to a manageable level to meet the standard of reasonable care. Ask yourself, how would a jury view your church's actions? In setting up a policy, you are attempting to act reasonably and with due care for everyone involved, especially the precious children in your ministry.

Example: How to Make a Bullet-Proof Emergency Plan that Reduces Church Risk (AG FINANCAIL INSURANCE SOLUITIONS)

In June 2017, the Federal Emergency Management Agency (FEMA) released its latest recommendations to churches for developing high-quality emergency operations plans (EOPs). This free 38-page resource is available for download on their website and blog: www.agfinancial.org/blog.

Developing an EOP can help **protect your congregation from harm** if the unthinkable happens. Furthermore, staying up to date on FEMA's recommendations is important for every church because the guidelines may serve as the benchmark by which a church's actions will be judged from a liability standpoint.

During emergencies, the typical reaction is to freeze as you watch the disaster happen and wait for someone to take action. While this is a normal reaction, the longer people remain frozen, the more likely they are to do nothing. In an emergency, doing nothing is the worst response. Having an EOP goes a long way to prevent that tendency.

Characteristics of an effective EOP:

- It is supported by church leadership.

- It is established and crafted by an emergency planning team of designated individuals who will communicate with first responders during emergencies. It is recommended this team be made up of people that you employ or from your congregation who have medical, human resources, law enforcement, or military experience. In addition, include attorneys, insurance professionals, and building supervisors. However, be sure to keep the team small enough to operate effectively.

- It is a written document that is reviewed and updated regularly, as team member and church needs change.

- It considers all threats that could affect your church. An often-overlooked threat is child abduction. Writing down the steps your church will take to prevent and respond to such an occurrence can help reduce liability.

- It takes a five-pronged approach of preventing, protecting, reducing, responding, and recovering from different types of emergencies.

- It clearly identifies the action(s) the church will take.

- It includes the perspectives of children, the elderly, and those with disabilities, as these groups often need special care during emergencies.

- It is shared with local first responders in your area who can add their input and recommendations for creating and implementing the plan.

- It includes practice drills for fires, tornadoes, and other threats. Drills do not have to take place during service times or involve everyone in the congregation, but make sure to include team members.

- Policies in the plan are shared with the congregation.

Additional recommendations:

- Put emergency exit and shelter maps in every room of the church.

- Invite first responders to assess your church property and identify safety areas. Give them a map of the church with entries and exits clearly marked.

- Inform the congregation of all safety areas.

- Have people monitor the weather during services.

Special Considerations in the Case of an Active Shooter

Very few patterns can be extrapolated from 27 church shooting incidents that occurred over the last 15 years. Only five of the shootings were from members of the church, making it extremely difficult to predict this type of threat. In such cases, FEMA simply recommends that congregations run, hide, and fight. However, we think more can be done to help in such a situation.

First, **conduct congregational meetings** to openly discuss the threat ahead of time. Active shooter incidents require an immediate response, so the importance of having a well-laid-out plan cannot be overemphasized. Your emergency team will have to act right away, so they need to know exactly what to do. Consider providing team members with radios to use during services so they can communicate with each other and direct people to safety areas.

Second, while fighting can be a viable option, churches need to carefully consider their policies regarding the **use of weapons**. Appointing a security team to include at least one uniformed law enforcement officer present at all services is a great idea and an effective crime deterrent. If you have law enforcement present and they respond to the crisis, it minimizes the church's potential liability. You may also decide to allow conceal and carry for people in your congregation. However, this option is not as desirable as a police officer. If they respond to the crisis, it won't minimize the church's liability because they would be acting as an agent of the church and not as law enforcement. In this case, any use of what might be deemed "excessive force" could put the church at risk for litigation. For this reason, try to choose people with extensive training and use the same training that your area law enforcement requires. Examine their experience, licensure, and history. To learn more about conceal and carry policies for churches, view the [Risk Mgmt LIVE video](#) on this topic on their website/blog.

Third, **compare your emergency plan** with what other local churches and schools are doing. With a solid plan of action in place, your church will be prepared to minimize damage and protect lives during an emergency.

Watch the full Risk Mgmt LIVE video about dealing with registered sex offenders on our website. Others resources include dealing with fraud, having appropriate child-adult ratios in each classroom, same-sex marriage, protecting church leadership against liability, church protection when allowing others to use your facilities, etc.

A resource of AG Financial Insurance Solutions

APPENDIX C

COUPLES EXERCISE FOR CREATING INTIMACY

(Take turns answering each question or by writing your answer and then sharing your response)

1. One way I make it difficult for you to give me what I need from you is _____ and admitting it makes me feel_____
2. One way I try to act self-sufficient is by _____ and it makes me feel _____
3. One way I detach from others is by _____ and it makes me feel_____
4. Sometimes I keep you at distanced by _____ which makes me feel_____
5. Sometimes I act superior by _____ , I feel _____
6. When I don't listen to you, I feel _____
7. I remember being hurt when _____ and I wanted to (or did) react by ____ and that made me feel ____
8. Sometimes I feel hurt when _____ and my hurt shows by _____
9. Sometimes I try to hide my hurt by _____ and it leaves me feeling _____
10. A better way to deal with my hurt would be to _____
11. When I feel angry, I often _____ and this leaves me feeling _____
12. One way I sometimes try to hide my anger is by _____ and I feel _____
13. A better way to deal with my anger would be to _____ and I'd feel _____
14. One thing I fear is _____ and when I think of it, I feel _____

15. If I ever honestly told you how fearful I feel, I think you might _____ and if you did I'd feel_____
16. A more positive way to deal my fears would be to _____ and I'd feel _____
17. When I know I've done something that makes you happy, I feel _____
18. When I am happy, I want to ____ because I feel _____
19. I would be happier if I'd _____ and I'd feel _____
20. I feel sexually attracted to you the most when _____

21. Sometimes I hide my interest in sex by _____ and it leaves me feeling _____
22. A better way to deal with my sexual interest is _____ and if I did, I'd feel _____
23. When I recall the ways my parents failed me, I feel _____ and want to _____
24. As a child, I never understood why they _____ and it left me feeling _____
25. If I could have told that young child (me) that I was _____ I'd have felt _____ and having been told then today I'd feel _____
26. The guidance my mother or father failed to give me was ____ and without it I felt____
27. As a child, it seemed that mother always _____
28. As a child, it seemed my father never _____
29. One way I get even with my parents for failing me is _____ which leave me feeling __
30. When I think about my mother's and father's painful experiences, I bet they _____
31. One of the ways I treat myself as my mother did is _____ When I do this, I feel____
32. One of the ways I treat myself as my father did is _____ When I do this, I feel ___
33. If I fully accepted that child (me) as a valuable part of me, I'd _____
34. One way I try to win my parent's approval is _____

35. If my mother/father was dying today, and I had one last chance to tell him/her something it would be_____ and I'd be left feeling_____ for having told her/him.
36. One way I try to deny they love me is by _____
37. One of my earliest happy memories is when _____. I felt _____
38. The thing my parents failed to do for me that I now do for myself is _____ and if I would do it, I believe I would feel_____
39. When I forgive the child I once was for not knowing what else to do, I can _____
40. Sometimes I contribute to my own frustration by _____ and it has me feeling_____
41. One thing I should do just for myself today is _____ because I would feel_____
42. The good thing about procrastinating is _____
43. If you could see the tears I hide, they would tell you _____
44. The good thing about pretending I don't like myself is _____
45. If I told you how much I actually do like myself, you would _____
46. If pursued my career in ways to become very successful, I'd _____
47. One way I block my emotional growth is by _____ and it leaves me feeling_____
48. One way I block my spiritual growth is by _____ and it leaves me feeling _____
49. One way I block my physical health is by _____ and it leaves me feeling_____
50. One way I block my relationship with you is by _____ and it leaves me feeling_____
51. One way I block being close to my parents is _____ and it leaves me feeling _____
52. One way I block being close to our children is _____ and it leaves me feeling_____

53. One way I can stop blocking others love is to _____ and this would leave me feeling _____
54. When I think of one of us dying and the other being all alone, I feel _____
55. If I were to allow myself to turn lose and love you with all my heart, I'd feel _____
56. The thing I try to convince myself that I don't care about is _____ and this leaves me feeling _____ If I change and show I care, I'd feel _____ and I'd show it by _____
57. If I would give myself permission to make mistakes, I'd _____ and I'd feel _____
58. If I could express my feeling better, I'd _____ and I'd feel _____
59. I'd be more ambitious if I'd only ___ and I'd feel ___
60. I'd take more risks if I'd only _____ and I'd feel _____
61. When I feel guilty I tend to ___ because I feel _____
62. If I really believed that I am NOT a bad person, I'd _____ and I'd feel _____
63. If I'd allow myself to occasionally be selfish, I'd like to _____ and I'd feel _____
64. If I stopped holding myself back, I'd _____, and I would feel _____
65. The one thing I no longer need to prove to others is _____ and this lets me feel _____
66. Letting go of my need to _____ has given me freedom to _____
67. Knowing God loves me no matter what, and I don't have to prove that I am a good enough, frees me to _____ and that lets me feel _____
68. Letting go of our children and allowing them to learn to do things on their own makes me feel _____ because I want _____
69. The way we work to be healthy is by _____ and that lets me feel _____
70. Another thing we could do to be healthier would be ___

71. One thing we should do to be healthier is _____
72. The ways we try to bond emotionally is by _____
73. One way we could bond closer is by _____
74. One thing we should do so we feel closer is _____
75. One way we work at managing money is _____
76. One thing we could do to manage our money better is _____
77. One thing we should do for having better control of our finances is _____
78. One way we can grow spiritually is _____
79. One thing we could do to be stronger spiritually would be to _____
80. What we should do so we are closer to the Lord is ____
81. One thing we could do so we argue less is _____ and that would make me feel _____
82. One thing we should do so we argue less and feel closer to each other is _____ and doing it would have me feeling _____
83. Happiness is something we deserve, and I will pursue it by _____
84. I will put a boundary around what makes me happy by _____ and I will enforce it in a loving way by _____
85. I will work to ensure you are happy by ____ and agreeing to do this makes me feel _____
86. If I am unhappy, I will _____
87. One thing we could do to communicate better is ____ and that would leave me feeling ____
88. One thing we should do so we communicate without hurting the other is _____ and agreeing to do this makes me feel _____
89. One way we can make time to be alone without others interfering is ____ and doing that would let me feel ____
90. One thing you could do to help me feel better about us is _____ and if you did it, I would feel _____
91. When I make a promise to you, I feel _____ and when I keep it, I feel _____

92. One promise I would like from you would be to _____ and your doing it would leave me feeling _____
93. The difficult thing about being a woman/man is _____
94. When I think, "You are the one I've chosen to spend my life with," I feel _____
95. If I fully believed in my goodness, I'd _____
96. If I took full responsibility for getting everything I want, I'd _____
97. If I stop blaming others and start living, I'll _____
98. To fully put God first in my life, loving Him with all my heart, mind, soul, and strength and fully depend on Him, I'd need to _____

APPENDIX D

PROBLEM: CLEANLINESS/HOUSEHOLD CHORES

The issue is the wife feels overloaded and wants him to help more with routine care of the house.

Cleanliness of the house falls on the bottom of many men's list. Of the long list of topics, on her list this likely falls #4-5 in importance, but she may rank it as a 7 or 8 for how much pain or discomfort it causes her. He is more likely a zero in both places, or close to it. Few men say complain about the condition of the home. Because she is the one drowning in pain, she initiates their negotiation and has the final say of what makes an acceptable resolution.

You ask her: What do you want? What could he do that would improve things in this area? What could he do to make things better? Ensure she is very specific about what she wants/what it would take for her to move this problem near the bottom of her list and become less of an issue.

Her: I wish he would clean the table after dinner, stack the dishwasher and turn it on, and then empty it once it's finished. I would like him to change our sheets weekly, wash them, and put them back on the bed.

You ask him: Can you agree to do these things?

Him: No way. I already assume total care of the car, changing the oil and rotating the tires. I pay all the bills and mow the lawn. I think I'm pulling my share of the load. She ignores all the ways I help. *(feels a lack of respect/ lack of value)*

You ask him: What is one thing you could do to help more?

Him: Well, I guess I could clear the table after we eat and stack the dishes in the sink. But I can't put them in the dishwasher because she never thinks I stack them correctly. *(feels disrespected by her criticism)*

You ask him: How do you feel when criticized for this?

<u>Him:</u> Like a little child who is being yelled at and having to go sit in the corner without dinner. It makes me angry and feel unappreciated for all I do.
<u>You ask him</u>: Is that what you did as a child?
<u>Him</u>: No, not in the corner, but mother did criticize me a lot, and I had to go to my room and sometimes miss dinner.
<u>You ask him</u>: How did doing without dinner and being isolate make you feel?
<u>Him:</u> Like they didn't love me or they would know I was hungry. I guess I felt abandoned and like a punching bag.
<u>You ask him</u>: When your wife criticizes you, how do you typically respond?
<u>Him</u>: I pout. I turn the TV louder. I try to avoid her for the rest of evening. I knows she's upset, and I just want to withdraw. I try to hide.
<u>You ask him</u>: Did withdrawing as a child, or now, help improve things?
<u>Him:</u> No it's just an escape that changes nothing.
<u>You ask him</u>: Doesn't it actually make your relationship worse?
<u>Him</u>: Yes, I guess it does.
<u>You say to him</u>: So you withdraw like you were made to do as a child when your mother was upset with you.
<u>You ask her</u>: How does knowing he deliberately avoids you make you feel?
<u>Her</u>: Angry, because I am only wanting more help. I shouldn't have to do everything by myself.
<u>You ask her:</u> (pick up on use of should) So you have an expectation that he should help you each day, or he is doing wrong and his not helping means he's not loving you. Is that right?
<u>Her</u>: Well, if you word it like that, it sounds bad. But yes, I do expect it. He eats like the kids and I do. He needs clean clothes, and we can't afford a maid. So one of us has to do it. And I'm the one stuck with it all. Yes, it makes me angry.
<u>You ask her</u>: So now you know you can be angry with and love the person, and do both at the same time.

Kirk: Counseling an Adulterer Saving a Marriage

Her: Yes, but it still hurts.
Ask her: How do you react when he avoids you?
Her: I slam pots and pans and yell at the kids. I take it out on them. Then I am disgusted with me for doing that. I know I am hurting them, and that's wrong.
You ask him: How do you feel about her directing her disappointment with you onto the kids?
Him: I never realized she did this. I don't want them hurt because she feels upset with me. I feel a little ashamed that my actions cause them to be hurt.
You ask her: He offered to clear the table and stack the dishes. What could you do so he felt appreciated, and no longer feel disrespected with criticism as he does this?
Her: I could show him how things best fit in the dishwasher and then thank him for helping. It's just that there are ways to load it so it holds more and we have to turn it on less often. That saves on our utility bill.
You ask her: So your goal is to save on the utility bill?
Her: Yes, I do try to help us save money where we can, and this is one way I try to help.
You ask him: What would you think about her showing you how to load it so you run it less often?
Him: I'd feel inadequate, like a child needing mommy to show him how to do things. *(fears feeling disrespected/ unequal as an adult partner)*
You ask her: Is his loading the dishwasher a certain way worth him feeling bad and disrespected and then withdrawing from you? It seems you are choose between his feelings and money
Her: No, I just never thought he took it like that. . *(She has been unaware of how she contributed to his not helping more)*
You ask her: Then would his suggestion of continuing to care for the car and clearing the table make the problem of house cleanliness bearable for you?
Her: No, not really. The car rarely needs the oil changed or the tires rotated, but the dishes have to be washed daily. I need help with things that must be done every day. (She

thinks: *He doesn't love me or he'd care how much I have to do and would offer to help more)*
You ask her: So you distort the meaning of his not helping more as his not loving you. But you do honestly know he loves you, don't you?
Her: Yes, I do, but I want him to care how much I have to do once we get home each evening. I feel used and overwhelmed most days, with the kid's homework, dinner to prepare, dishes, laundry. Some days I don't sit down until I go to bed. (Resentment)
You ask him: How do you feel knowing she has so much to accomplish each evening that she can't even take a break?
Him: Like I am a heel for not helping more. I come in tired too, and just want to forget about doing more work.
Her: Your're not a heel. I just need you to become more aware of what has to be done. I would also like to be able to sit down and watch a movie at night too. (feels used/overloaded/but resentment is melting)
You ask him: What could you offer to do so she felt loved because you supported her daily? What could you agree to do every day to reflect "I am doing this to help because I love you. I care how hard you work, and I want you to have more free time too?"
Him: How about if I pick up the kids toys before going to bed, unload the dishwasher every morning before breakfast and help prepare the kid's school lunches? I fear I'd never remember to empty the washer at night and then you'd be upset with me. I want to help, but not if it means I end up in the doghouse. But I will notice if our cereal bowls are still in the washer in the morning. (*I would feel disrespected when you complained/unequal, unappreciated*)
Her: That sounds fine, but would you also agree to help me fold clothes each night if I bring them to the sofa to fold so we can both watch TV?
Him: I could do that. Sure, I'd be glad to do that. In fact, if you continue putting a load in the washer each morning as we

leave for work, I will move it to the dryer when I come home and fold them while you prepare dinner.
Her: If you would also put them in the drawers where they belong, that would be a great help and a giant relief for me. *(feeling more love coming from him/relieved)*
Him: I could do that too. Sure. Provided you don't complain if I put things in the wrong place for a while. *(fears being disrespected/criticized)*
Her: I promise. Why not make the kids help you take them to the bedrooms? They know where most things go. At least they know where their things belong. It would good for them to learn to help more too.
Him: I can agree to do that.
Document and date what the problem was and what each agreed to do to resolve it. Have both sign. They should both leave with a copy, and you put one in their counseling file. Ask how they can celebrate putting this problem behind them. Insist that they do something special each time they resolve an issue that's been causing one or both hurt or distrust.

Kirk: Counseling an Adulterer Saving a Marriage

PROBLEM: MOTHER-IN-LAW SETS UP COMPETITION

The issue is how his mother deliberately competes with his wife, and he allows his mother to always win which means the wife always loses.

For the wife this issue ranks a 10 and causes her pain that's a 10. For him, it is little more than an annoyance of a 3 or 4, until his wife explodes after the fact, and then it becomes a 10. She is the one drowning in pain so she has the final say of a resolution.

<u>Ask her</u>: Explain what happens to cause you such pain.

<u>Her</u>: Let me give you an example. His mother does nails, and I let her do mine last week. My husband picked me up at her shop, and without asking me, he invited her and his dad for dinner. I had nothing prepared, but I didn't think I could object because she had just done my nails free of charge. Once home, I pulled hamburger meat from the freezer and when I discovered I didn't have any buns, I asked him to go to the store to get some, and he said he didn't want to go, that I should just make spaghetti instead. His mother listened quietly and then said she wished we had soft drinks to go with it. When I told her we didn't have any, but was making tea, she asked him to go to the store and get her a coke. He immediately left and came back with a coke for her but no buns.

The week before, I asked if just the two of us could go to Dan's, a nice, but expensive restaurant to celebrate his birthday. He said we couldn't afford it. But the very next day, his mother phoned and said we should all go out together to eat. We did, and guess who picked up the entire check? We couldn't afford for just the two of us to eat out that week, but he found money to pay for us, the kids, and his parents. No matter what his mother wants, she gets it, even when it's the very same thing I wanted, and he has told me no. *(feels unloved/second place).*

You ask her: How does his mother getting her way when you were refused the same thing make you feel?
Her: Unimportant and unloved. Like he loves her a lot more than me. Like I'm second fiddle and never first. It makes me angry and feel hate for her. I want to blame her but it's him who lets this happen. If he didn't participate, she couldn't do it.
You tell her: Hate comes from feeling vulnerable, and we want to destroy the object we hate. But when we find a way to stand up for ourselves and no longer feel vulnerable we stop the hating.
Her: I could tell his mother what I think about how she treats me and tries to come between us, but I know if I do, she might never speak to me again. That would harm our marriage. I think he can stop her interference and there still be a relationship.
You explain: You are correct. When there's in-law issues, the child of those parents needs to be the one to resolve the issues. Otherwise, there's always friction.
You ask him: How do you feel when you see your wife is hurt and jealous of your mother?
Him: I feel trapped in the middle of two women I love. It's like one is pulling at one sleeve and the other is tugging on the other sleeve. I hate being caught in the middle.
You ask him: So how do you cope when this happens?
Him: I usually take mother's side because of the guilt I have if I don't.
You ask him: Did you mother make you feel guilty if you didn't do as she asked when you were a child?
Him: You bet she did. She'd cry and I'd cave. If I didn't cave, I knew a long-term grounding was coming. It was easier to do what she wanted than to protest. By doing as she wanted, I could be back to doing my thing much sooner. So I just always took the easier way out.
You ask him: Who does the Lord say you are to be one with?
Him: I know it's my wife, but when we're all together I just want things to be peaceful, and I try to find a way to keep

everyone happy. My wife's anger isn't nearly as difficult for me as my mother's guilt. Mother can still give me that look that lets me know I did wrong.

You ask him: How is that working for you?

Him: I see your point. It's not working well at all.

Ask her: What is it you want your husband to do?

Her: I want him to say no to his mother – until she learns she will lose if she asks him to do something he refused to do for me. Each time she sets it up a request as competition I want him to take my side. If she loses each time she does this, she will finally stop. *(feeling unloved/ second rate)*

Ask him: Can you say no to your mother if it's for something you have already told you wife no, so you wife doesn't feel unloved and less important to you?

Him: My mother asks so little of us. We rarely see her so I feel guilty saying no to her. But, yes, I can try to do more of that. (feels shame for disobeying mother as if he's still a little child)

Ask her: Is that satisfactory to you?

Her: No. I don't hear a commitment. I want to know that the next time she sets up the competition that he takes my side, not hers. I want him to say no to her and yes to me in her presence. I want this loser-winner thing to stop, and only he can stop it by showing her she's not going to have her way and I'm the one he supports no matter what she asks. If he refuses to do what she asks then she will stop playing her mean game. (feels second-class/ unloved)

Ask him: Can you commit that no matter the situation or what the subject is that if you have already told your wife no then you will tell your mother no?

Him: Okay, if I've refused to go to the store for her, then I will refuse to go for mother. Or if I have told her we can't afford to eat out, I will tell mother we can't afford to eat out right now.

Ask her: Is that acceptable to you?

Her: No. Not quite. The next time it will be a different topic. When she asks him to do something, I want him to tell her no, and then let me ask him and him do it for me. . . no matter what it is. Otherwise, his mother will never see that he will do things for me that he won't for her or anyone else. *(feeling less/unloved because she's not first with him, jealous)*

Ask him: Can you agree to prove to your mother that your wife comes before her by saying no to your mother and then letting her hear you say yes when your wife asks you to do something, even if it's similar? Or if your mother asks you to do something that you have already said no to your wife, can you say, "Mother, Sue and I agreed not to do that at this time." Or, "Sue and I agreed to cut back on spending for a while. So maybe we can later, but we need to decline for now?" If your mother wants something that requires you to run an errand you didn't want to run for your wife, could you say, "Sorry but we don't have any cokes. Next time if we know you are coming, I'll try to have some on hand, but I'm not up to making a special trip right now." Can you do this to stop your mother's competing and to prove that your wife ranks first of all women in your life?

Him: I will do my best.

Ask Him: What can you say to your mother?

Him: I guess I can say I don't feel like doing it.

Ask Him: But what if that's not the truth and you do feel good? And how will you explain you then feeling okay to go for your wife?

Him: So you are saying my excuse would be a lie?

Ask Him: Only if it is. What could you say that would be honest and let your mother understand?

Him: I really don't know. I've never stood up to her before.

Ask Him: Do you think your dad always put your mother first, before other women?

Him: Yes, I think so.

Ask Him: Then could you say something like, "Mom, God tells us to put our spouse before others and I've been guilty of doing things for you when I should have only been doing them only for my wife. I need to change that and I am sure

you want me obeying the Lord. So, I can't do as you ask this time." Could you put something like this in your own words?
Him: It will be difficult but I will practice it. Yes, I will practice. I will do my best.
Ask her: Is that an acceptable solution?
Her. Only if he's really commits to doing it. Doing his best is not a firm commitment. *(lacks trust)*
You ask Him: If that doesn't work, could you make a list of ways she has set up competition and go talk privately with your mother about the damage she is doing to your marriage? Could you explain how this is interfering, and it has to stop?
Him: I honestly am not sure I could do that. I mean I could tell you I would, but I know it would end up a real battle. She would cry and then give me that look that makes me crumble and just want to escape. I've never stood up to her before. I fear I might cave. But it almost sounds like you want me being rude to mother.
You tell Him: To protect your wife, there may be times you have to be rude to someone, but God expects you to protect your relationship, not let another control it.
You ask Her: How do you feel about him standing up to his mother?
Her: I just want the competition to end, and end by me being consistently the one he puts first, not second-place. We are to be one, not him and his mother. God says so. And if you are asking if I trust him to do this, I guess I have no reason to. (Jealous/unloved).
Him: But you are first with me. I rarely see mother.*(feeling disrespected).*
Her: But when we do, she consistently sets up competition and you do things for her you won't do for me. I can't stand how deeply that hurts. It makes me do my best to avoid being with her. I don't invite them to visit because I know the day will end with me being hurt. I don't want things to be like that. (feels unloved, second rate, and has to protect herself, because he doesn't).

Him: If I could promise to put you first every time – without fail, would you invite them a little more often? If can learn to do this, would that be okay? Just know it's really difficult for me to take a stand with her.

You explain: Most people try to hide their vulnerability and just express it with hate or dislike of another. When we do, the hurt never goes away, and we dislike that person forever. To let go of her pain, she has to feel she has some power, enough so she's no longer vulnerable and mistreated. She has to know things will be balanced in the relationship and know you will always protect her in your mother's presence. She doesn't trust you to protect her from your mother's deliberate painful competition.

Him: I want to do that. Really I do. I just haven't known how to do things right. I live my life never wanting anyone to be hurt, but you are saying that one is probably going to be hurt in this situation, and God says it must not be my wife. I get it.

You tell him: Your mother will be annoyed and probably frustrated that she's losing control over you, especially the first time or two, but she won't want repeats once she is convinced of what your response will be. Remember she has used control over you for years. It's going to be difficult for her, but she will adjust. We know because it has you doing as God commands. Remember we are to leave parents and become on without spouse. You have just never fully left her control, and you can't become one with your wife until you do.

You ask her: With his commitment, are you now comfortable inviting his mother to your house?

Her: Sure, I'd like being with any woman who tried to compete with me for his time, attention, and money if he showed her that I'd always be the one first with him. In fact, when it's just she and I, we get along quite well. It's just when he comes in that I know hurts on its way. In fact, it might help if he would spend one-on-one time with her. Why don't you invite her for lunch on the days she is in town shopping? Maybe she sets things up this way because she is

fearful you no longer love her like she used to. Maybe to invite her to have time with just you would help too.
Him: That's a good idea, and it might help. Then, yes, I commit. I will see that you are first in my life, no matter the issue. I promise to always take your side. If I should think you are wrong, I will still take your side and tell you only after we are alone. But in front of others, especially in front of my mother, you will always be first. I won't let her tell me what to do unless it's something you would also want.
You ask her: Then how often can you invite his mother to your home?
Her: How about once a month or every six weeks for dinner or to go with us to a play or to one of the kid's ball games.
Ask him: How is that offer for you?
Him: That's plenty. To be honest, I don't like being with my parents that much anyway. In fact, once every two or three months is plenty, because they tend to always argue, and I don't' like them doing that in front of our kids. So once every couple of months or so is enough for me not to feel guilty. I just wish she would sometimes be the one to invite them and it not always fall my place.
Her: I agree to do that.
Have them sign a sheet stating the problem, its solution, date it, and decide how to celebrate their success at deciding on a workable solution.

Kirk: Counseling an Adulterer Saving a Marriage

www.ingramcontent.com/pod-product-compliance
Lightning Source LLC
Chambersburg PA
CBHW070136100426
42743CB00013B/2716